Heartfelt Praise for

Dear America

LETTERS HOME
FROM VIETNAM

"*Dear America* is more than correspondence from homesick GIs. It is a collective letter to the nation and its government, a plea that asks: Why did you do this to your children? To America? For the sake of our country, don't let this happen again."

—*San Francisco Chronicle*

"This riveting anthology . . . is extraordinary by its very ordinariness, a collection of 208 letters written to wives and friends and lovers by 125 of the men and women who were there. They are, for the most part, neither deep nor philosophical, only very, very human."

—*Los Angeles Times*

"*Dear America* tells of an ache as ancient as time—adolescents off to war with high expectations, who soon change greatly. Ambiguities abound—from pain, disillusionment and sorrow for dead comrades to a hard-earned measure of individual strength and survival."

—*Washington Post Book World*

"*Dear America* is painful, but it must be difficult to be realistic and entertaining about war. . . . Reading it, I felt I was listening to the voices of the men and women who lived and fought in Vietnam."

—*Baltimore Sun*

"In the recent special issue of *Newsweek* about Vietnam, Gloria Emerson suggested that the politicians who conducted the war be chained to the Vietnam Memorial in Washington and forced to read, slowly, every name on it aloud. They should also be required to read these letters [in *Dear America*], slowly, one by one."

—*Philadelphia Inquirer*

"Not a history book, not a war novel. . . . *Dear America* is a book of truth. Really."

—*Boston Globe*

"Closing *Dear America*, the best of the new books, late at night, with my two sons asleep in the house, I thought, 'Nothing is worth that.' Bernard Edelman, a Vietnam veteran and member of the New York Vietnam Veterans Memorial Commission, has exercised tact, restraint and skill in editing this collection. . . . *Dear America* is a work of art."

—*San Jose Mercury-News*

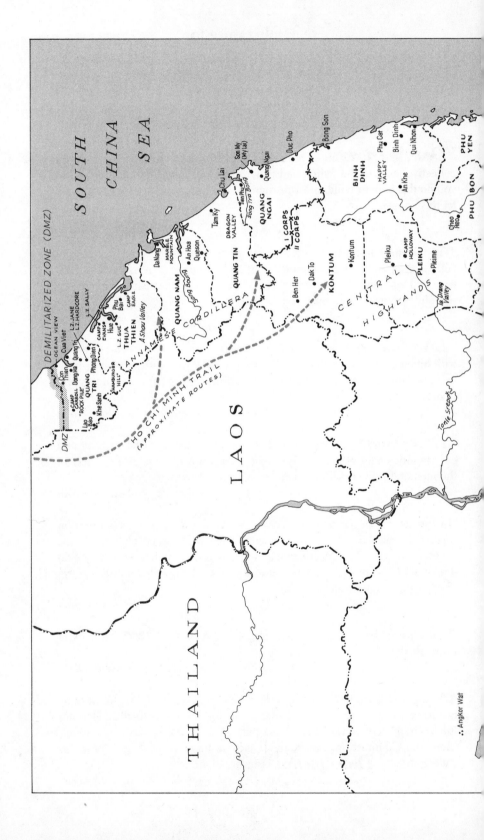

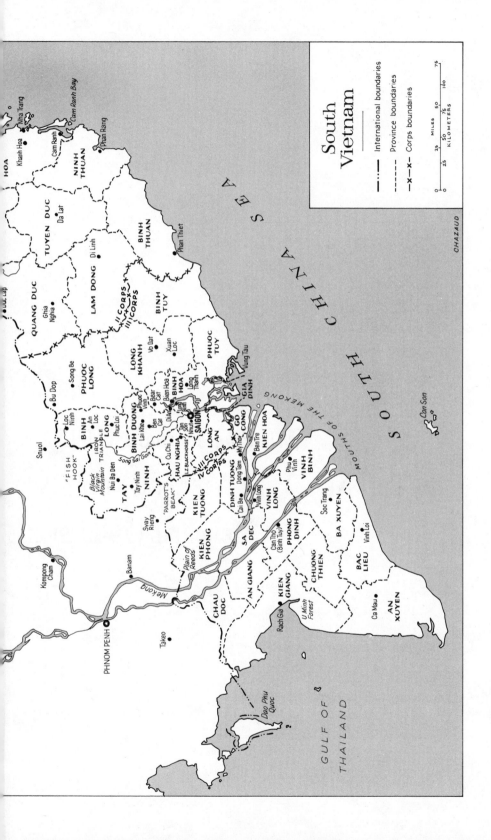

South Vietnam

- ····· International boundaries
- ------ Province boundaries
- –x–x– Corps boundaries

MILES
0   25   50   75   100
0 25 50 75 100
KILOMETERS

CHAZAUD

SOUTH CHINA SEA

GULF OF THAILAND

MOUTHS OF THE MEKONG

II CORPS
III CORPS
IV CORPS
III CORPS

HOA
NINH THUAN
TUYEN DUC
Nha Trang
Khanh Hoa
Cam Ranh Bay
Cam Ranh
Phan Rang
Da Lat
Dak Lap
QUANG DUC
Ghia Nghia
LAM DONG
Di Linh
BINH THUAN
Phan Thiet
PHUOC LONG
Bu Dop
Song Be
Snuol
LONG KHANH
BINH TUY
Vo Dat
Xuan Loc
Loc Ninh
An Loc
BINH DUONG
BINH LONG
Phuoc Loi
PHUOC TUY
Vung Tau
"FISH HOOK"
IRON TRIANGLE
Black Virgin Mountain
Nui Ba Den
TAY NINH
Tay Ninh
Ben Cat
Lai Khe
Phu Cuong
Ben Cat
Di An
Bien Hoa
BINH HOA
Long Thanh
GIA DINH
Cu Chi
Di An
SAIGON
Tan Son Nhut
HAU NGHIA
LONG AN
GO CONG
KIEN HOA
"PARROT'S BEAK"
Svay Rieng
Z BLACKHORSE
Duc Hoa
My Tho
Ben Tre
DINH TUONG
Dong Tam
VINH BINH
Phu Vinh
KIEN TUONG
Cai Be
Vinh Long
VINH LONG
Phu Vinh
Soc Trang
Plain of Reeds
KIEN PHONG
SA DEC
PHONG DINH
Can Tho (Binh Tuy)
BA XUYEN
Vinh Loi
Kompong Cham
Banam
Mekong
Takeo
PHNOM PENH
CHAU DOC
AN GIANG
KIEN GIANG
Rach Gia
CHUONG THIEN
BAC LIEU
AN XUYEN
Ca Mau
U Minh Forest
Dao Phu Quoc
Con Son

Song Sai Gon
Phuoc Vinh
Long Binh
Phuoc Vinh

CHAZAUD

edited by Bernard Edelman

for THE NEW YORK VIETNAM VETERANS

MEMORIAL COMMISSION

Dear America
LETTERS HOME FROM VIETNAM

PUBLISHED BY POCKET BOOKS NEW YORK

To those who served
and those who sacrificed,
To those who wept
and those who waited,
Because of the Vietnam War.

POCKET BOOKS, a division of Simon & Schuster, Inc.,
1230 Avenue of the Americas, New York, N.Y. 10020

Contents

Foreword

As I read the letters in this book I could see the men I served with in Vietnam fifteen years ago, their faces dirty and sweaty and plastered with big grins that hid the fear. And I could hear the true voices of Vietnam again—not filtered by the media, not smoothed out in recollection, but direct, raw, personal: the way it was. These letters made me sad, they made me laugh, they made me proud; many were hard to read without tears. Like the young Americans who wrote them, these letters are variously naïve and wise, sentimental and bitter, frightened and boastful, noble and ordinary. I doubt if anyone who reads this remarkable book—who listens to the voices—will ever think the same way about the Vietnam War or its veterans again.

With the possible exception of his rifle, nothing was more important to an American in Vietnam than his mail. In 1969 I was a Marine lieutenant commanding a platoon in the mountains west of Da Nang. Twice a week a helicopter would bring out the red mail sack. The squad leaders would pass out the mail to their men along with a running commentary: "Hey, Rinaldi, your girl changed her perfume—what's the matter, she don't love you no more?" Each package would be shaken, its contents the subject of often obscene conjecture; if it contained cookies or other edibles, etiquette required that it be immediately shared and given a rating. Men who received consistently low ratings were encouraged—not subtly—to instruct their correspondents to improve the quality of their mailings. Everyone knew who was getting mail and who wasn't, who was having trouble at home, whose girlfriend was trying to let him down gently. It was a special time, private but also communal.

Usually we wrote our letters late in the afternoon, after we had made our way to a new position and dug our foxholes, in that violet hour before the patrols went out and the night became the enemy. When I came in from the mountains to work in division headquarters I was able to type my letters neatly; in the mountains I scrawled on paper so damp from humidity and sweat that the pen went right through the paper. Sometimes paper was not available; I remember writing letters on C-ration cartons.

Since buying stamps in such conditions would have been inconvenient, and carrying them around in the jungle would have made them useless in any case, we were given the privilege of sending our letters without postage. Next to the extra $65 a month we received for bearing the risks of combat for our nation, it was the greatest benefit (the list was not long) of being in Vietnam. We simply wrote "Free" where a stamp ordinarily would be affixed, and the letter would speed on its way. That little bit of power always made me feel special, as if the vast resources of the government were, for a change, at my command. Some of the men in my platoon let that power go to their heads. They would write five, ten, even twenty letters a day, with twenty-seven, I recall, being the record. When I left Vietnam, I was glad to take a real bath, to wear tennis shoes instead of boots, and to watch the scars from my leech bites fade away. But it took a while before I accepted having to buy stamps.

We addressed the letters to Peach and Darling and Red and Widu; and to Mom and Dad and to Folks. We wrote a brother or sister, or maybe a buddy. One of the most poignant letters in this book was written by Marine Lieutenant Tyrone Sidney Pannell to his newborn daughter. If we didn't have a wife or regular girlfriend, we might simply pick out any girl we knew and write to her constantly. The important thing was to write. In my platoon, for example, most of the men were still teenagers, unformed and vulnerable, away from home for the first time. Letters were the bridge between Vietnam and America, between what the war had made them and what they had been before. At times those two worlds were so dramatically different that it was nearly impossible to span the gap.

I remember once, after an operation deep into the mountains, my platoon returned exhausted and numb, that unfocused stare in our eyes. I sat down on the ground, my fatigues soaked and filthy, and began responding to a letter asking for suggestions on who should get what Christmas presents. But instead of resenting such an incongruous task, I welcomed it. The more mundane the details, the more absorbed in them I could become. My parents, like everyone with a child or a husband or a father in Vietnam, were hostages to the war, waiting and not knowing, half expecting the phone call at night or the knock on the door that would mean their worst fears had come true. Letters were the one way to keep up their own defenses against that fear, and so they filled letter after letter with the details of their daily lives. At times they would apologize for boring me with such "little things," but it was the little things that kept all of us planted on the ground. We were caught up in war, a very big thing, and only the little things made sense.

The letters in this book were not meant to be their author's last letters (as were those in *Last Letters from Stalingrad,* an equally memorable collection from the doomed German Sixth Army in World War II), but some of them turned out to be. They were not intended for a larger audience; they are unselfconscious and intensely specific. And they are constantly filled with plans, as if we believed that if we talked enough about the future we would have one. "When I get out," wrote Private First Class Louis E. Willett, who was later awarded the Congressional Medal of Honor, "I guess I'll take it easy for a couple of months and just mess around. Been thinking of buying a car and just riding around the country to see what there is and forget the Army."

These letters are so powerful in part because we know what the author does not: we know what Fate has in store. Louis Willett will never get to ride around the country. Tyrone Pannell will never see his newborn daughter again. But these simple dreams have a fresh power, even some twenty years later. Some things don't erode with the passage of time. The honest, fundamental human emotions of men at war is one of them.

Not all the letters are so poignant. Some letters contain tales of heroism, told matter-of-factly, in language that underscores the uncommon nature of the deed. There are wonderfully improbable moments, like this description by Thomas Pellaton, a Sp/5 with the 101st Airborne Division, of a village clinic: "I went along as security and got to help treat some of the children. We played games with them, went for a walk to the beach, took pictures, in general just loved them up. They stole my watch, but it really didn't matter, because just before leaving I sang for them the 'Largo al Factotum' from the *Barber of Seville*—you know, 'Figaro, Figaro'. . . ."

Other letters, like those from Marion Lee Kempner, a Marine Lieutenant who was killed in 1966, have a high-minded literacy that is reminiscent of letters and poems from World War I. Kempner wrote his great aunt about a red flower, the first plant they had seen all day without thorns. It reminded him of Vietnam, "a country of thorns and cuts, of guns and marauding, of little hope and of great failure. Yet in the midst of it all, a beautiful thought, gesture, or even person can arise among it waving bravely at the death that pours down upon it." But in a few letters the madness at the core of war bursts through, as in this one to the mother of a dead soldier: "The guns don't bother me—I can't hear them anymore. I want to hold my head between my hands and run screaming away from here. . . . I'm hollow, Mrs. Perko. I'm a shell and when I'm scared I rattle." After reading lines like these even Michael Herr's *Dispatches,* with its superbly tuned ear for the reality of the war, seems thin in comparison.

We were far from home, and we felt forgotten by the country that had sent us. And we were scared—of death, certainly, but also of being abandoned. It was considered bad luck to talk about the fear of death, so it tended to be absorbed into the other fear, into worrying about the women we had left behind. Each mail call, like the trails we walked down, could be booby-trapped; a Dear John letter was as feared as a mine. Both of these fears came together in this letter from Marine PFC Raymond Griffiths, who was killed in action a few weeks later: "Oh, and one more favor. I'd like the truth now. Has Darlene been faithful to me? I know she's been dating guys, but does she still love me best? Thanks for understanding. See ya if it's God's will. I have to make it out of Vietnam though, cause I'm lucky. I hope. Ha, ha. Miss ya, Love, Ray." In a few short sentences that letter says everything, explains what made all of us whistle in the dark: "I'm lucky. I hope. Ha, ha."

To help calm those fears, we had only each other or our superior officers, who often were no older than we were. Marine Lieutenant Don Jacques, who was later killed at Khe Sanh, wrote home describing how he had counseled a Marine, who was nineteen, about his wife, who was eighteen: "If he knew I was only twenty, I wonder if he would have come." I spent hours trying to explain to my young Marines why they were in Vietnam and most of their friends weren't. It was not easy, but it was no more difficult than explaining why their girlfriends had left them. They were both variations on the soldier's eternal question: "Why me?"—why have I been brought to this, why has this happened to me and not to everyone else? These were among the mysteries we contemplated on watch late at night, when the stars were clear and now and then a satellite would streak across the sky. We did not often share those questions in our letters; only someone who was there, with us, would have understood.

The emotions of war often swing wildly from comradeship and exhilaration to shame and guilt. Sp/4 George Olsen reflects on the extreme demands of combat: "The frightening thing about it all is that it is so very easy to kill in war. There's no remorse, no theatrical 'washing of the hands' to get rid of nonexistent blood, not even any regrets. When it happens, you are more afraid [than] you've ever been in your life. . . . You kill because that little SOB is doing his best to kill you and you desperately want to live, to go home, to get drunk or walk down the street on a date again."

But in other letters it becomes clear that the battles going on around us were matched by the battles we were fighting with ourselves. In two of the letters that Lieutenant Jim Simmen wrote to his brother, a parish priest, he first compares war to hunting. "I know I'm after souls, but I get all excited when I see a VC, just like when I see a deer. I go ape firing at him. . . . Last night I killed and everyone has been patting me on the back. . . . It isn't all that horrifying." A few months later Jim felt differently: "[I] feel kind of ashamed of the way I've thought and acted over here. I realize that I've actually enjoyed some of the things I've done which would be repulsive to a healthy mind. . . . When one starts to enjoy the sickness of war, he is sick. . . ."

For young officers the responsibility could be an agony. When I first joined my new platoon I was afraid that I might be wounded or killed, but mainly I was afraid I wouldn't be able to do my job. Everyone on the hill where the helicopter deposited me knew more about Vietnam than I did, but I was supposed to be their leader. Nothing in civilian life mattered. I couldn't show them my résumé. Marine Lieutenant Brian Sullivan, who now teaches history, captured this feeling of helplessness in a letter to his wife: "Oh, Darling, it's been so unreal. . . . These last days were just so filled with fighting, marching, thinking, all the time thinking, 'Am I doing it right? . . . How can I be sure I haven't led us into a trap?'"

In some letters the sense of duty is palpable. Most of the men in my platoon had volunteered. They didn't believe in the war, the way policy-makers might have. They were simply patriotic young Americans; there was a war going on, and they decided to do their part. This is Marine Captain Rod Chastant describing to his mother why he decided to extend his stay in Vietnam by another six months. "It is not easy to say I opt for six more months of heat, sand, and shooting. . . . Here there is a job to be done. There are moral decisions made almost every day. My experience is invaluable. This job requires a man of conscience. . . . I am needed here, Mom. . . . The incompetency and the wrongs committed in Vietnam are staggering. But through it all I see a little light."

Rod Chastant never made it home; he was killed a month into his extension. But that light, that not so little light, shines again in *Dear America.* He and the other Americans in this book were the best we had, doing the best they could in a difficult and unpopular war. Many of those who came back have done well in the world: in this volume are letters from, among others, a Yale professor, a deputy New York City parks commissioner, a managing director of Shearson Lehman/American Express, and a maître d' at the Carlyle Hotel. Other veterans have had a harder time putting the war behind them, and still need help and understanding. Almost 60,000 young Americans died there, and their voices will never be heard again. This book reminds us how they sounded, and what they thought. They gave no less than their ancestors at Gettysburg, Normandy, or Iwo Jima. Who knows what they might have accomplished, the families they might have had, the lives they might have led?

So long, good buddies. And thanks for leaving a bit of yourselves behind, to remind us of who you were. We really miss you.

William Broyles, Jr.

Preface

Of the 2.9 million men and women who served in Vietnam during the war, New York City provided one of the largest contingents. They came from every neighborhood in the city, from all ethnic groups and all walks of life. The service that they saw was as varied as their backgrounds, and the vast majority of them performed their duties to the best of their ability.

How, then, could we fail to recognize the contribution of our relatives, neighbors, and friends who sacrificed so much? Understandably, many Americans wanted to forget about the war once it was over, but in the process they forgot about those who were sent to fight it. Yet our common responsibility to these veterans remains clear, and as mayor of New York City I decided it was time to do something about it.

In 1981, I appointed a task force of 27 leading citizens of this city to develop a framework for a fitting memorial to our Vietnam-era veterans. This task force recommended a twofold tribute: first, a physical memorial to honor the service and sacrifice of those who answered their country's calling during the difficult time of the Vietnam War, one that would combine an acknowledgment of those who fell with a celebration of life for those who returned; second, a jobs program, which we call our "living memorial," to address the continuing employment problems of many of our Vietnam veterans, tailored to their specific needs.

To implement these recommendations, I established the New York Vietnam Veterans Memorial Commission in the fall of 1982. One hundred citizens from New York City, over half of whom are Vietnam-era veterans, volunteered their time and effort to raise $1 million from private donations to realize these two elements of a truly significant memorial. In fact, in excess of $3 million was raised.

The commission sponsored a design competition which attracted over 1,100 entrants from 46 states and 6 foreign countries. The winning design was submitted by a three-member team from New York City. It survived the rigors of a two-phased blind competition, including scrutiny by a distinguished professional jury and final approval by the commission's Design Committee, almost all of whom are Vietnam veterans. This design is a translucent glass-block structure 66 feet long and 16 feet high, etched with excerpts of letters sent to and from servicemen during the Vietnam War. This beautiful and moving monument was built in Vietnam Veterans Plaza—formerly Jeannette Park at 55 Water Street— and dedicated on May 7, 1985, the tenth anniversary of the official end of the Vietnam era. On that day, New York City opened its heart to the country's Vietnam veterans. More than 25,000 vets paraded across the Brooklyn Bridge and down lower Broadway—the "Canyon of Heroes"— to the cheering of a million New Yorkers who paved the route with tons of "ticker tape." This welcome home was long overdue.

In addition, the commission sponsored a detailed study of the unemployment and underemployment problems of the city's Vietnam veterans. From this study, a model for the jobs program was developed with achievable goals and with opportunities for expansion and refunding in the years to come. Proceeds from this book will go toward funding this program.

The New York Vietnam Veterans Memorial Commission will remain as an extraordinary example of how a community can begin to heal the wounds inflicted by the Vietnam War and to pay back the debt it owes to those who have suffered and sacrificed in its service.

As mayor of this city and as a veteran of this country, I am proud to have been a part of this effort.

Edward I. Koch
Mayor

Acknowledgments

This book is the product of a unique collaboration of many individuals who contributed freely of their time, talent, and energy. Those who worked at the core of the process should be commended for their patience, sensitivity, and belief that this book could and should be published. All involved warrant mention. (It should be noted that commission members and friends worked without compensation, and often around the clock, in order to see the book completed in the time allotted.)

Our thanks go first to Edward I. Koch, mayor of the city of New York, who established the task force from which the New York Vietnam Veterans Memorial Commission was born. Without his interest and initiative the commission, the memorial, and this book would not have been created.

We thank our fellow members of the commission's Executive Committee, who gave unselfishly of their time and talents to bring the goals of the commission to reality: Donald Trump and Scott Higgins, co-chairs of the commission, for their leadership and overall support; Jim Noonan and Bob Patterson, co-chairs of the Program Committee, for pulling together the employment study and jobs program; Jay Connolly and Steve Mann, co-chairs of the Finance Committee, for raising the money to pay for everything; Catherine Saxton and Ed Vick, co-chairs of the Communications Committee, who, along with the creative minds at Ogilvy & Mather, continue to get the word out about what we are doing; Marina Kellen-Gundlach and Bob Ptachik, co-chairs of the Adminin-stration Committee, for overseeing the day-to-day operations of the commission; Frank Havlicek, our counsel, not only for his work on our legal matters, but for being instrumental in setting up the mayor's task force; and Steve Mersereau, our treasurer, for keeping track of our money.

The collective wisdom and energy of the members of the commission cannot be overstated. Particular mention goes to William Broyles, Jr., and Andrew Phelan, both veterans of Vietnam and members of the jury for our National Design Competition, who were the first to recognize the importance of the letters themselves and the possibility of a book during the competition.

To the winning designers of the memorial—architects William Fellows and Peter Wormser, and their literary consultant/writer Joseph Ferrandino, himself a Vietnam veteran—we are indebted for the quality and ingenuity of their vision.

Several people played key roles in transforming this book from idea to reality. Commission member Neil Leinwohl designed the posters announcing the competition and calling for material for the book. David Dunlap and his editors at the *New York Times* printed a generous article which not only helped announce the quest for letters but sparked interest from several publishers. One of these was W. W. Norton & Company, our hardcover publisher, which discerned the potential for a significant volume and has been more than generous in permitting most of the profits from this book to go to the commission. Our special thanks to Bob Patterson, who represented the commission during the negotiations that led to the selection of that publisher.

Three individuals who should be singled out are Bernard Edelman, a member of the commission and editor of this book, Peter Mahoney, then the commission's deputy director, and Kathleen Anderson, our editor at Norton. Bernie devoted his time and editorial abilities to mold the raw material of letters into a workable manuscript; he did beaucoup work in titi time and didn't didi when asked to do this job. Peter was the administrator who coordinated the entire process. He ensured that the letters kept coming in, that they were logged, and that the information was verified. It was his persistant and sensitive research that gave form and perspective to the letters. Kathy gave selflessly. Her editorial competence, judgments, and exhortations not only helped pull this book together but added immeasurably to its texture and flow. *Dear America* could not have been completed without their dedication, insights, and commitment to the intrinsic value of these writings.

Thanks go also to Bob Ptachik, whose comments and research—and wisdom in recommending our editor—cannot be minimized, and to Jim

Hebron, then the commission's executive director, whose judgments and suggestions added to the substance of this book.

We also acknowledge other members of the commission not previously mentioned who participated in all phrases of the memorial competition, from determining the philosophy to choosing the winner, and those friends who, along with commission members, read through the manuscript and offered all manner of constructive criticism: Patrick Antiorio, Michael Cunningham, Herb Dubose, Paul Friedberg, Bob Georgia, Chaim Gross, Tim Gunn, Patti Harris, Martha G. Hernandez, John Hightower, Bob Holcomb, Margaret Hunt, Edmund Janiszewski, Darylynn Kenny, Annette Kuhn, Bill Lacy, Leon Littles, Phil Moulaison, George Raustiala, Jim Resti, Barry Rosen, Nancy Rosen, Arthur Rosenblatt, Lelia Ruckenstein, Margaret Ruddick, Larry Schultz, Stuart Schwartz, William Simon, Robin Smith, Susan Smith, Howie Spielman, Randy Stein, Mark Stewart, Pam Tice, Jose Velez, Ursula von Rydingsvard, Bob West, John Willenbecher, and Gary Zarr. We particularly appreciate the contributions of those veterans who traveled back in time and relived some of their own experiences in Vietnam as a result of this process.

Henry J. Stern, commissioner, and the employees of the New York City Department of Parks and Recreation deserve a special note of thanks for their encouragement, especially those who provided administrative support during the preparation of the manuscript: Priscilla Baber, Suzanne Bachman, Donald Bloiso, and Michael Stewart. From Norton we are grateful to our manuscript editor Carol Flechner for her expeditious work on the manuscript; to Safi Newman for her careful readings, to Milly Matacia, our typist, and to Mary Cunnane for coming up with the title. We also acknowledge the efforts of Mary Flynn, the commission's secretary; Marnie Nicoll, our photo researcher; Russell Burrows, for his kindness and generosity in providing us with photographs taken by his father, Larry Burrows; and Gerard White, of the Medal of Honor Society, for his interest and assistance.

We extend our special thanks and appreciation to Joseph Bresnan, our technical adviser and mentor at the Parks Department, whose enthusiasm and advice during the entire process were invaluable; to Pat Mulhearn, counsel to the mayor, for his advocacy and unwavering support of our goals; to Herb Rickman, special adviser to the mayor, for his quiet yet significant contributions; and to Ellen Leary, for her aid and comfort, particularly to our editor, during the editing process.

Our very special thanks go to those men and women who shared their letters, their poetry, their emotions, and their memories with the commission so that others may better appreciate the human dimensions of the Vietnam War.

Robert D. Santos
Stewart G. Long
Co-Chairmen
Design Committee

Introduction

Darling, believe me, I try my best not to skip a day in writing to you. If my mail means as much to you as yours does to me then I know how you feel when the mailbox is empty. Whether or not I get a letter determines if it's a good day or not.
> —Captain Joseph Bush, Jr.,
> in a letter home to
> his wife, 25 June 1968

Please, my son, try to write as often as you can—even just a few words from you will help me and ease my tension and my mind. Every day I look for mail from you and every day I don't receive any is a disappointment. I know when you are out you can't write, but yet I keep looking for word from you.
> —Mrs. Anne Bramson, in
> a letter to her son in
> Vietnam, 9 August 1970

There are no simple truths about the Vietnam War. It was a war that embodied the turbulence and ferment of the '60s. Young men fought an elusive enemy for a cause that wrenched apart the nation the longer it dragged on, a cause obscured, finally, by the absence of victory. In Vietnam, the illusion of American military omnipotence was shattered. It was our longest war, costing 58,000 American lives and 300,000 wounded. It succeeded only in leaving a legacy of bitterness and unacknowledged sacrifice.

For the soldiers, correspondence to and from home—contact with the World—was an outlet and a refuge. "Your letters are sanity in an insane world," one GI wrote to his pen pal. "How much I've relied on getting a note of concern, a phrase that conveys a thought of interest, a word that asks of well-being."

In base camps and foxholes, in sandbagged bunkers and air-conditioned offices, soldiers wrote about what they saw and what they did, what they felt and what they yearned for: the physical trials and travails of combat; the psychic torment and turmoil of loss; the divisions over strategy and tactics; the distress borne of dislocation and loneliness. They wrote to mothers and fathers, brothers and buddies, sisters and sweethearts and wives. Their observations are honest, more likely to conceal than reveal, to downplay than dramatize the gore and the carnage they experienced. "Don't worry, Mom," they'd write, just before going on a combat assault. "This will be a 'hot' LZ tomorrow, so everyone is writing letters home," Lieutenant Fred Downs wrote to his wife. "Not only won't we get a chance to write for a while, but there is a good chance some of my men won't come back."

In their letters, GIs might describe a fire fight almost matter-of-factly, listing KIAs and WIAs—those killed and wounded in action—like so many baseball scores. They might recount treks through the jungle, the caches of enemy arms and materiel recovered, or their night drinking "Saigon Tea" with a bar girl on Tu Do Street. Whatever their theme, these writings evoke the war in a way other media do not, offering exuberance and weariness, courage and confusion, bravado and fear. While some soldiers give graphic accounts of the spillage of combat, most ruminate on its emotional aftermath. They relate the routines in base camp, the uncertainties of patrol, and the hazards of weapons modern and primitive. Even in what they withheld they are telling: "My letters are mirrors of what I see," one GI wrote to his mother. "If you see death in my letter, multiply it 10 times—that's what I see."

For most soldiers, news from home supported and sustained them through their tour. "Mom, I appreciate all your letters," Rod Chastant, a Marine later killed in action, wrote. "I appreciate your concern that some of the things you write about are trivial, but they aren't trivial to me. I'm eager to read anything about what you or the family are doing. You can't understand the importance these 'trivial' events take on out here. [They] help keep me civilized. For a while, as I read your letters, I am a normal person. I'm not killing people, or worried about being killed. While I read your letters, I'm not carrying guns or grenades. Instead I am going ice skating with David or walking through a department store to exchange a lamp shade. It is great to know your family's safe."

It is difficult, if not impossible, to estimate how many millions of pieces of corresondence were written by the men and women who served in Southeast Asia. In response to publicized requests from the New York Vietnam Veterans Memorial Commission for material from veterans, excerpts of which are etched onto New York's memorial to Vietnam veterans in lower Manhattan, some 3,000 letters, tapes, poems, newspaper clippings, petitions, journal entries, and even a sound track of the 1968 Tet Offensive were submitted by 600 individuals—veterans, their families, their friends, even former girlfriends and ex-wives. The overwhelming number of them were letters sent home from Vietnam—hence the title of this volume. Considerably fewer were letters sent *to* Vietnam, perhaps because few of these—and certainly not the "Dear Johns"— survived the war.

After weeks of sifting and culling, 208 pieces written by 125 people were finally chosen. One-third of these authors are deceased. They were either killed in combat or died subsequent to their service in Vietnam; because they died, their letters were cherished perhaps all the more by their loved ones, who chose to share them with the commission. Just fewer than half the letter writers either grew up or now live in New York; the rest come from exactly half of the states of the union, with California, New Jersey, Connecticut, Pennsylvania, Massachusetts, and Texas particularly well represented. No pretense is made that these represent a complete account of the concerns, opinions, and perceptions of soldiers in the war zone; letters from doctors and nurses alone, few of which were submitted for consideration, could probably run a volume.

To ensure that publication of this book would coincide wtih the tenth anniversary of the official end of the war—7 May 1975—and the dedication of the New York Vietnam Veterans Memorial, the editing process was compressed into 10 weeks. Two parameters were set in selecting the material: all correspondence must have been penned during the war; each should provide descriptions or psychological insights that would in some way amplify the human dimensions of Vietnam experiences.

In editing the letters, the desire always was to retain their immediacy and essence while eliminating repetitious, private, and tangential information. To avoid cluttering the text and at the same time to promote its flow, elipses have been used only when more than two sentences from the original piece of correspondence were deleted. Editorial license was exercised to standardize spelling (*Vietnam*, not *Viet Nam* or *Viet-Nam*; *Da Nang*, not *DaNang* or *Danang*), to correct spelling (the misspelling most encountered: schrapnel), and to indent paragraphs where appropriate.

As affinities between letters began to emerge, chapters suggested themselves. The chapters were put into a sequence that would relate a year's tour in Vietnam. The letters were then arranged to create allusive connections between them. Biographical notes, which identify the writer, appear at the end of each letter or poem; the amount of information varies according to what the commission has been able to obtain. In the case of writers who have several letters in the book, biographical notes have been given at first mention and then, to avoid repetition, in abbreviated forms thereafter. Due to the nature and organization of the work, these decisions were made on an individual basis; it was impossible to establish a single rule for the book as a whole. To aid the reader, an index of contributors has been provided.

Throughout this volume, words perhaps unfamiliar to the general reader frequently appear. Vietnam offered a new language—a marriage of colloquialisms, military terminology, and bastardized Vietnamese: *hooch* and *Huey*, *body bag* and *boom boom*, *medevac* and *track*, *gook* and *dink*, *didi mow* and *dinky dow*. These words, if not explained in the letter itself, are defined in the glossary. Other terms and acronyms that appear only in the context of a single letter are defined in brackets.

"I just realized today I've learned a whole new language over here, and I don't mean Vietnamese," Captain David Forrest, a psychiatrist stationed at Long Binh, wrote to his wife, "A GI had come into my office and was expounding his difficulties, and I was wondering if anyone back home would comprehend.

> *I'm with the Lurps at Bien Hoa, extended for my didi early out, and been humping the boonies titi time since I got back from leave in the World. Been humping an M-60 with the grunts, blowing claymores at the gooks, and can't sleep because of the incoming. I just can't hack it. NCOs are all messing over me. They say I'm stoned with the soul brothers beaucoup times. Every time I didi for a short-time girl, I get harassment, but same-same if I don't. My CO gives me an Article 15 and a bust for titi reasons and says he'll see me in LBJ. Now the dude wants to 212 me!*

Translated, this reads: "I'm with a Long Range Reconnaissance Patrol unit based at Bien Hoa. I increased the length of my tour of duty in Vietnam in order to get released from the military a few months earlier than I'm supposed to. I've been on patrol in the jungle a little since I returned from leave in the United States. I've been carrying a machine gun with the infantry, setting off antipersonnel mines at the enemy, and can't sleep because of the motars and rockets being fired at my position at night. I just can't do it any more. Noncommissioned officers are harassing me. They said I get high with black soldiers many times. Every time I leave to go to a prostitute, I get hassled, and I get hassled even if I don't. My commanding officer gives me nonjudicial punishment and a reduction in rank for small reasons and says he'll see me in Long Binh Jail. Now he wants to give me a psychiatric discharge!"

It should also be noted that much of what was communicated orally in Vietnam, especially the humor and some of the more expansive idioms, did not make it into letters—at least not those received by the commission. "Don't mean nothin' ," GIs would mutter, perhaps about the death of a buddy, when, of course, it meant everything. "Nevah happen," they'd say, when they knew something wouldn't happen but hoped that it might. "There it is," they'd say, pointing out a truth so obvious, so inclusive, that it didn't require explanation.

Today, 10, 15, even 20 years since these letters were written, Vietnam veterans still slip into the language. The war hardly seems so long removed. For those still affected by Vietnam, and for those who, as the girlfriend of a veteran wrote to the commission, "were either too young to fully understand what was going on, or old enough to know all too well," it is hoped that this volume is true to its sources and that it adds some illumination to "the human side of the war. Perhaps," as Debbie Bernfeld wrote, these letters "will help to answer so many questions about it, so many years later. At least we can hope to elevate the level of consciousness of a war that touched, and will continue to touch, so many lives."

While the conduct and strategies of the war are still being argued, and will be for a long while, there is little disagreement that its veterans were treated shabbily upon their return. "[They] marched home to furled flags and silent drums," wrote Joan Henn in a note accompanying several letters from her brother. Indeed most veterans felt scorned. Perhaps worse, they felt ignored by all but their families after one of the most intense experiences of their lives. In the jungle one day, they were back home 48 hours later. Little had changed since they'd been gone—except them. Most returned in isolation, quick to shed their fatigues and Class A uniforms and try to forget the war which, of course, they couldn't. There was no "detroxification" from the stresses of combat, from the sheer presence of death and devastation. Institutional response to their needs was sluggish at best, nonexistent at worst. There was no period of national mourning for those who died, no outpouring of thanks for those who returned, no welcoming embrace by a grateful nation. Some were ashamed of their service and wouldn't, or couldn't, talk about it. Instead, "Vieterans" became a symbol of the many conflicts and controversies surrounding America's involvement in Vietnam. The burden of their untold hurts and unexpurgated emotions often fell only on those they loved, who bore the equal weight of helplessness.

The Vieteran was quickly stereotyped. Because the war was so warped, the illogic went, its soldiers must have been, too. In movies and on television shows, the drug-crazed baby killer, consumed by guilt, filled with anger, unable to love, become the model for the combat vet. He was a victim out of control. This image was buttressed by too many newspaper headlines blaring, "Vietnam Vet Slays Wife and Self," as if Vietnam alone accounted for all subsequent actions. In certain cases, it may have. For the majority, however, no one knows for sure.

There can be little argument that "emotonally, the Vietnam War has been our toughest war," as Pete Dawkins, the soldier and scholar who distinguished himself during two tours in Vietnam, recently told the *New York Times*. "It really tore at the fabric of society. We're only seeing part of the healing process now. There is a growing perception that, regardless of your view of the wisdom of it, many served proudly and loyally." The reality, as another veteran, Bill Becker, put it in a letter to the commission, was that "we were just a bunch of kids hoping that we had a life ahead of us."

Certainly, there are veterans with problems—severe and lingering problems—which stem at least in part from their service in Vietnam, in part from their reception when they came home. Studies have been conducted attesting to the dimensions of personal tragedies induced by the war, the eruptions of rage and self-destruction, from what one psychiatrist calls "sub-clinical malaise" to post-traumatic stress disorder, from criminal acts to suicide. The purpose here is not to recite case studies; these are documented in other sources. But what should be noted, because it is so often overlooked, is that most veterans have been able to build on their experiences in Vietnam. Their lives belie the stereotype. For every Vieteran who has had difficulty readjusting, dozens of others have thrived.

None, of course, has forgotten. Vietnam is not easily erased from memory. Dick Strandberg, who served as a Navy lieutenant commanding a river patrol boat in the Mekong Delta, is now an artist living and painting in Arizona. "I guess I came to believe I was invincible, having escaped death as many times as I did," he reflects. "It's a wonder I wasn't killed over there. You would never believe some of the absolutely insane chances I took." Today, he writes, "there are two people in this body of mine—the crazy young fool back there in 1967-68, who keeps that year alive—vividly alive—17 years later; and the older man, now 41, trying to live a life separate from the Vietnam experience. Rereading these old letters triggers all sorts of things in me. But most it leads me to wonder what I would say to that kid now—*now* that I am old enough to be that kid's father."

Perhaps because we have been so long caught up in arguing the wisdom of the war, as a nation we have only belatedly come to recognize the sacrifices of those who were sent to fight. To this end, the letters and poems in this volume are tools for contemplation, of value in part because they illustrate, without artifice or exaggeration, what it was like to be a soldier—a "grunt," a medic, a clerk or a nurse—in Vietnam; in part, because they express what it is like to be a soldier in *any* war. They are, perhaps, more telling, more revealing, than the many histories, novels, and memoirs of the Vietnam era.

I would like to conclude with a personal note. First, my thanks to Robert Santos for his trust and confidence in me and his vision for this volume, and to Peter Mahoney for the significance and sensitivity of his contributions. Second, I am a member of the commission, a veteran of Vietnam. I did not spend my tour "humping the boonies." I traveled through Vietnam in 1970, collecting material for stories for the information office to which I was assigned. Most of these were censored. But I saw and felt a lot of the hurt and anger and confusion that seemed to fill the ranks of GIs there, and I see how Vietnam continues to permeate the lives of its veterans and their loved ones. It is for them that I have devoted my efforts on his book.

Bernard Edelman

If you are able,
save for them a place
inside of you
and save one backward glance
when you are leaving
for the places they can
no longer go.
Be not ashamed to say
you loved them,
though you may
or may not have always.
Take what they have left
and what they have taught you
with their dying
and keep it with your own.
And in that time
when men decide and feel safe
to call the war insane,
take one moment to embrace
those gentle heroes
you left behind.

—Major Michael Davis O'Donnell
1 January 1970
Dak To, Vietnam

Michael O'Donnell, from Springfield, Illinois, was a helicopter pilot assigned to the 52nd Aviation Battalion, 17th Aviation Group, 1st Aviation Brigade, based at Dak To and Pleiku. On 24 March 1970, attempting to rescue eight soldiers, his chopper was shot down. He and three crew members were declared missing in action. In 1977, he was promoted to major. A year later, he was officially declared killed in action. He was posthumously awarded the Distinguished Flying Cross, the Air Medal, the Bronze Star, and the Purple Heart.

Dear America

1
"Cherries":
First Impressions

We came 10,000 miles, almost 3 million of us, to fight America's longest war. When we arrived—on the beach at Da Nang, at the bustling air terminal of Tan Son Nhut, in the baking heat of Cam Ranh Bay—we were trim and eager, jaunty and scared. But mostly, we were young. White and Black, Hispanic and Native American, Guamian and Hawaiian, the majority of us were not yet out of our teens. "Cherries" we were called, and "Newbies" and "FNGs"— "Fuckin' New Guys"—by troops hardened and made less sanguine, perhaps, by just a few months in the bush. Like them, we would age —bust our cherries—quickly.

During the rapid build-up of American forces in the wake of the 1964 Gulf of Tonkin resolution, entire units were shipped to Vietnam. Some were greeted by "friendlies" bearing wreathes of flowers, others by sniper fire. Later, though, most of us cherries were sent as replacements, to be assigned individually to units after arriving in country. Once assigned, we plunged into the routines of our jobs, slogging through jungles and rice paddies; skying over land cratered and defoliated, lush and green, in helicopters and jet fighters and bombers; saving lives of the traumatically injured in evacuation hospitals; cooking and clerking, writing reports and clearing land from the Delta to the DMZ.

We soon found ourselves caught up, as Lieutenant Robert Salerni put it, "in a war of contrasts in a land of contrasts," where few things were as they seemed. The Vietnamese were at once friendly and deceptive, alluring and treacherous. The weather was broiling and chilling, dusty and muddy. Even the language was different: titi and boo koo, claymores and bangalores, dust-offs and flechettes, Hueys and Willy Pete, AK and AO.

We would get to know our unit's AO—area of operations— understanding the war in terms of our time and place in it. And 365 days later—30 more if you were a Marine—as we were about to head back to "the World," to the United States, aboard our Freedom Birds, we'd look with empathy at the cherries who were taking our place.

18 April 67

Dear Dad,

I am writing this letter to you at your office because I want you to tell Mom in your own words. I didn't think writing home would get anything straight. Well here it is—

We have been told that our whole company will be shipping to Vietnam after AIT [Advanced Infantry Training]. We will get a two-week leave, of course, and after that we will go.

We are in the third training brigade. It is the only brigade at Jackson training for Vietnam. Our company commander and our battalion and brigade commanders told us that there is no sense trying to fool ourselves, we are going for sure. The only thing that makes me mad is how do they expect you to tell your parents. They act as though it is an everyday experience, and that we should feel that way. I don't mind going, but there are some guys here who just won't make it, and I don't think they will make it out alive. Tell Mom I wished I could have told her myself, but I just didn't know how.

Your son,
Bob

P.S. Tell her not to worry. It's nothing I can't handle.

Sp/4 Robert Devlin served with the 71st Infantry Detachment (Long Range Reconnaissance Patrol), attached to the 199th Light Infantry Brigade, based at Long Binh, from July 1967 to July 1968. He is now associate director of Open Arms, Inc., an outpatient program for alcoholics. He lives in Haverstraw, New York.

— ☆ —

Wednesday
[25 February 1970]

Dear Pete—

After you hung up last night I felt very bad because [I] could tell from your voice that you were way down. And it made me feel bad that there was nothing I could do to help but offer advice—and advice is something you can do without.

But please, Pete, don't do anything foolish. You are like me and have a very bad habit of doing foolish things to help ease the hurt. Do as her mother says. Ignore her, hard as it seems—one thing a girl can't stand is being ignored. Maybe she just doesn't want to tie herself down while you're over there.

And, too, God forbid anything should happen to you. Maybe she feels she'll be less hurt this way. Give it time. Things will work out; they always do. What is the old saying, "Time heals all wounds"?

Enough advice and lecture. Seriously, though, Pete, please take care of yourself and don't be a hero. I don't need a Medal of Honor winner. I need a son. Take care and write often.

Love,
Mom

Peter Mahoney, a first lieutenant with Mobile Advisory Team 1-44 from March 1970 to February 1971, trained and advised Vietnamese popular and regional forces in Thua Thien province, I Corps. He has been active in veterans' affairs since his discharge. He lives and works in New York City.

— ☆ —

December 5, 1966

Dear Folks,

Arrived at Oakland, California, in good shape. Took regular Army bus to base. Mom: the chow we ate, gulped, is oily, tasteless and mean to me stomach. Went through some processing till Friday and then abruptly left for the trip over.

Stopped at Anchorage, Alaska, for a cool hour, and then a long hop to Tokyo before landing at Saigon's airport: Tan Son Nhut.

The first thing you notice going down the ramp is a heavy, lousy, sweet smell that floods your nose, along with a somewhat dirty feeling all around. Inside the makeshift customs building, the heat you didn't notice before begins to flush your head as sweat starts to flow. Answer a few questions, surrender any guns, knives and drugs, and be quiet, we are told. Ants scramble up the dirty white pillars as we wait.

We then left by bus for Long Binh, 22 miles northeast of Saigon, for more processing. A cruddy place, typical of an Army camp put up in a hurry. Passed through sections of a town that are something like our Coney Island, "honky tonk" with dirt everywhere. Sanitation seems non-existent. Hope better awaits.

Regards,
Rick

Sp/4 Richard Loffler spent November 1966 to October 1967 as a drafts-man and supply clerk with the 36th Signal Battalion, 2nd Signal Group, in Long Binh and Bear Cat. He lives in Little Neck, New York, and works as an architectural draftsman.

— ☆ —

0945 hrs.
Saturday
22 Feb. '69

Dear Mom, Dad & Tom,

I'm now sitting on a bench in the 90th Replacement Battalion compound, waiting for transportation to take me to my unit. I've been assigned to the 20th Engineer Brigade, and may be on my way there by the time I finish this letter.

I arrived at Bien Hoa airbase about noon (Vietnam time) yesterday. The flight over was long, 19 hours air time with stops at Honolulu, Wake Island, and Okinawa. At each stop we were told the correct local time, and were continually setting back our watches. . . .

I'm now waiting at a BOQ [Bachelor Officer Quarters] near Brigade Headquarters, just a short ride away from the replacement center. A Vietnamese woman is ironing fatigues. In about 10 or 15 minutes I'll go to eat chow, after which further transportation is supposed to come to take me down to my smaller unit. It could be anywhere in the III and IV Corps areas of South Vietnam, roughly the area just north of Saigon and extending southward to the Mekong Delta. I won't know till I get there.

1230 hrs.

I've just finished eating, and I'm waiting for transportation. Waiting again—there's plenty of that in the Army every time you report to a new station. Waiting to cash our currency. Waiting to draw equipment. Wait-

ing to be assigned to a unit. Waiting for transportation. And waiting for
further transportation, which is what I'm doing now. . . .

The most immediate evidence of a war going [on] is the presence
everywhere of barbed wire and sand bags, the artillery rounds which you
can hear in the distance, the ever-present helicopters flying overhead. You
see many Vietnamese on their motorcycles, Lambretta scooter-carts, and
bicycles. While riding here on a truck, we passed another army truck
which was loaded with small children who smiled and waved to us.
The kids were accompanied by a GI—I have no idea where they were
going. . . .

This morning I brushed my teeth with a special flouride tooth paste
which is supposed to retard tooth decay for six months. Last night I took
my first weekly anti-malaria pill, and was warned of possible side effects,
which haven't materialized.

Well, in 360 days I'll be home. . . . As I've said already, I'm fine.
Try not to worry too much about me. I know that will be difficult, but
it doesn't do anyone any good. I'll write more often once I know my
address.

Love,
Bobby

*1Lt. Robert Salerni, from Astoria, New York, was a platoon commander
assigned to the 554th Engineer Battalion, 79th Engineer Group, 20th
Engineer Brigade, based at Cu Chi and Nui Ba Den, from February
1969 to February 1970. He is an architect and lawyer in New York
City.*

— ☆ —

7/30/69

Dear Folks,

I'm still here at the 22nd Replacement Center. I'll probably ship out
tonight or tomorrow, where to I don't yet know. Things are still quiet—
no trouble whatsoever. It's really funny seeing guys going home and I'm
just getting here. It's just one big cycle. All the guys I talked to were
infantry. They seem very sad even though they are going home. I guess
they saw a lot. The clerks on the other hand are completely opposite. They

just don't know what the war is really like. As one guy said, "You got to fight it to know it." I hope you are all well. I'll write again when I get a chance.

Billy

Sgt. William Nelson, born and raised in the Bronx, New York, served with Company A, 2nd Battalion, 502nd Infantry, 101st Airborne Division, operating out of Phu Bai, from July 1969 through September 1970. He is an accountant and lives in Putnam, New York.

— ☆ —

27 March 1968

Dear Mom and Dad,

Would you believe I am now officially assigned to a unit? It's taken so long that it's quite a relief. I have a new address that should be permanent. It is:

Company A, 4th Battalion, 3rd Infantry

11th Light Infantry Brigade, APO San Francisco 96217

I don't know if you've sent me any mail yet, but if so it hasn't gotten to me and I doubt that it ever will. But with this address everything should reach me, so no sweat. . . .

I am told that our AO is quite a good one. There is almost no contact with Charlie, and what little there is rarely turns into much of a fight because he runs away. The principal danger here is from mines and booby traps.

From the people I've talked to I've come up with some new ideas on the war. For the most part nobody is particularly wild with patriotic feeling. There are, of course, those who just get a real charge out of killing people. One lieutenant I talked to said what a kick it had been to roll a gook 100 yards down the beach with his machine gun. But most people generate their enthusiasm for two reasons: one is self-preservation—if I don't shoot him, he'll eventually shoot me—and the other is revenge. It's apparently quite something to see a good friend blown apart by a VC booby trap, and you want to retaliate in kind.

While I am able to read *Stars and Stripes* and listen to AFVN radio newscasts, I still feel very cut off from the world outside of Vietnam. I would love it dearly if you would subscribe to *Newsweek* for me. Also, what do you think of Bobby [Kennedy] for president? What about [General William] Westmoreland's new job? What does everything mean?

I now have one last editorial comment about the war and then I'll sign off. I am extremely impressed by almost every report I've heard about the enemy I am about to go and fight. He is a master of guerrilla warfare and is holding his own rather nicely with what should be the strongest military power in the world. But it is mostly his perseverance that amazes me. He works so hard and has been doing so for so long. You've heard of his tunnelling capability? A captured VC said that in coming from North Vietnam down to Saigon, he walked over 200 miles completely underground. Anyone who would dig a 200-mile tunnel and who would still do it after being at war for some 30 years must be right!

> All love,
> Mike

2Lt. Robert C. ("Mike") Ransom, Jr., raised in Bronxville, New York, arrived in Vietnam in March 1968. He was a platoon commander with Company A, 4th Battalion, 3rd Infantry, 11th Light Infantry Brigade, Americal Division, operating out of Chu Lai. He died after two months in country, eight days after he was wounded by shrapnel from a mine. He was 23 years old.

— ☆ —

> Jan 30, 1968

Chris,

I finally got to my unit yesterday . . . what a life!

I have been assigned to A Battery, 2nd Battalion, 40th Artillery, and further attached to E Company, 2nd Battalion, 3rd Infantry as a forward observer. My job is to advise the company commander on artillery matters and to direct the guns onto enemy positions when we find them. Right now we are positioned on the bank of a beautiful river. The men have been swimming and keeping cool for the last two days.

There are absolutely no comforts in our job. I carry nothing but a razor and a bar of soap for comfort, wear the only clothes we have and wash them in rivers and streams as we cross them. Our mission is to find

VC and kill them. I should be operating like this for the next two months before I get a chance to take a shower and sleep in a bed. . . . At least it is something unique. You were right, I managed to get myself right in the middle of it all.

It was about 100° yesterday, and that sure baked me like a lobster. . . .

I miss you.

Love,
Alan

1Lt. Alan Bourne's unit operated in III Corps, where he served from January 1968 through January 1969. Christina Haskin is his "ex-girlfriend and present friend." He is a real-estate broker in New York City.

— ☆ —

Jan. 25, 1967

Hi, Mom, and all the rest of you lucky people,

. . . I received your writing paper today, as you can tell by this paper. Thank you, you're a doll.

During some training we took before we came down here to the Delta, two men from my company drowned. They got stuck in the mud and couldn't get out because of all the equipment they had on. What a way to go. . . .

I'm writing this letter by moonlight, as my soda is being chilled in the water about me. We are finding ways to give Charlie less and less opportunity to use our things against us. One of his biggest weapons against us is a small can of peanut butter, which he makes a beautiful booby trap out of. At first he used to get a lot of it because a GI won't eat it [since] it makes you thirsty. Well, we now save all we can get because if you add insect repellent, a small can of peanut butter can heat a whole squad's chow. You see, peanut butter burns and insect repellent burns slow—add them together and it will burn for about 10 minutes. Smart. How is everyone? OK I hope. Give everyone my love, and tell Cathy if she wants to marry me, it's OK with me. I'll wait five years if she will skip five. Better make that 10 years. . . .

Love,
Johnny

PFC John Dabonka, from West New York, New Jersey, arrived in Vietnam in December 1966. He served with Company B, 3rd Battalion, 60th Infantry (Riverine), 9th Infantry Division.

— ☆ —

Red,

It was nice to hear from someone for a change. Believe it or not yours was the first letter I got here in Nam so it's something of a landmark. Not that I'm going to pull one of those "lonely soldier away from home through no wish of my own" kinds of crap because I'm where I want to be, quite voluntarily doing what I think is right and am far from being homesick. Still it's nice to get mail—I guess I really am human (sometimes).

Right now I am sitting in a bunker on a radio relay station about 15 miles inland from Chu Lai in the middle of two NVA regiments which are scattered in and around the surrounding area. I'm up here with about 15 other Rangers on the highest hill in I Corps area maintaining radio contact with our teams on the other side of these mountains. It's a bit of a hairy proposition as the hill is expected to be overrun soon.

I've been over here a month and have been in training for this unit ever since getting to Chu Lai. Right now I'm on my first combat operation, which is more or less my graduation exercise as when I come off this hill I officially graduate as a Ranger LRRP [Long Range Reconnaissance Patrol]. This unit is about as different from a normal "grunt" unit as an M-16 is from a blunderbuss, and it would probably shock your delicate little "Peace and Prayers"-type soul to know half the stuff we do. I'm not being sarcastic because all little girls should be like that, but the only reason they can be is because they haven't seen anything like what goes on over here and haven't been exposed to a lot of what really goes on in this world—which is as it should be and I hope it never changes. What we do is wage Charlie's war against Charlie and play holy hell with the Geneva Convention doing it. We operate in from 6- to 12-man teams, with six being the norm and 12 the absolute maximum, deep inside NVA-controlled territory with no friendlies for miles around. Operations range from hunter-killer ambushes to recon patrols to POW snatches. One team of eight actually pulled off an ambush in the middle of an NVA base camp and got away with it. Charlie doesn't like this company, and many men in it are known by name to the VC-NVA, who have actually put prices on their heads. Charlie'd give a lot to get his hands on some of us, but so far he's had no luck as no man from Company G Rangers has ever surrendered.

I'm real proud of the unit, and it looks like I'm going to get into it. I started with 20 men, and 10 of us will graduate. The course is three weeks and is really brutal. When people think of the Army, they think of men being beaten by sergeants, forced-march brutality and hell in general, which is simply not the case. The regular Army is a bunch of clerks doing the same job in the Army that they did outside the Army, but not over here, and not for this outfit. The training is designed to break you if you can be broken, and is amazingly tough. I ran 56 miles in seven days with 65 pounds of equipment and rifle on me. There is no real way to give you a conception of what this is like, but the only reason I'm not out on a hunter-killer strike like some of the students is that I have been effectively crippled for two or three weeks by the training, having worn the skin off my feet so that now I'm hobbling around on bare muscle, which has become infected. Since it would be impossible for me to keep up the pace on a hunter-killer operation, they've given me a support role in a static defensive position for a few days. And to date that has been the extent of my activities in Vietnam.

Yes, I do think our landing on the moon was quite an achievement and internationalism be damned. I'm glad to see the Stars and Stripes up there first. It really gave me quite a thrill, and I sure as hell admire the courage of the men who went. I really sweated out the time between the landing and the takeoff once they were up there. I only hope man doesn't go off and louse up the rest of the solar system with his pollution and family quarrels like he has Mother Earth. . . .

The light is getting bad now—and for obvious reasons there'll be no light after dark, so I've got to sign off. I'll mail this when I get off the hill in two more days. If you've got time and want to, I'll let you write me (honest). All letters accepted cheerfully and answered when possible. When not possible to answer all letters, I'll answer in spirit.

George

Sp/4 George T. Olsen wrote this letter to Rosemary Dresch, a college friend at St. John's University, which was then in Brooklyn, New York. Olsen, who arrived in country in August 1969, was a Ranger with Com-

pany G, 75th Infantry, operating in the area around Chu Lai. He was killed in action on 3 March 1970. He was 23 years old.

— ☆ —

4/21/69

Hi Honey:

Well here I am. We left our training site at Long Binh Saturday afternoon and went to our unit's headquarters. There we received our rifles, ammo, etc. From there we were trucked about 20 miles, through Saigon, and came to a riverbank where boats picked us up and took us downstream. That's where our company is located, along the river's edge.

As soon as I got here, Sunday, I was put in a platoon and found out that my squad was going on an ambush patrol. We [stayed] out that whole night and came in at seven in the morning. We had breakfast, and by 8:30 we had another operation, called a sweep. The whole company goes out looking for VC. Today we went through the rice paddies, and I never saw so much mud in all my life. I was covered with it. We got back about an hour ago, and I took a bath in the river.

I know I might have made you think that I'm really having a hard time, but it really isn't that bad. I took a few pictures, but have to find a place to develop them. . . .

Honey, I miss you more than anything in the world. I'm constantly thinking of you. It seems like I did my whole year here already. I can't wait for the day that I come home to you. Remember, honey, you're my everything.

> Love You Dearly,
> Michael

Sp/4 Michael Romano, raised in New York City, was based at LZ Black-horse in III Corps, where he served as an infantryman with Company B, 2nd Battalion, 3rd Infantry, 199th Light Infantry Brigade, between April 1969 and March 1970. He currently works as a maintenance man for Pepsico and lives in Holmes, New York.

— ☆ —

23 Dec 67

Dear Tom,

Hi! How are you? I hope all is well at home. Everything is OK here. It is now about 4:30 P.M., and it is as hot as hell outside. I am sitting in the squad bunker that we just put the finishing touches on this afternoon. It is nice and cool inside.

We arrived at Qui Nhon the morning of the 19th and took a truck convoy up to Duc Pho the following morning. It was a 4½-hour ride. Snipers shot at us all the way up. . . .

Last night was my first in this bunker on the perimeter. There aren't much VC in the area besides a few snipers which fire at us every night. They never hit anybody—lousy shots. They shot the hell out of a bunker last night with a machine gun. Nobody got hurt, though.

As I look out from my bunker there is about 250 feet of bush and tall grass. It slopes down, as we are on a hill. Then there is a river only about 80 feet wide, and after that rice paddies for a mile. After that you can see the Central Highlands, which is booming all the time. It's safe in the daytime. We stand out in the open or work on the bunker. We can run up and down the hill with no worries. But at night we got to stay in the bunkers as snipers sneak in. They usually shoot from the other side of the river. Last night, while [it was] my turn on watch, I saw one duck behind a bush on this side of the river. I shot once at him and he disappeared. He must've gone back to his tunnel on the other side. The first squad found the tunnel this afternoon. All the VC do around here is try to keep us from getting too much sleep. I sleep soundly when I'm not on watch anyway. I thought this crap would bother me, but it doesn't. He could shoot at this bunker all night for all I care.

My whole squad is in this bunker, and they are all a bunch of screwballs. Eddie is running around now with an insect bomb, cursing the bugs. The mosquitoes that come out at night are man-eaters, but the insect repellent keeps them off. I got a head net too. . . .

Take care and enjoy the holidays. I'll probably be knocking out some beer on Christmas. A pleasure gravely earned.

Dennis

P.S. Send some Kool-Aid. Water here taste like hell.

Cpl. Dennis W. Lane, from Brooklyn, New York, landed in Vietnam on 19 December 1967 with Company A, 4th Battalion, 3rd Infantry, 11th

Light Infantry Brigade. His unit, a component of the Americal Division, operated along the coast in I Corps. He was killed by fragments from a mine explosion on 21 May 1968. He was 21 years old. This letter was written to his brother.

— ☆ —

Ocean View
20 May 68

Dear Folks—

Hope you are well and enjoying springtime in New York. I am having more or less an Arabian summer here. It is 110° today, and a brisk wind is blowing sand all over the place. After this there will only be pools for me, no beaches!

We sleep out on the dunes, and I awoke this morning with about four inches of sand covering me completely. The insects are really unbearable—I have about 42 mosquito bites on my left forearm.

I killed my first "gooks" last night—about 20 of them. I spotted them about 800 meters in front of our position by using a starlight scope, and called in artillery on them. I only had to make one adjustment, and then they were blown away. I took a patrol out and found a lot of blood, but no bodies—for these NVA carry off their dead and wounded. It didn't bother me at all, because self-preservation is the name of the game over here. If I didn't get them, they would have gotten me or somebody else.

Thank God we only have two more days at this place before we go back to Cua Viet for a shower and a cold Coke or something. C-rations three times a day gets very old very fast.

We had a treat yesterday and let the men (and, of course, ourselves) go swimming. No, not in the ocean, but in a crater made by a 2,000-lb. bomb dropped by a B-52 a month ago. The water was cooler than the air by a few degrees. It is not secure enough up here to use the ocean yet, but perhaps after we get our barbed wire in. . . .

This war is so damn frustrating and boring at times that it would try the pope's patience. It is made up of extended periods of boredom interspersed with periods of utter mayhem. . . .

Have to run (would you believe a slow walk?) now. Well, keep in touch.

Love,
Des

Desmond Barry, Jr., was a lieutenant with the 2nd Battalion, 7th Regiment, 1st Marine Division, in northern I Corps from March 1968 through April 1969. He is now an attorney in New York City specializing in aviation law.

— ☆ —

3 April 68

Dear Mom and Dad,

Well, your eldest is now a combat leader. So far I haven't even fired a shot, nor have I been under any sort of fire. Our company is currently involved in an operation to prevent the local rice harvest from falling into VC hands. Our tactic is to remain in a company base during the day, since it is too hot for any long, arduous movement. At night each platoon sends out two or three squad-size ambush patrols.

Two days ago we went on a heliborne combat assault. Our mission was to cordon a village that was suspected of having a platoon of VC hidden in it. It was an extremely well-executed mission. We were airlifted out of our defensive position and then were dropped in around the village about 15 miles south. Once we were in position, a group of Vietnamese Popular Forces moved in through our lines searching the village. It was an all-day operation that netted one VC killed, six captured and three weapons captured. It is in operations like this that we hurt the VC most. As you know, the local VC are terribly underequipped. So when we capture two or three weapons, we put 10 or 15 enemy out of commission, at least for a while. At the end of the day we were again helilifted back to our company base. It was basically a simple school problem, but for me, since it was really the first operation I had been on, it was quite exciting.

The first night I spent in the field an ambush patrol from the first platoon had three men wounded when they set off a booby-trap grenade. This morning, the second platoon took 14 casualties, including one killed, when they set off two mines while on a road-clearing mission. So far, my platoon, the 3rd, hasn't had any trouble, but these booby traps are so well hidden that no matter how good you are, they'll get you. . . .

I heard Johnson's speech on AFVN Radio last night and think it to be the best one of his career. I am heartened by his bombing reduction and pray, as does everyone else here, that Hanoi will respond. What do you make of it? Also, how about his not running for president? I was beginning to think that the only way for this war to end was to have Johnson reelected in November.

Things aren't all bad—I've got a really good company commander and a good platoon sergeant. In my job these are the most important people in the world to me. Also on the bright side, I'm getting the best suntan I've ever had.

Dear Mom and Dad,

I just got my first letter from you plus the clippings on Johnson and my pictures. I can't tell you how great it is to be back in touch with you again. . . .

I lost my first man last week. He was killed by accident by another man in the platoon. I had sent a squad out on the night ambush. They had been set up in position for a few hours when the flank man crawled away to take a leak or something, and as he was crawling back to position another man mistook him for a dink and shot him. He died on the chopper that dusted him off.

Of course it really tears me up to lose a man, especially like that, but I must not show any emotion over it. I've got to press on, keep doing my job. Even among my men this is universal. They are saddened by the death of a buddy, but he is gone. The concern among the team (for that is what we are) is how it will affect the man who shot him. Will he fall to pieces over this and be unable to perform his function? This is what we're worried about first and foremost. War Is Hell!

You know that joke about how hard it is to tell the good guys from the bad guys over here? Well, it's funny in Bronxville or Dorset, but it isn't over here. The enemy in our area of operations is a farmer by day and VC by night. Every male is required to register at his provincial capital. He is further required to carry an ID showing his picture, fingerprints, age, etc. But anyone with a VC background is supposedly denied an ID. Simple, you say? All we have to do is come to a village and police up everyone without an ID, right? Well, about three months ago we captured a VC printing plant that manufactured ID cards. Every man we pick up says, "Me Vietnamese Numbah 1, VC Numbah 10," so we have to let him go. But more than once we have captured or killed people with weapons whom we recognized as one of those smiling faces we had picked up and released earlier. It's maddening because we know damn well that they're dinks but we can't do anything to them until we catch them with a weapon or actually shooting at us.

By the way, Number 1 means real good and Number 10 means real bad in pidgin Vietnamese-English. Other handy phrases, just in case you're planning a vacation in this tropical paradise, are: titi—very little; boo koo (a bastardization of beaucoup)—very much; boom boom—whore; didi mow—get out of here. What more do you need to know? . . .

More soon.

Love,
Mike

2Lt. Robert Ransom, Jr., platoon commander, Co. A, 4/3rd Inf., 11th LIB, I Corps, wounded 3 May 1968, died 11 May.

—— ☆ ——

17 Sept. 69

Red,

Thanks for the letter, but now you've made me self-conscious about my writing. You used some words that rather jolted me: Morbid, Chaplain, and a few others. [They] belong to another world about which I've forgotten an amazing amount as it's irrelevant to anything going on now. I've just about forgotten what college was all about, though there are a few memories that stick in the back of my mind.

Yesterday we took to the bush to recon a river crossing on one of Charlie's major supply routes coming in from Laos. . . . It was an uneventful patrol, but I committed the mortal sin of small-unit patrolling: I broke contact with the man in front of me and split the patrol into two elements, something that could easily prove fatal in the event of contact with the enemy. We'd just crossed the river at a ford to join the team reconning the other bank and were going through fairly green stuff when the man in front of me dropped his lighter. I bent to pick it up and by the time I straightened up he was out of sight and hearing. Had we been hit then, it would have been a bad situation made worse by my stupidity. I've picked up most of the patrolling tricks—taping metal parts to prevent their making noise during movement, wearing bandoliers so the magazines are on your chest and stomach and form makeshift body armor, and other tricks that stretch the odds a little more in your favor and give you a little more of an edge in combat—but I'm still new and yesterday I really loused up. . . .

The fact of the matter is that I was afraid—which I am most of the time over here—but I allowed my fear to interfere with the job at hand, and when that happens to someone, he ceases to be a good soldier. It's all right to be afraid, but you can't allow that fear to interfere with the job because other people are depending on you and you've got responsibility to them and for them. From now on I'll be keeping that in mind and I won't louse up so badly again. Had that happened under fire, people might have died unnecessarily due to me.

One other impression from that patrol is that anyone over here who walks more than 50 feet through elephant grass should automatically get a Purple Heart. Try to imagine grass 8 to 15 feet high so thick as to cut visibility to one yard, possessing razor-sharp edges. Then try to imagine walking through it while all around you are men possessing the latest automatic weapons who desperately want to kill you. You'd be amazed at how such a man can age on one patrol.

We're supposed to go on a very hard sortie soon which, unless it's canceled, virtually guarantees some hard fighting. I'm not trying to be mysterious or anything, but common sense precludes giving too many details before the operation. We're going to raid one of Charlie's POW camps and attempt to free some GIs, but that's about all I'll say till we pull it off, if we do.

I may have played up my unit here a bit too much, but I'm proud to be in it and might be inclined to brag. We're not supermen or anything like that, and we're not about to walk into bars, where the music automatically stops at our entrance, and proceed to demolish anybody and everybody in the place. But as far as being soldiers, we're proud of our outfit and its history, and are definitely among the best troops over here. . . . Men have gone on operations here with broken ankles in order not to let their buddies down. So you see, we take our business seriously.

I'm going out now for a run in the sand to toughen my feet up. So I'll be signing out. . . .

George

Sp/4 George Olsen, Co. G, 75th Inf. (Ranger), Americal Div., Chu Lai, 1969–1970, KIA 3 March 1970.

—— ☆ ——

May 8, 1968

My Dearest Bev,

For the last week we have been waiting for an attack, and last night it came in full force. Honey, I was never so scared in my life. We got hit by 12 mortars and rockets, and some even hit our ammo dumps, which really hurt the battery. A mortar landed about 30 feet from me and I was lucky enough to have my head down, but the sergeant next to me didn't, and we think he lost an eye. We got three men seriously hurt and four others shaken up by the blast. This was my first real look at war, and it sure was an ugly sight. I helped carry some of the wounded away, and boy, I sure hope I don't have to do that again. It was an experience you can never explain in a million words.

The noise from shooting is enough to drive a person crazy. Even after the attack last night, we had to stay up and wait for a ground attack which, lucky for us, never came. We expect to catch a lot of hell through May because it seems that the VC are really putting a big push on.

Bev, I was so surprised last night to see that the men here were willing to risk their own lives to save a buddy's. It really makes you have faith in people again, but I hope I don't have to go through what we did last night in a long time (like never!).

I take your picture out quite often and just look at it, because it's such a relief from this pitiful place to see such a beautiful being. I am thinking of you always.

All my love,
Al

Allen Paul was a sergeant with Company D, 2nd Battalion, 5th Cavalry, 1st Cavalry Division (Airmobile). His unit operated in both I and III Corps during his tour, April 1968 to April 1969. He is now information coordinator for Indiana Technical College, Richmond, Indiana.

—— ☆ ——

June 9, 1967

Dear Mom,

Well, I finally made it into the air. Boy, was it some experience, though.

To start off with, I got up at 6:00 this morning and had to be on the flight line by 7:00. We only waited around for five minutes when the phone rang three times. That's the signal for emergency medevac. So off we went—the pilot, co-pilot, [two door] gunners, me and the other corpsman.

What a ride. It's certainly not like a plane. All the noise and shaking and swaying. Finally we got to the zone. There were two Marines wounded in the head by sniper fire. The pilot noticed that the patrol was receiving intense mortar and small-arms fire. So he decided to circle overhead. All of a sudden, out of nowhere, two U.S. jet fighters came swooping down and bombed and rocketed the VC positions. At this chance, we went down—that was the scariest part of all.

Before I knew it, we were down in the zone with the VC firing all over the place. No sooner, the wounded were hustled aboard. Both were alive and didn't appear in real danger, but head wounds can be tricky.

When they were aboard, we swooped up and cut off the trees in the way. Then the bird started swaying back and forth like crazy. That's to keep the enemy from hitting us.

Well, after that I finally caught my breath and checked one patient over. He asked me for a cigarette so I lit one and gave it to him. The poor kid looked scared, but didn't cry or scream once. He was really a brave boy. All the time back to the hospital I kept holding his hand for comfort, and wiping some of the blood off his face.

When we got there and I started unloading him, he looked up and smiled and said, "Thanks, Doc." Then he shook my hand.

Boy, Mom, I felt like crying to see the way he acted. This may sound crazy to you, but all the time I wasn't really as scared as I thought I would be. In fact, I didn't even feel one bit scared. I just kept thinking to myself, this is only a job and I'm trained to do it, and I did.

Now that you're all upset (I hope not really), I told you all this because I think you'll understand better what's happening over here. I know you worry an awful lot, but I don't think there's any use in lying or holding back on you because you are my mother—I love you very much.

I was surprised later on to find out that a CBS newsman was coming aboard to take films. He didn't get me in, but one of these days you'll see an air/evac helicopter on the news and it might be me on that one, so watch.

The one he went on was when a little girl got her leg blown off, so maybe he'll say something about it.

Well, Mom, it's been a long, hard day and I have the duty tonight, on top of it all. Boy, did they really screw me up. I'm not supposed to have the duty when I fly, but I'll take it anyway. This way I can stay up and write some letters.

Before I forget, last night was a miserable experience. About 2 A.M. it started to rain like hell. Then the wind started blowing too. Remember what I told you [about] the huts . . . old rusty tin, full of holes. The rain came in and got us all soaked. I didn't care, though, I just laid in bed and took it like everyone else.

Well, that's the news for now. I'll write again when I get a chance.

All my love,
Gary

P.S. XXXX—for Lisa.

Gary R. Panko, from Yonkers, New York, was a Navy hospital corpsman attached to the Medical Department, Marine Air Group 16, 1st Marine Air Wing. He flew medevacs—medical evacuations by helicopter of injured and wounded Marines—out of Da Nang from June 1967 through early 1968. He died in Houston, Texas, in 1983.

— ☆ —

Dec. 23, 1966

Dear Mom and Dad,

Everything is just fine—in fact it's better than I thought it would be. They have us in a big base camp. We're going to be staying here for a month. This area is perfectly safe. While we're in base camp, we aren't allowed to carry ammo or even keep it in our tents. . . .

Besides the platoon leader, I'm the next most important man in the platoon. All the talk I hear from the guys who have been here awhile make it sound pretty easy over here. We eat three hot meals a day. I heard when we go to the field, they fly hot meals to us in the morning and night, and for lunch you eat C-rations, and you're allowed two canteens of water a day. When you're in home base you drink all you want, plus while you're in the field you get a beer and soda free every other day.

Last night I had a little trouble falling asleep because of the artillery rounds going off. It's a 175 [mm gun], and it has a range of miles, but when it goes off it sounds like a firecracker going off in your ear. All in all things look pretty good. They have PX's where you can buy whatever you want or need, which is doing me no good because I'm broke. Don't send me money because it's no good here. We use scrip for money which looks like a Sweepstakes ticket, and besides I'll be getting paid in a few days. You should be receiving a $150 in about a week. If you need it, you can use it, but if you don't, then put it in a bank, OK?

The people live like pigs. They don't know how to use soap. When they have to go to the bathroom, they go wherever they're standing, they don't care who is looking. Kids not even six [years old] run up to you and ask for a cig. The houses they live in are like rundown shacks. You can see everything—they have no doors, curtains. I'm real glad I have what I have. It seems poor to you maybe, and you want new things because you think our house doesn't look good, but after seeing the way these people live, there's no comparison. We are more than millionaires to these people —they have nothing. I can't see how people can live like this. It seems funny, in one of your letters you write about the TV going on the blink. At the same time, I almost had to laugh. These people don't even have the slightest idea what a TV is even.

Right now our big guns are going off and it sounds good knowing it's yours and they don't have any. . . .

It takes me a day to write one letter, and every chance I have I'd rather write to you than anyone else. Tell Susan I'm sorry, but I just don't have the time to write as much as I would like to. . . . Mom, the least of my problems now are girls. That's one of the things I don't have time to worry about.

One thing I don't do is worry—it doesn't pay. If I worried about everything over here that there is to worry about, I'd have a nervous breakdown. I'm very fortunate, because I have a cool head. Things that make other guys scared or shaky don't seem to bother me. Also I'm fortunate because my platoon leader, Lt. Sanderson, also keeps a cool head. This man is really sharp when it comes to this stuff. I have already learned a lot about human nature from this man. He's only 23 years old, but his knowledge is really something. A person can't go wrong following his example.

Well, it's about time. I thought you would never send those onions. I can't wait for them to arrive. . . .

For sure, now, I'm going to close this short novel.

With all my love,
Your grateful son,
Johnny

On 2 February 1967, less than two months after he arrived in country, PFC John Dabonka was killed in action near the Mekong Delta town of My Tho. He was 20 years old.

— ☆ —

2
"Humping the Boonies"

They were called grunts, and most of them, however grudgingly, were proud of the name. They were the infantrymen, the foot soldiers, of the war. They "humped the boonies" in their own special nightmare, hacking their way, as the narration of an official Army slide show described,

through triple-canopy jungle, where the three layers of foliage are so intermeshed that whatever sunlight penetrates is but a diffused glow. After the heaviest downpour, rain doesn't even drip; it's absorbed by the overhead cover. The soldier fighting in this terrain is surrounded by the fetid, claustrophobic jungle, so that only the men immediately to his front and rear are visible. The infantryman finds himself slogging through foot-gripping mud with water lapping at his armpits, or enveloped in a cloud of dust, or stumbling across craggy mountains.

In the guerrilla war that was Vietnam there was no "front." Pitched battles were the exception. "The way we move without contact," wrote Marine Lieutenant Don Jacques, "you begin to wonder if the VC are even out there. And all the time you know they are. The great frustration is that they don't come out and fight." So the grunts humped, sweeping the countryside on search-and-destroy operations, setting up ambushes, seeking to make contact with an elusive enemy, the Viet Cong—the VC, also called Victor, Charlie, Victor Charlie, Chuck, and Mr. Charles—and the NVA—the North Vietnamese Army. Even more pernicious than the enemy were the booby traps he set and the land mines he planted and the mortars and rockets with which he bombarded American positions. In a war that seemed without end, in engagements that seemed without strategic purpose, territory won one day was contested the next, and again the next month, and the next year.

A grunt's best friends were the medics who tended him, the firepower that supported him, the helicopters that rescued him. But he was tightest with other grunts. Theirs was a closeness forged by the dependency of their shared experience. For months on end, they lived in the bush, eating C-rations, bathing rarely, sleeping without comfort, filled with fears of the shadows in the night that only the dawn could dispel. They might return to base camp for a few days or a few weeks to "stand down"—take a breather from the bush. But the boonies was their home, and they spent the bulk of their tour in the thick of it, humping.

Jan. 14, 69

Hi [Connie],

This is to let you know that I'm OK. I want to tell you about that 12-day mission so that you can keep Mom from worrying. Don't show her this letter because the following is what I'll be doing for the next 11 months.

First it rained for six days solid, I got muddy and wet. My hands are covered with cuts. The jungles have thousands of leeches and mosquitoes of which I think I have gotten bitten almost all over my body. I personally had to dig up two dead gooks. The smell was terrible. I just about got sick. About three or four guys got hurt through accidents. Only two got shot chasing a gook.

Actually the fighting is not heavy yet, but the rumor is we're moving south on to the A Shau Valley. I walk up and down mountains with a heavy pack on my back. But if everyone else does it, so can I. It's not so hard, actually, but one thing is for certain: you surely learn to appreciate some of the finer things you once had. Don't get me wrong, I'm not complaining or expecting sympathy. All I want to do is lay the line on what I'm doing. . . . In return you must tell Mom that I'm probably out in the field doing hardly a damn thing at all.

Feb. 19, 69

Hi [Connie],

Mom wrote me in a letter and said you worry a lot too. Please don't. I'm taking care of myself and every chance I get to get out of danger I do. By the way, you know this is not to be shown to anybody. So don't worry. I still haven't gotten fired at directly. I haven't even fired my weapon.

A week ago five guys went out on LP [listening post]. One got killed and the other got shot and is going home. Two days ago four guys got killed and about 15 wounded from the first platoon. Our platoon was 200 yards away on top of a hill. One guy was from Floral Park. He had five days left to go. He was standing on a 250-lb. bomb that a plane had dropped and didn't explode. So the NVA wired it up. Well, all they found was a piece of his wallet.

By the way, don't worry about [what] Tia Louisa or anybody else says. Here in Nam a point man (the first man in a line) is bound to at least get wounded. . . . Don't get the wrong idea. It's not battle time all the time. You always hear our artillery wherever you go. Even right now they're firing 81-mm mortars in the background. It becomes a part of your life. I'll tell you, the worst part of it all is that you walk all day with a 70-lb. pack on your back, up and down the hills. After a while you don't let it bother you. Well, you wanted to hear exactly what I do. Regards.

Love,
Sal

Sp/4 Salvador Gonzalez served with Company D, 1st Battalion, 506th Infantry, 101st Airborne Division, which operated in I Corps, from December 1968 through December 1969. An electrical engineer, he is on the board of directors of Queens Chapter 32 of Vietnam Veterans of America. Connie is his sister.

——— ☆ ———

5 Nov. 67

Hello My Darling,

Here I am setting down to write of my love for you and the horrors of war. Right now I'm pretending that I'm talking to you.

I can picture your face in front of me, and our home and our children. Oh! How much the things we take for granted can mean so much. The smell of cut grass, the wind blowing over the lake and making the trees and grass sway. The smell of autumn, the bareness of the world during winter. All of this means so much, and how little it is appreciated.

In the mornings I put on my fighting gear: web belt with ammo pouches, hand grenades, smoke grenades, first-aid pouch and canteen. Then I put two bandoliers of ammo around my neck so that it crosses my chest.

Then comes my pack containing poncho, poncho liner, five C-ration meals, rain jacket, sweater shirt, extra canteen, extra ammo, gun-cleaning kit, extra smoke grenade, an extra bolt for my rifle, a camera and some cigarettes. Then I pick up my weapon and put on my helmet. With that on, I call my squad leaders and explain what my plan for the day is, based on what the captain passed down to me. Mud, I never knew how much mud I could hate. We live in mud and rain. I'm so sick of rain that it is sometimes unbearable. At night the mosquitoes plague me while I'm lying on the ground with my poncho wrapped around me. The rain drips on me until I go to sleep from exhaustion.

This continues day after day until one wonders how much the human body can stand. . . . And yet it is my job, and I do it willingly, knowing that war is a constant factor in this world and has been since the beginning of man. There is something that keeps us fighting past the time when we feel like quitting.

We go in tomorrow, for sure. Everyone's morale is high, including mine. I'm looking forward to getting clean and relaxing. Most of my men will be drunk as lords by tomorrow night.

There should be some mail for me. I surely hope so. Letters mean a lot.

You know something, honey? I love you lots and lots. Only you know how much.

I'll write when we get in.

With all of my love,
Fred

2Lt. Frederick Downs, Jr., from Kingman, Indiana, was a platoon leader assigned to Company D, 1st Battalion, 14th Infantry, 4th Infantry Division, operating out of Duc Pho, from August 1967 until January 1968, when he was wounded in action. Linda was his wife.

— ☆ —

2 September, 1966

Dear Mom, Dad, Shrub, the Egg and Peach:

Sorry to be so long in writing, but I have just come back from an abortion called Operation Jackson. I spent a three-day "walk in the sun" (and paddies and fields and mountains and impenetrable jungle and saw grass and ants, and screwed-up radios and no word, and deaf radio operators, and no chow, and too many C-rations, and blisters and torn trousers and jungle rot, and wet socks and sprained ankles and no heels, and, and, and) for a battalion that walked on roads and dikes the whole way and a regiment that didn't even know where the battalion was, finished off by a 14,000-meter forced march on a hard road.

My God, the epic poems I could write to that ambrosia of Marine Corps cuisine—peanut butter and/or hot coffee after three days of that! The only person in the whole battalion to see a VC was, of course, me. I was walking along a trail doing a village sweep all alone, and here comes

Charlie, rifle in hand, with not a care in the world until he sees me, and then it's a race to see if he can get off the road before I can draw my .45 and get off an accurate shot (he won). Of course, there was an incident when four snipers took on the battalion, which promptly, more to release the weight of all that unexpended ammunition than anything else, threw everything at them but the Missouri; and that would have been there too, except it could not get up the Sang Tra Bong [River]. So goes about $50,000 worth of ammo. They probably played it up as a second Iwo Jima at home, but it wasn't.

Then, two days after we got back, we played Indian Scout, and my platoon splashed its way through a rice paddy at 3:30 in the morning in a rainstorm to surround a hamlet, which we managed to do somehow without alerting everyone in the district, which is surprising as we made enough noise to wake up a Marine sentry. It was "very successful" since we managed to kill a few probably innocent civilians, found a few caves and burned a few houses, all in a driving rainstorm. There's nothing much more, I'm afraid.

Love,
Sandy

2Lt. Marion Lee ("Sandy") Kempner, born in Galveston, Texas, in 1942, was a platoon leader with Company M, 3rd Battalion, 7th Regiment, 1st Marine Division, operating in I Corps. He arrived in country in July 1966. He was killed by shrapnel from a mine explosion on 11 November 1966.

— ☆ —

Jan. 13, 1969

Dear Mom,
    We've been running around these mountains every day without a break. We finally got a day of rest today.
    On the fifth of January, we went out on a patrol and found a rather large weapons and ammo cache. It consisted of 166 Russian carbines and SKSs [Soviet semi-automatic rifles], 300 82-mm mortar rounds, 4 mortar tubes, 4 122-mm rocket launchers with rounds, 2 tripods for a 75-mm recoilless rifle and rounds, plus many other items. It's one of the largest caches anyone has found in the last couple of months. It was really great finding all this stuff, but getting it out was another thing. As you can well

imagine, we couldn't hump all of that stuff out, so we had to wait for choppers to come in and drop nets to us so we could have it all choppered back out.

That all sounds quite simple, but the whole thing took four days. It was raining, and we had to sit on all that junk until the choppers could come in. (They won't fly in rain unless it's for a medevac.) I needn't tell you it was pretty miserable being wet and hungry for four days. There were only 30 of us, and we were afraid the gooks might try to overrun the place to get all that stuff back. They probed our lines every night with Chicom [Chinese communist] grenades, and kept everyone on his toes. The only time we got any sleep was during the day.

Finally we got all that gear retroed and got the heck out of there. All I did that night when we finally got back to the hill was eat. You can imagine how hungry we were.

Two days [later] we went out and got into a fire fight with two gooks. We trapped them in a cave, but it took two hours to get them out. In the process, one man was shot and killed and a couple others were wounded. I caught a small piece of shrapnel in the arm, but it wasn't serious enough for a Purple Heart. . . .

There are so few men left in the company that we're about due to go in pretty soon. The company is operating on about 70 men instead of about 170. A few days ago the 2nd Platoon was operating with 15 men. Everyone has been catching malaria or some kind of fever. There is no such thing as a squad-sized patrol any more, because all we have is two 5-man squads. Things are pretty bad out here.

I sure am getting tired. Humping these mountains is bad news. We really need a little rest. It's really nice in the rear when you can sleep a whole night without having to stand watch.

I've been keeping up with my diary. Actually, I could send the 1968 diary back, but I think I'll keep it because I've been keeping a list of how much I've been paid and KIAs and WIAs and a few other things.

I haven't got much more to add at this time, except that when I get to the rear, I'm going to sign up for a CAP (Civil Action Program) unit. If I get into that, I go to Da Nang for a two-week schooling program, and then I'll get assigned to a unit. It has to do with helping teach the children and the people new and modern ways of doing things. I think I'd be much happier helping the people rather than fighting the gooks. I would have signed up before, but you have to have three months in country before you can. I hope I can get in right away. I'll let you know what happens. . . .

Much love,
Cam

Cameron MacDonald was a lance corporal assigned to Company F, 2nd Battalion, 5th Regiment, 1st Marine Division. From October 1968 to November 1969, his unit patrolled the areas out of Da Nang, An Hoa, and Chu Lai. He now lives in Lake Mary, Florida, where he builds custom furniture.

— ☆ —

Sept. 23, '69

Red,

I never made it down to Nha Trang for extra recondo training. A rear-echelon sergeant took me off the list and put his name there, so he went in my place and I went into the field for a three-day recon in the monsoons. Someday climb into the shower with all your clothes on, stay there three days under the water, shutting it off every now and then, but always turning the water back on before your clothes can dry out, and you'll have a reasonably good idea of what it's like in the boonies during the seasonal rains. I looked like a prune by the time we came back.

For two days we staggered over ridgeline after ridgeline trying to get to our AO (area of operations) since our chopper pilot became slightly confused and inserted us two miles south of the area we were to recon. On the last day we stopped for a break when two NVA walked by making enough noise for a platoon. I've read statements from NVA POWs claiming the American soldier is too clumsy and noisy in the jungles, but 12 of us followed both of them for over a half mile and they never knew we were there until it didn't matter—for them. They led us right into a platoon-sized base camp, and we made the biggest haul ever for Chu Lai Rangers.

The platoon was having a siesta-fiesta break, and we crawled within six feet of one group and then charged, and all hell broke loose. It had to be a tremendous shock. I've never seen such panic and pandemonium. NVA tumbled out of hammocks, hit the ground running, and took off leaving all their equipment. One man went down fighting, shot our point man in the ankle at fistfighting range, and then was blown apart by the sergeant leading us. I won't go into detail, but it is unbelievable what an M-16 will do to a man—particularly at close range. The only conceivable comparison is swatting a bug with a chain-mail glove. Enough said—too much perhaps. The whole thing lasted less than 30 seconds, then we were alone, standing among piles of food and equipment, blood trails and corpses. We brought back weapons ranging from a mortar to AK-47s, clothes, medical kits and documents and were mentioned on radio and TV over here for that day's work.

It was a very successful patrol, and everyone seemed happy with it —everyone but the point man, that is. His wound, of itself, wasn't serious, but the power and shock of a modern rifle bullet is absolutely unbelievable and within two minutes of being hit he was fighting for his life in shock. There was a foulup in the extraction, and for half an hour we were stuck in a wide-open rice paddy, in a valley, with helicopters trying to find us but not having our radio frequency, while the hills all around [were crawling] with communists who, if they had come back, could have wiped us out. The wounded man stopped breathing three times on the LZ but was revived via mouth-to-mouth resuscitation and a few punches on the chest. He is now on his way home by way of Japan, where his ankle will be taken care of, so maybe, in a way, he was the luckiest one out there. He's going home to his wife in one piece, with his eyes and all his limbs, and will probably not even have a limp, while we'll be going back out until either our time or luck runs out. He'll never take to the field again. He's home safe—we're not. In that distinction lies the difference between those who have luck, and those who aren't yet sure [if] they have it or not.

George

Sp/4 George Olsen, Co. G, 75th Inf. (Ranger), Americal Div., Chu Lai, 1969–1970, KIA 3 March 1970.

—— ☆ ——

Ambush

One night we wandered far and long
To kill young men who, brave and strong
And precious to their loved, their own,
Were coming to kill us.

Aching, filthy, weak, afraid,
Creeping through the dripping shades,
Searching forms through jungle haze,
We stalked those men as prey.

A stinging, steaming, humming hell
Tried our flesh and pride and will,
But we walked and watched and waited, until
We froze—and saw them coming.

Quietly picking their way along,
Far from their loved ones, far from home,
They seemed to be dreaming. One muttered a song,
And they carried their weapons slack.

I fired first! The shattering blast
Unleashed a deafening force that smashed
And ripped and shook, and seemed to last
Till the very Earth was torn.

Then, silently, coldly, on command,
We plucked among that gory band
And left, with a simple wave of the hand,
The offal to the leeches.

Now jungle covers the stench and sight
Of the wrecks we left behind that night.
Yet we, too, die, while winning such fights,
From a sickness caused by slaughter.

And when we next go out again
At night to kill more killer men,
Or else be hunted to our end,
Will it prove The Cause is ours?

How can we ever "know we're right,"
Lost in this dark, primeval Night?
Must we kill them, as beasts must fight,
Until the Earth is torn?

—James McLeroy
1967

*1Lt. James McLeroy, whose tour in Vietnam began in May 1967, spent
six months with Company C, Team A-104, 5th Special Forces Group,*

operating in the mountains of I Corps. He is now vice-president of a trade finance corporation in Coral Gables, Florida.

— ☆ —

July 6, 1967

Dear Dad,

I have a rough one to tell you about this time. Yesterday my squad plus one machine gunner, one rocket man and a Navy corpsman (medic) went on a patrol into a real bad area. We were short of men, so there were only 10 of us. I haven't been carrying the radio the last two weeks, but yesterday I did because our regular man (just got here two weeks ago) was going to mine school in Da Nang. Having that thing on my back helped save my young ass.

The VC set off 10 mines, which were spread out on the trail under us. When they all went off at once, every man in the patrol was hit. A large chunk of metal hit me in the gut, but only gave me a good size lump and some bumps and bruises. My belt was smashed up, but I was OK. I went into the aid station to see the doc, who said I will be fine. I will get a Purple Heart for it. I'm great now and back in the field.

The corpsman who was behind me was killed instantly. [The] squad leader right in front of me will lose both his legs from the knees on down. One man lost an eye and will have a couple of real bad scars on his face, also a smashed hand. The man behind him had his leg broken in three places and shrapnel in a few others. My buddy Mike had his left leg broken, and shrapnel tore his ass and back up pretty well. The other four guys and myself had to take care of the wounded while fighting off the gooks at the same time; they were throwing grenades at us as well as firing automatic rifles. Dad, it was hell!! I have never been so damned scared in my life. I had to call in help and a medevac while trying to fix my rifle, which jammed up on me after firing only 60 rounds. Help got to us in a half hour, but it seemed like hours.

My buddy Harry brought his squad out the quickest and then destroyed that whole damned village. Those slant-eyed VC farts knew what they were doing. They almost got us all. They want to put us up for medals. This will be the second time for me. I don't care. I'm just glad I made it out of there in one piece. I hope this letter doesn't shake you up too much, but I did tell you that I would tell you everything that happens over here.

I am fine and healthy and wanted you to know the whole story in case you are sent a telegram about my Purple Heart. They don't usually send it for things unless the wound draws blood. Mine didn't. Tell Mom only what you think she should know.

So long for now,

Love,
Bob

P.S. (Those little runts can't get me!!!)

PFC Robert C. Wilson, from Dobbs Ferry, New York, arrived in Vietnam in May 1967. He died on 8 January 1968 when the aircraft in which he was a passenger crashed into a mountain approximately 18 miles south of Dong Ha. He served with Company B, 1st Battalion, 1st Regiment, 1st Marine Division. He was 21 years old.

— ☆ —

5th or 6th Oct. 67

Hi Honey,

I had a hell of a day yesterday. I'll explain it from the time I started out on patrol with my platoon until yesterday evening. . . .

We were going up this valley, and I got a report that approximately 60 VC were spotted on the ridgeline next to my location. I told my point man to change direction towards that position. We came to a river that was deep and wide due to all of the rain we've been getting. We were looking for a way across when six VC took off out of a hut across the river.

We immediately opened fire, and my front element jumped into the river to try and head them off. I went across the river and told my platoon sergeant to take control of the rear element and to provide cover fire. After I was across, the dinks divided into two groups and took off up the mountain to our front.

My platoon sergeant crossed with his element and gave chase on the right flank. I took control of the left flank, and we took them under fire. We hit one, but he dropped into a tunnel and we lost sight of him.

Meanwhile, on the right flank, a VC popped out of a hole and threw a grenade. My M-79 man stood his ground and fired at the dink [at] the same time he threw the grenade. My M-79 got hit in the leg with shrapnel from the grenade, and the dink that threw it got knocked down with the blast from the M-79. My man crawled into the bushes. His helmet, wallet, pictures and letters were scattered all over, not to mention his weapon. He started yelling "medic," so I ran over to him with the medic and called in the dust-off.

My right element chased the dinks up into the brush and wounded two more. They left two big blood trails in the brush as we tracked them down, but they got in their tunnels and we could not get them. I told the men to throw grenades into those tunnels, which they did.

Meanwhile, the track unit that we are attached to came up in their APCs [armored personnel carriers], and I had them rake the hill with their 50s.

At about the same time, I was comforting the man who had been hit. It was raining, and his blood was mixing with the water in the puddle he was lying in. He wanted to hold my hand because it was hurting him so bad. I held his hands and told him he had a million-dollar wound. He was in pain so bad he was clenching his teeth, but he tried to smile at that. Everyone in the field wants the million-dollar wound so they can be sent back to the States.

The dust-off came in at that time, and I "popped" smoke so he would know where we were located. The chopper landed about 15 feet way, and one of the men in [it] jumped out with a collapsible stretcher. When we picked the man up, he cried out in agony and passed out. We put him on the chopper, and they took off.

I took my left element up the left side and sent the right element up the right side of our hill. We found tunnels, spiderholes, [and] straw mats where [the VC] had been sleeping, and food cans. We found medical supplies in a hut at the bottom of the hill plus canteens, propaganda and—get this—at one of the tables, six hands of cards. One hand was thrown all over the floor but otherwise they had been so surprised they had left all six hands on the table.

All of the tracks got stuck in the damn rice paddies, and we had to pull back and guard them, so the rest of the dinks got away. When the tracks finally got loose from the mud, it was getting dark, so we had to pull back to our bridge.

On the way back we searched this hut and found a VC gas mask and a clip of ammo for a carbine rifle. We took [four women] prisoners and brought them in. They will have some explaining to do about that equipment they had.

I told my men that the first squad to kill a dink with a weapon, I would buy them a bottle of whisky. They can't wait to kill one of them now.

I just heard an explosion down the road. From the radio I hear that an Army vehicle hit a mine and the dust-off has been called. The mine demolished the truck and blew a three-foot hole in the road. This is some war. A man can't feel safe anywhere in this whole country.

I'll never forget the look on that man's face when I was holding his hand.

Well, my love, one of these days, I'll get some mail and I'll read those sweet words "I Love You."

With All My Love,
Fred

2Lt. Fred Downs, platoon leader, Co. C, 1/14th Inf., 4th Inf. Div., Pleiku province, 1967–1968, WIA 11 January 1968.

— ☆ —

15 Nov '69

Red,

Due to the incredible industry of our new hooch maid, your last letter has gone out with the trash after I read it once under somewhat peculiar conditions, and I don't remember too much what was in it. . . .

I had thought that we'd slow down somewhat during the monsoons but, if anything, the tempo of our operations has been drastically stepped up. My team by the day after tomorrow will have gone out 10 times within 40 days, which is counting the time it takes to get one's equipment in shape—a real accomplishment. The mission before last we set up next to a waterfall in a 360° perimeter, making a hell of a racket doing it, I might add. It would appear that the noise of the water killed our noise because when one of our men looked over the boulders we were in, into a hollow next to us, there was Victor in blissful and fatal ignorance that we were less than 20 feet away from him and 15 feet above. We had all the time in the world to get ready, and the surprise was total. After a short and absolutely one-sided fire fight we went through a large base camp which had been hurriedly evacuated, marked it for the Cobras [assault helicopters], then lit out 800 meters to an LZ [landing zone] with one Victoria

Charlie and her three-month-old baby as POWs. We'd just made her a widow, and with all the steel flying in that hollow she was lucky to have escaped unscathed. But I will say that there wasn't a man among us who wasn't glad the child wasn't hit as nobody'd seen either of them during the fight. We'd shoot a female out there without blinking an eye as a woman with a rifle can kill you just as dead as any slant-eyed Hector or Ulysses. But a baby is nobody's enemy, and, as I said, it made us all feel better that it hadn't been hurt.

I've just come in from one mission that started out terrible. [We had] to hump three clicks [kilometers] over the most abominable terrain I've ever had the misfortune of encountering. It has become my opinion that the national flower of Vietnam should be an immense thorn. On the second day we heard Victor laughing, talking and raising cain in general, which are sure signs of a nearby base camp—you'd be amazed at the racket Charlie will make when he thinks he's safe in his rear areas. We also heard people in back of us and to our right. We took off for an LZ —you don't go after base camps with seven men and when you're [being] followed unless [you're] sure of surprise. There's no doubt that Charles knows you're there and is waiting to get enough men to overrun you. With noises getting closer and closer, [I] turned around and waited, hoping Victor would blunder and get close enough to see—no easy accomplishment when visibility is less than 20 feet. I was rear security (last man), and it was a hairy thing listening to people moving all around you and having nothing to fight back at.

At one point there was a violent commotion in bushes about 20 feet from me, and I almost cut loose. But then whoever it was took off the other way, so I guess either he saw us without our seeing him, or the lack of movement noises from us tipped him off at the last minute as to what we were doing. I got a few white hairs out of that one, and maybe it was the noise of my teeth chattering that gave our place away, but if I'd ever caught a glimpse of anybody back there, I'd have stitched him from ankle to ears in a heartbeat and been relieved at the prospect. The worst thing in the world is [having] to wait for a rifle bullet to smash into you [before you can] fight back and influence the final outcome of your little duel. We took scattered potshots on the LZ extraction but got out safely with the help of some Cobra gunships. When we extracted, we could hear our friends in back of us yelling and scrambling for cover as the Cobras lined up for their runs. You'll never know how much a man can fall in love with a machine till you've stood on the ground with your head in a noose and had the rope cut at the last minute by a Huey's rotor blades. I'd marry one of those helicopters if it could scratch my back and cook a respectable meal. The day after tomorrow we're going back with 11 men and try for that base camp again, and I sure as hell hope that area has quieted down some or we could definitely wind up in a bind.

George

Sp/4 George Olsen, Co. G, 75th Inf. (Ranger), Americal Div., Chu Lai, 1969–1970, KIA 3 March 1970.

— ☆ —

Jan 31, 1968

Chris:

I guess letters are going to be a long time writing over here . . . there is so much going on.

Yesterday afternoon we were given an emergency mission to move about 10 miles to a new position. We got there about 6:30 and deployed the men. About midnight all hell broke loose. We were sitting right in the middle of the boondocks [when] rockets, flares, machine guns, and planes started shooting. The VC got Bien Hoa airport and Long Binh province about 24 hours after I got out! Chris, someone said a prayer for me. . . .

We just had a Vietnamese man come into our position with a terrible cut on his leg. "Doc" took a look at it and said that "gang green" had set in. We called in a helicopter and had him lifted to a hospital. One minute we're killing them, the next we're saving their lives.

I miss you.

Love,
Alan

1Lt. Alan Bourne, A Battery, 40th Artillery, attached to 2nd Battalion, 3rd Infantry, 199th Light Infantry Brigade, wrote this to his then-girl-friend Christina Haskin during the Tet Offensive. He is now a real-estate broker in New York City.

— ☆ —

Sunday
July 3rd [1966]

Dear Mom & Dad,

I don't know how I can say this without alarming you, but I know I'll have to tell you about it because NBC News was there and I'm afraid you might have seen me on film or read about the dreadful fighting.

When I think about the hell I've been through the last few days, I can't help but cry and wonder how I am still alive. My company suffered the worst casualties—I believe something close to 50 dead and wounded. Friends who I took training with at Ft. Polk have been killed, and some are seriously wounded. In my squad of nine men, only four of us survived.

This was the worst battle as far as losses are concerned that this company has experienced. I'm not able to go into details now. I'm still in a slight state of shock and very weary and shaken from the last three days.

I just wanted you to know that I'm OK. How I made it I don't know. Perhaps you didn't read about it, but in case you did I just wanted to tell you I'm OK.

I can't help crying now because I think about the horror of those three days. I was carrying the bodies of wounded and dead onto helicopters that were in a clearing when I saw, I believe, Ron Nessen, of NBC, and they were taking pictures.

Yesterday (I thought they'd never come for us) we were evacuated from that area by helicopter. The area is less than two miles from Cambodia, where VCs have regiments, and they ambushed us.

I received your letter dated June 25th and will answer at a later date. Try to hold up. By the time you receive this, I hope to be somewhat recovered and at ease.

Love,
Kenny

Sp/4 Kenneth Peeples, Jr., served with Company A, 2nd Battalion, 18th Infantry, 1st Infantry Division, operating in III Corps, from June 1966 until he was wounded in February 1967. He lives in South Orange, New Jersey, and is a librarian at LaGuardia Community College in New York City.

— ☆ —

Nov 17 [1966]
Near Cambodia

Happy Thanksgiving!

Hi Ronnie,

How are you doing? Did you ever get that letter I wrote you? How's your daughter doing? Can she walk yet? Say hello to your wife for me, and have a cold beer on me.

Well, things have been pretty hot around here lately. November 12th about 300 of us got hit by a regiment of NVA troops and got the worst mortar attack of the war. They also shelled us from Cambodia with 120-mm mortars and artillery. It was the first big attack I've been in, and it was something else. The mortar and artillery shells just kept coming in, and it seemed like they'd never end. The Charlies were jumping around in the thick brush around us and shooting and chucking grenades at us a lot.

Every once in a while you'd get a glimpse of one and let him have it. I think I might have got two and maybe three or four others but can't tell since they dragged most of the bodies off. But I'm pretty sure I got those two. We were expecting any minute for a wave of them to jump up from bushes and charge us. But [they] never did. Our Air Force and supporting artillery broke up the moves before they could get to us.

In the morning we swept out to see what we had got. In open areas where they couldn't get to them, we found a lot of bodies and weapons. Sweeping a few hundred meters out from the perimeter we found lots of abandoned gear, blood pools, and bloody bandages. We took six dead and 40 wounded ourselves, and one artillery gun in our LZ was knocked out. The ammo for it kept exploding all night, shells and casings landing all over the place. In the morning we dug a lot of shrapnel out of our bunker. A 105 dud landed right in front of our bunker, [so] I got out, ran around to [the] front, and picked it up and threw it in an old bomb crater. Didn't realize how crazy that was till I got back to bunker. Could easily have got it. Also [had] to leave [the] bunker and go through fire a couple of other times to get ammo. Then went out to set up [a] claymore and grab a rifle some guy left there. That was pretty stupid, too. But if they had charged us, the claymore would have got a lot of them. A lot of guys did asshole things and didn't think nothing of it at the time—later on realized it. Those dead Cong didn't seem like people [as] we dragged them into piles and cut their equipment off them. They felt like a pile of rags or something, can't really explain it. We shot all their wounded [the] next day.

The official body count was 79. They've seen around 300 from planes in the area and the estimate is they might have lost two to three times that many. They really got creamed. From the few prisoners [we] found out the 88th Regiment, fresh from Cambodia, had hit us.

Felt real bad though when [I] found out one of the dead was my best friend, a guy I'd known since Basic and always hung around with. Wished the whole thing hadn't happened in a way. He was married and had three kids—never should have been drafted. Intend to get some Charlies for him. Hope I run into some of those peace demonstrators when I get back. Like to knock their heads in.

Cut a canteen off one Charlie for a souvenir, got an aluminum spoon from a knocked-out mortar position. Would have liked to have got a weapon or knife, but guys who didn't go on sweep grabbed them all up. When [we] came in [we] had a whole poncho full of gear, but none was worth keeping. Some of the Charlies were just kids, 14 or 15 years old. They must be crazy or something.

Our company is quartering artillery now until we get some replacements to make up our losses. Three choppers got shot down the day before. Some of the guys in them lived, but can't see how since they were just balls of flame when they went down.

Well enough about this lousy place. What have you been doing lately? In a couple of days I'll have a year in the Army and four months over here. Will be great to get back to the States and out of the Army. It's probably starting to get cold out now in [the] States. Has there been any snow yet? When I get out, I guess I'll take it easy for a couple of months and just mess around. Been thinking of buying a car and just riding around the country to see what there is and forget the Army.

May try to get into choppers, as you get flight pay and don't have to walk, which I don't like at all.

If you get a chance, drop a few lines. Like to hear how you're doing. Next time I hope to have something more cheerful to write about.

Louie

PFC Louis E. Willett served with Company C, 1st Battalion, 12th Infantry, 4th Infantry Division. He was killed in a fire fight in Kontum province on 15 February 1967. For his actions he was awarded the Congressional Medal of Honor, the nation's highest military award. His citation reads in part: "PFC Willett covered [his] squad's withdrawal, but his position drew heavy enemy machine gun fire, and he received multiple wounds. [He] struggled to an upright position and, disregarding his painful wounds, he again engaged the enemy with his rifle to allow his squad to continue its movement and to evacuate several of his comrades who were by now wounded. Moving from position to position, he engaged the enemy at close range until he was mortally wounded." PFC Louis Willett, born in Brooklyn, New York, and raised in Richmond Hill, was 21 years old when he died. This letter was written to his friend, Ronald Zimmermann.

8-17-68

Dear Mrs. Carlson,

I received your letter and I'm very sorry about the death of your son Richard. I often wonder if it was worth the sorrow and the pain which so many of us fret over now each day. I guess this is a [situation] nobody can explain.

Richard and I were very good friends, as [we] were the two medics attached to Delta Company. During the month of May our company was on a search-and-destroy mission in the South Vietnam National Forest. We had been searching the area from the beginning of May up until the 20th without making any contact with the enemy. On the 21st day of May we met enemy resistance consisting of heavy automatic weapons fire, which caused our company to pull back and call in artillery and air strikes. Our commanding officer received reports that we were up against a regimental-size force, so for three days we called in artillery and air strikes before moving back into the area of contact.

We advanced without any contact whatsoever when our lead element spotted two enemy soldiers and killed them both. As we continued on farther, Charlie had concealed himself and set up an ambush, which he let us walk right into before he sprung the trap. The enemy opened up, hitting one of our men in both legs. At this time we pulled back, but in the excitement we didn't know that we had a man laying back there wounded until we heard his shouts.

At this time we couldn't get to him because the firing was so heavy, so I crawled forward and aided the man, but I couldn't pull him back because they had me pinned down. A five-man team was sent forward to provide a base of fire for me while I carried my wounded buddy back. But those five men never made it to my position. They were all shot down and wounded. So I left the other man and began applying aid to the other wounded members of my company. Richard crawled up to my side and began patching up the nearest man to him when he was shot in the leg. He was bleeding badly and in great pain. I applied morphine to his wound to ease the pain.

He finally told me the pain had subsided a great deal, so I told him to lay there until I could drag him back. But he saw that an officer had been hit in the head and was losing a lot of blood. Richard rolled over several times until he was by the officer's side. He then began to treat the man as best he could. In the process he was hit several more times, twice in the chest and once in the arm. He called me, and I went to his side and began treating his wounds. As I applied bandages to his wounds, he looked up at me and said, "Doc, I'm a mess." He then said: "Oh, God, I don't want to die. Mother, I don't want to die. Oh, God, don't let me die." We called a helicopter to take him and the rest of the wounded to the hospital. Richard died before the ship arrived.

I did everything in my power to save Richard. Every skill known to me was applied. I often wonder if what we're fighting for is worth a human life. If there is anything that I can do please, call on me.

Sincerely,
Charles Dawson

Charles Dawson wrote this letter to the mother of Cpl. Richard A. Carlson, a fellow medic with Company D, 2nd Battalion, 8th Cavalry, 1st Cavalry Division (Airmobile). Carlson, from San Francisco, California, had been in Vietnam four months when he was killed on 24 May 1968. He was 20 years old. His last letter home is on page 291.

— ☆ —

Only the crickets
Are bold enough to speak
Suddenly they stop
The rapid respiration
Of frightened men remains.
You think of home and wait
Mostly you just wait.
The mortar lands nearby
Ringing in your ears

> Leaves you deaf
> For the rest of your life
> But just how long
> Will that be?
>
> —George T. Coleman

Sp/4 George Coleman, from Mercerville, New Jersey, was assigned to the 303rd Radio Research Battalion, Long Binh, from May 1967 through June 1970. He is assistant manager of the Hyatt Regency Hotel in Princeton, New Jersey.

— ☆ —

Khe Sanh, located in the Annamese Cordillera, the mountain range in the northwest corner of South Vietnam, was one of the anchors in a series of American defensive strongpoints positioned along the length of the DMZ. Its remoteness, six-month cloud cover, mist-filled valleys, and triple-canopy jungle offered the North Vietnamese Army an ideal infiltration route into the northernmost provinces of South Vietnam. For 77 days in early 1968, Khe Sanh was the focal point of a contest of will and arms between the NVA and the Marines.

This battle, the longest of the war, became known as the Siege of Khe Sanh. Two NVA divisions and support elements comprising over 20,000 men ringed the combat base and hill outposts, effectively sealing in 6,000 Marines and South Vietnamese Rangers. To many, the situation at Khe Sanh was reminiscent of the infamous battle of Dien Bien Phu, in which French forces suffered the humiliating defeat that resulted in the termination of French involvement in Indochina.

Khe Sanh held. Official estimates put the cost to the NVA at 10,000 to 15,000 killed or wounded. Marine casualties were put at 1,800 killed and wounded.

(Biographical notes for the next five letters appear together.)

30 Jan. '68

Dear Ellen,

Please forgive me again for not writing sooner, but since I've gotten back from R&R I haven't had much time for such luxuries. We've really been preparing for this all-out offensive by the gooks on [Hill] 881 and Hue. This is the largest troop movement the NVA has made in the Vietnam conflict to date. They say this battle could be the key to bring Hanoi to the peace table on our conditions.

I guess you might have read about it in the papers. The guys here all have newspaper clippings from home about the mortaring and rocketing of Khe Sanh. That was the worst I've seen since I've been in Vietnam. I lost quite a few buddies that day, and all I hope for now is the chance to get back at them and make them pay for it. I'm sorry for writing like this. I try not to write home about any action I've been in, but I just can't help feeling bitter and vengeful toward them. There is supposed to be a truce in Vietnam during the Chinese Tet New Year. Khe Sanh is the only area not observing it because of the build-up. . . .

I just can't thank you enough, Ellen, for your help and kindness in the past four months. A guy comes to realize that he couldn't have made it through this mess without someone back there pulling for him and keeping him aware that all is not lost and restore his morale and faith in America. . . .

They just dropped six rockets in on us. Another buddy of mine got hit. Jeff Culpepper got his arm gashed. Well that's about all the news for now. I'll try to write again soon.

Love,
Jim

29 January 68

Dear Mom and Dad,

I guess by now you are worried sick over my safety. Khe Sanh village was overrun, but not the combat base. The base was hit and hit hard by artillery, mortars and rockets. All my gear and the rest of the company's gear was destroyed. Right now we are living in bunkers just like the Marines at Con Thien did last fall.

I am unhurt and have not been touched. I skinned my knee on the initial assault, but other than that I am OK. My morale is not the best because my best buddy was killed the day before yesterday. I was standing about 20 feet from him and a 60-mm mortar exploded next to him. He caught a piece of shrapnel in the head. I carried him over to the aid station where he died. I cried my eyes out. I have seen death before but nothing as close as this. Junior, my buddy, had 67 days left in country and then he was to return to his wife and daughter. His death really hit me hard. Two days before that four other Marines in my company were killed by a rocket exploding on the floor of their bunker. They were killed instantly, but their bodies were horribly mangled. I think with all the death and destruction I have seen in the past week I have aged greatly. I feel like an old man now. I am not as happy-go-lucky as before, and I think more maturely now. Payback for my buddies is not the uppermost thought in my mind. My biggest goal is to return to you and Dad and Ann in June or July.

The battle for Khe Sanh is not over yet. Since it began, we (Bravo

Company, 3rd Recon Battalion) have lost 14 men KIA and 44 men WIA. Our company is cut down to half strength, and I think we will be going to Okinawa to regroup. I hope so anyway because I have seen enough of war and its destruction. I am scarred by it but not scared enough to quit. I am a Marine and I hope someday to be a good one. Perhaps that way I can be worthy of the friendship Junior and I shared. It bothers me to think of these so-called Americans who shirk their responsibility to our country. If I even get close enough to a peace picket, he will see part of the Vietnam War in my eyes. They cannot compare to the man Junior was. I will miss him greatly. He was with me since June of last year, and we went everywhere together. We have so little over here, but we share it all.

Please pray for us all here at Khe Sanh and also for my buddy Junior Reather. I hope he is happy where he is. Take care and God Bless.

Your Son & Marine,
Kevin

31 January 68

Joe—

Greetings, old buddy. This is gonna be a half-serious (that's serious for me!) attempt at letting my handwriting speak for my mind.

I guess we're in a pretty bad situation over here. The gooks are hell bent on trying to take over this area—and it isn't over by a long "shot" (pun!) yet. Sometimes it gets pretty hairy in this motherfucker—and I've come close a few times. Not close enough, though.

Anyway, I want to say I'm not afraid of dying. I'll just feel sorry for my folks. Brothers and sister and you. There's no way I can describe how good friends we two are and how much your ugly presence means to me. I'll feel sorry about "pulling out" so early, Joe—kinda like I let you down. Without being *too too* clichéd I'll say there's so much to say and do and no time or place to attempt it.

If, if I should go, I'll have to say it's been a fantastic nine years. Full of the best of everything, with no regrets. A barrel of laughs. Good times and bad, happy and sad, etc., etc. . . . I wouldn't have wished it any other way . . . and I'll feel most shitty for you, man. So much we got planned —so much we're gonna do. Hell, I'm only taking it one day at a time now —leaving it up to the Big Referee in the Sky. He's the one who makes the rules and takes out players and sends in subs. Nothing else really counts.

I feel shitty just writing this mess—but it's been on my mind constantly in the last 12 days and I had to let you know the score, just "in case." I think you know what I mean.

Now that that's over and done with—come October '68 I'm gonna stand in your driveway and watch you put a match to this piece of crap —and that's "no lie."

I gotta hustle—sun's almost gone. Another month shot to shit.

See ya pronto—
Dennis

P.S. What's this I hear about Anderson (#44) being offside (but not detected) on the Dallas 6-inch line? Why? Why? Why? Why?

8 Feb 68

Dear Dad and Mom,

Well, they haven't gotten me yet. I'm sitting here in my new bunker underground with many sandbags and metal skids between me and the surface. But the men and I will be all right no matter what comes. We are all well and morale is high. I really will get on it and get a note off to both the girls.

I hope Dad isn't working too hard and is keeping up with the rest of the crew at the old watering trough. You know I've never really regretted coming over here, even yesterday when my favorite turd got it. The little guy was my platoon sergeant's radio man. His name is Pietro Osimanti. A cuter little guy you've never seen. He was originally from Rome, Italy, and wrote letters to his Mama in Italian. I really loved the kid. He was the hardest little worker and never complained. Do anything for you.

I moved my CP [command post] from my old bunker to the new one two days ago. I sent Pietro down to get something—I can't even remember what now—and I myself had just walked out when a rocket came in and hit right in front of the old CP. Pietro got hit, and I knew he had at the instant he did. I held his head for 15 minutes while my corpsman worked on him. Then they took him to regimental med. He is down in Da Nang now and will be all right, thank God.

But you know, after they had taken him away, it almost "kicked my ass," as the saying goes. I almost cracked. But there are 75 others to worry about, and I snapped myself out of my cheap civilian bull and got back to work. Poor little guy (just turned 18). All he could say was "God, why me?" over and over. I'm going to write a letter to his mom and dad and tell them what a good little guy he is, and how much they have to be proud of. . . .

Well, you learn every day the mistakes you are making, and the biggest one is to get too attached to any one person. Not over here at least. Things happen so quickly, and one minute he's fine the next he's not.

But old Don is pretty lucky (knock on wood), and home I'll come, I'm sure. They have been hitting all around us pretty much, and a lot of good men have gone down, but we are getting our share. We have gotten over 1,000 confirms in the Khe Sanh area alone since the 21st, and more every day. I hope it is over soon. It looks like this might be their last big push. Maybe after we wipe them up here they'll go to the bargaining tables and we can come home. All of us!

I'm sure you are both fine and well as I am, and so I'll close with love in my heart for both of you.

Love,
Don

16 Feb 68

Dear Family,

As you probably already know, we are now at Khe Sanh surrounded by 20,000 NVA troops, so now they can't get away. I never thought incoming artillery sounded so terrible—it just screams out of the sky.

So far my two squads have killed 21 NVA. We killed 15 the day that small outpost was overrun 750 meters away from my gun position. We have a new experimental shell that produces air bursts of darts and can be set for any range. Two days later we killed six more with one shot. This was done at night with a starlight telescope.

Every now and then a Marine will be killed or wounded by an incoming mortar, but every day fewer come in. We've been having B-52 strikes around the clock, and combined with close air support the NVA are having a hard time getting close enough.

Khe Sanh is in a valley surrounded by high mountains, and the NVA are said to be planning another Dien Bien Phu–type operation on us. But we aren't making the same mistakes the French made. At any rate, by the time they get enough artillery into the mountains around us, I'll be on my way home. Also the highest hills are held by Marines, 881 and 861, and they'll never push us off them.

It's a lot different up here fighting NVA instead of VC. Up here anyone who isn't an American is an enemy, and they are as well equipped as we, with helmets and new assault rifles and body armor.

I take good care of myself, always in my hole, and I'm armed to the teeth—knives, pistol, rifle, grenades, everything. Around us we have all kinds of barbed wire and mines, and we've dug trenches all over the place.

The battalion is still rumored to go afloat in March, and we're supposed to leave Khe Sanh on the 27th of February for Dong Ha to prepare. But you know how rumors are. If we do, I'll be too short to go along so I'll probably go to Okinawa. If that happens, it'll mean I only have a few weeks left in the field.

The weather is very cold up here, a lot like California in the winter, with thick fog and cold wind. We have wool shirts and field jackets, but you still get cold standing watch at night.

I live in an underground bunker with a roof made of huge logs we cut with a machete and with a double layer of sandbags on top of that. Inside it is lined with a camouflaged parachute. The airstrip is closed for repairs so all our supplies are dropped by parachute, and we keep all the damaged ones.

That's about all there is to say right now. The next time you hear from me, it'll probably be in person. I've got less than two months left in Vietnam.

Your son,
George

PFC James Hebron, assigned to Company B, 1st Battalion, 26th Regiment, 3rd Marine Division, ended his tour in Vietnam on 18 February 1968. One week later, a patrol from his platoon, led by 2Lt. Don Jacques, was decimated in an ambush while seeking an enemy mortar. Twenty-five of the 29 Marines on patrol were killed that day, 25 February 1968, the day Hebron landed in New York. Long active in veterans' affairs, he lives and works in New York City. This letter was written to a friend from high school, Ellen Raspitha.

Kevin Macaulay, a corporal with Company B, 3rd Recon Battalion, 3rd Marine Division, from June 1967 through June 1968, was at the combat base at Khe Sanh during the siege. He now works for the New York City Board of Education as a school custodian.

Dennis Mannion was a lance corporal with K Company, 3rd Battalion, 26th Regiment, 3rd Marine Division, from September 1967 to October 1968. His unit was positioned on Hill 861 during the siege. He is now an English teacher and football coach in Cheshire, Connecticut. This letter was written to his friend Joe Doherty.

2Lt. Donald J. Jacques, from Rochester, New York, arrived in Vietnam in October 1967. Assigned to Company B, 1st Battalion, 26th Regiment, 3rd Marine Division, he commanded the third platoon, positioned on Hill 881 and at the Khe Sanh combat base, until 25 February 1968, when he was killed.

Sgt. George W. Storz, from San Anselmo, California, assigned to H & S Company, 1st Battalion, 9th Regiment, 3rd Marine Division, was killed in action on 8 March 1968, one month before he was due to return home. He never got to see his second son. He was 23 years old.

In a letter to the commission, Macaulay quoted the executive officer of Company B, 1Lt. C. J. ("Pappy") Schlack, as saying that, when he returned to the World, he was going to open a saloon for the survivors of Khe Sanh, and if it ever got more than two deep at the bar, he'd know somebody was lying.

—— ☆ ——

Bong Son   11/17/68

HEAT
FIRE
EXPLOSION
IS THIS DEATH?
HELP ME! HELP ME! HELP ME!
HE HOLDS TO ME FOR LIFE
AS WE MOVE TO SURVIVAL
FEAR AND CONFUSION
GUILT AND JOY
I'M ALIVE

—John Campbell

Sgt. John Campbell, Company E, 2nd Battalion, 503rd Infantry, 173rd Airborne Brigade, wrote this after four members of his recon team were killed "in the blink of an eye" by a booby trap at Bong Son on 17 November 1968. He served in Vietnam from October 1968 to October 1969, operating in northern II Corps. He is now president of Conserve Energy Group, Inc. in New York City.

— ☆ —

20 Mar 68

Hello Folks,

Here I am in sunny Da Nang—the only R&R area where you don't have fun. We've been operating around Hue now for the past two months and are now moving towards the A Shau Valley. We've done well so far —have made a lot of kills, have a good body count and make contact quite often.

My men have done an outstanding job so far—we've captured quite a few weapons and have been put in for quite a few awards. But with awards, you don't know about them until they've been okayed.

I'm sorry I haven't written, but we have so little time to do anything. Since I've been here I haven't seen a bed till my R&R. I've taken one shower in two months, wore the same clothes for two months, and have been sleeping on the ground in water. I guess that's why they say war is hell—cause people in hell don't even get wet.

Right now I'm sitting on a veranda overlooking the ocean, watching the waves break on the shore beneath me, and in 24 hours I'll be back out fighting the NVA. . . .

Well, I guess I better get going. I've lost Dad's address—I've lost just about everything.

Love,
Rob

1Lt. Robert Santos, one of the most decorated combat veterans of the war, was a rifle platoon leader with Company C, 2nd Battalion, 501st Infantry, 101st Airborne Division, from November 1967 through November 1968, operating in I Corps. Four days after he wrote this letter, he was hit by shrapnel from a hand grenade. He lives in Brooklyn and is now deputy parks commissioner for the New York City Department of Parks and Recreation.

17 Feb [1967]

Hi La

I'm fine—the cast is off my leg—scar healing fine—no permanent damage whatsoever. [The] frag went inside and bounced off my bones of steel and slid down in flesh. They dug it out, let the wound drain, sewed me up and now I'm walking. Stitches come out in about 10 more days and when I return to base camp and A Company I'll stay behind for at least a few more weeks and rest or pull light duty. Scar is about 8″ long. Sewed me up with wire. "Docs" are real good. [They] work like dogs— you may very well be here when you're one.

The company lost 5 KIA about 40 wounded. We fucked up at least two times as many Charlies as far as KIA, but we have more wounded. We "estimate" [that the] main problem was Charlie was dug in and of course we weren't. Wherever Charlie is dug in he has claymore mines set up, which caused 50% of our casualties. The cruits are coming in fast. Two went out—only here four days and got wounded. We're all hoping to get Charlie out in the open where we can kill 10 to 1 instead of 2 to 1. The fragments I caught from the grenades, I could have cut myself worse shaving. One in chest and one in back. In all honesty they were only the size of a freckle. The total casualty list for [the] 2nd Platoon was 17 wounded, 1 KIA.

Of course I haven't seen my close buddies killed—but it surprised me the way in which I and everyone accepts the fact that we did and will lose some troopers. It's sad. But the worst part about it is the fact of the family at home. We accept death as part of the risk of being a trooper. When a guy is not *seriously* wounded it's time for laughs etc. because he knows he's in for a rest and "ghost time." The worst part of getting hit is when they sew you up. When I got hit I wasn't even sure I was until I saw the blood. Of course this was "beauty to mine eyes." Just made me shoot harder and faster. After all, the infantry is "baptised in blood." . . .

After everyone finds out that all [our] buddies aren't too bad off we start joking etc., and in my case, picture taking. All this I guess is a means of keeping your minds off the troopers that aren't breathing and wrapped up in their ponchos. One of the saddest things I saw was when I woke to see three feet from me the jungle boots sticking out of ponchos of two troopers from Weapons Platoon. I knew both of them. We mourn for them only once at the memorial ceremony back at base camp. After that we talk of them only in good spirits in reference to the good times we had in Bien Hoa, or possibly a funny incident that took place in the field. . . .

Well, what else can I say. I told Mom I'm fine. Leg is healing perfectly. If she doesn't believe it, "that's the breaks," as we say. I can't emphasize enough I'm OK. Healthy, eating good, sleeping good, and there is no damage to my knee or anywhere else. Say hello to John and your buddies at school. Just finished *Beau Geste*. If there was still a French Foreign Legion I think I'd have to try that next. Damn good book.

Brother John

Sp/4 John Kane served with Company A, 1st Battalion, 503rd Infantry, 173rd Airborne Brigade, based at Bien Hoa, from June 1966 until February 1967, when he was wounded. He is vice-president of a direct mail advertising firm in Long Island City, New York.

— ☆ —

5/2/69

Hi Sweetheart:

First of all, you'll have to excuse the dirty paper, but right now I'm on a landing craft. I'll explain that later. Today I didn't receive any mail from you, but I did receive one from my mother.

Last night we went on an ambush patrol. The moon was so bright that I read four of your letters before it was my turn to guard. I've been going on the ambushes practically every night since I'm here. This morning, when we came back in, they told us we had to be security guards on this LCM [Landing Craft, Medium]; it's these big boats that transport people. They used to use them during WW II to land GIs on beachheads.

Well, anyway, we went way downriver to pick up some ARVNs [soldiers of the Army of the Republic of Vietnam], and from there we went even farther down to pick up some Vietnamese people, about 200 of them. Now the whole reason for this was to clear out a certain area of all the villagers. The only people that would be left would normally be VC. Well, we took all the people to a certain point, and as they left the boat their IDs were checked, and would you believe there were three VC women on the boat. Right away they were bound, blindfolded and questioned, but they denied everything. The ARVNs then put them in water up to their necks and held them underwater. One guy even stepped on [one woman's] head while [she was] in the water. Then they took them out and beat them with bamboo sticks. Meanwhile they were still bound and blindfolded. It seemed like they still denied everything, so they brought them down the road to a house.

About two hours later they came out looking beat-up and led the ARVNs to a case of ammunition. Even though you think their tactics are cruel, they work. That ammo was used to kill GIs. Altogether today they caught 20 VC. One guy was caught with an AK-47, 20 mortar rounds, 3 mines with detonating cord, 15 magazines of ammo. That's a good catch for one day. I took a few pictures and hope they came out. Right now we're docked on a shore along the river. The captain won't bring the boat downriver back to base camp in the dark. But don't worry, there are 13 of us with all kinds of weapons.

Well, honey, it's getting kinda dark so I'll have to leave off by saying I Love You and Miss You More Than Anything in the World. No one could ever take your place.

Always,
Michael

Sp/4 Michael Romano, from New York City, was an infantryman with Company B, 2nd Battalion, 3rd Infantry, 199th Light Infantry Brigade, based at LZ Blackhorse, from April 1969 to March 1970. He is now a maintenance worker for Pepsico and lives in Holmes, New York.

— ☆ —

29 Jan '68

Dear Dick,

Saw your letter to 153 crew this week. I passed it on to Pulliam and McPherson. I'm sure you know by now, but just in case you don't, I'll fill you in [on] the details of 18 January.

Hotel Patrol was proceeding west to the Cai Be station when 153 picked up two evading sampans about two miles west of Island #10 outpost. They were making it for a canal on the south bank and naturally Goldy took off after them. He called in to Dewey in 112 who turned back to cover him. When 153 was about 75 meters from the south bank, the VC opened up from the treeline. 153 took two rocket hits almost simultaneously. The first hit the radar dome and blew shrapnel all over the boat. The second hit the venture area in front of the coxswain stand and set the boat afire. Goldy was thrown to the deck, jerking the throttles into reverse as the blast knocked him down. Pulliam, the forward gunner, got off ten rounds with the 50s after he was knocked to his knees by the first rocket. Then the second one hit and knocked him down a second time. He got up slow the next time. Caufield was perforated with shrapnel and lay in the bottom of the boat, bleeding.

McPherson, on the after 50, was also wounded but got off a good blast of return fire with the after gun. Then he saw the boat was backing into the south bank—so he left his mount and jumped into the coxswain flat, which was burning pretty hot by then. He pushed the throttle ahead and drove the boat out into the middle of the river. If it hadn't been for Mac, we might have lost everyone and the boat too. PBR [River Patrol Boat] 112 got between 153 and the beach and laid down some suppressive fire. Then they pulled out and went alongside 153 to evacuate the wounded. All the time Charlie was shooting at them with automatic and small arms from the ambush. About that time 132 and 147 got there and made three firing runs which finally suppressed the fire. Seawolfs showed up a few minutes later and provided cover while all three PBRs pulled off the wounded. Everyone on the boat got it, including the Vietnamese cop. The cop died later that night.

It was a sad sight to see 153 all smashed up. I went out with 151 on an emergency scramble, but everything was under control by the time we got there. We took 153 in tow and brought her back. What a mess—the canopy was in shreds, and the inside of the boat was a horrible shambles from the blast and fire.

What was such a damn shame was Goldy getting it on the main river after all those canals he'd run. Pulliam, Caufield and MacPherson will recover after a short convalescence. Mac wasn't bad at all, but a little shaken when I last saw him. Pulliam and Caufield will be going home. Pulliam almost lost his left eye, and Caufield really caught a load of shrapnel. Nothing serious, I don't believe.

Goldy is in the worst shape of all of them. When I saw him last Tuesday, he was still on the critical list and only semiconscious. He suffered multiple fragment wounds to the head and upper body. His left arm is in very bad shape, but they have been unable to do anything about it because of his head wounds. The nurse I talked to said he suffered a skull fracture (right front) and probable brain damage. Goldy will be many, many months recovering. It was the most disturbing experience I've yet come across out here. You really wonder what the fuck this is all about.

Needless to say the guys on 112 were really down in the dumps after it happened. They were the ones who pulled all the people out. Mead went back into the smoke three times to try and get Goldy out of the coxswain flat. You can imagine what a psychological shock it was for them to see those people so torn up. They are better now, but all of them need some R&R.

Not much else has happened. I am counting the days now that I have only a little more than a month to go. Christ, I've had enough after the last 10 days. Good luck and keep in touch.

Bob

Lt. J.G. Robert Moir served with River Patrol Section 533, part of the Navy's River Patrol Force, from February 1967 through February 1968. Based at My Tho, his unit patrolled the Mekong River and its canals. He is now a corporate lawyer in Denver, Colorado. This letter was written to Dick Strandberg, a fellow officer in 533.

—— ☆ ——

30 Jan '68

Dear Sue,

I'm still in a state of half-shock. PBR 153, my old lead boat in 533, was hit with two B-40 rockets and a round of 57-mm recoilless. The whole crew was wounded, and the VN cop was killed. . . . I tell you, I'm just numb inside. 153 was the boat I was on when we took that rifle grenade.

I was really pissed after I heard about it. Last night—Tet, the Vietnamese New Year—I had my chance, but because of the cease-fire I couldn't do a thing. The VC had come into this village near the river and strung VC flags everywhere. There must've been 50 of them. One flag was about 30 feet from the perimeter of the outpost there. I saw about 10 to 15 of the bastards, ranging in age from 13 to 18, standing in front of one hooch, smoking and drinking beer, like a gang of hoods on a street corner in the States. They were in civilian clothes. I called in a helo fire team to look over the area and try to draw fire, and with them covering, I moved in close to see. That's when I saw them—two at first, just like the pictures in *Life* and *Look*—black pajamas, bandoliers strung across their chests, hand grenades on their belts, carrying carbines or M-1s. And they just looked at us. The helos swept down and a couple more ducked into a hut. I had them dead to rights, but I couldn't do a thing. Not until they fired the first shot—and they didn't.

God, I wanted to shoot them! We stayed in the area all night, but they didn't do anything.

Early this morning, however, the VC attacked Da Nang and that broke the cease-fire. This morning the helos from Vinh Long went out and greased 95 of the SOBs, moving down a canal in sampans. That tally, along with the 78 (body count—26 additional graves were found) the Navy helos (Seawolves) caught in the open last week and killed, washes away a little of the taste for revenge.

I guess it isn't *nice* to say, but if I had any compunctions about killing them before, I don't now. Give me another chance like last night and I'll drill a round into one of those yellow heads.

Geez, I hate Vietnam.

Love,
Dick

Lt. J.G. Richard Strandberg, from Minneapolis, Minnesota, served with River Patrol Sections 533 and 522 from May 1967 to May 1968. This letter was written to his wife. The curator of "The Vietnam Experience" art exhibits in St. Paul, Minnesota, in 1980 and in New York City in 1981, he is now an artist living and working in Mesa, Arizona.

— ☆ —

7 Dec 67

Hi Honey,

I received your letter today saying you got my ring. I figured it was too small, but you can get it made to fit your ring finger. I'm glad you like it. I was hoping you would. It's the nicest personal present I've ever given you, I believe.

I wish you weren't sick, honey. I know how you must feel, and I hate to be sick. With those two small tornadoes around the house I would imagine your nerves are shot.

I lost two of my men today to a booby trap. As usual, my luck stuck with me and I didn't get hurt. We had been checking through this village by the ocean and we had found quite a bit of explosives and rifle ammo. I had my platoon in rifle teams abreast with squads in column. I walked in between my two point men so there were three of us walking in front.

We were crossing a corn field with a thick hedgerow around it. There was one place that looked like we could get through, so I told my point man to go through there. I turned and headed for it. Just as my point man went through, he heard a click and jumped. I was five meters from him, and one of my squad leaders stepped in front of me to go through next. Just as he did, the point man jumped and the squad leader started to turn to me. There was a tremendous explosion, and I was knocked down by the force of the blast. My ears were ringing like hell, and my squad leader staggered to me. I jumped up and yelled for Bell, who was the point man. He was halfway through his jump when the explosion went off and threw him into the next corn field. My squad leader, Hunter, had caught the full blast of the explosion and shrapnel. His face, body, and legs were completely cut to pieces by the shrapnel. His clothes were blown to rags, and he was bleeding like hell. One of the pieces of shrapnel had penetrated his can of shaving cream, and it was spewing shaving cream about five feet in the air over both of us.

My RTO, who was also knocked down by the blast, and I yelled for the medic, who rushed up and probably saved the man's life by his fast action. Meanwhile, I crawled through the blasted area and ran over to Bell, who was lying on his stomach with his pack blown over his shoulders.

I got him out of his pack and turned him over. He took shrapnel in the left arm and hand plus his left leg, but he wasn't too bad off.

Captain Sells, who has been with my platoon, ran up to me right after the explosion, but I was too dazed to remember exactly what happened. He took over for about five minutes until I regained my senses.

It was a pretty exciting day. Someone up there knows I have a beautiful wife and two wonderful children to go home to.

I love you very much, Dearest.

With Much Love,
Fred

2Lt. Fred Downs, platoon commander, Co. D, 1/14th Inf., 4th Inf. Div., Pleiku province, 1967–1968, WIA 11 January 1968.

— ☆ —

13 March [1968]

Hi Vern,

The shit has been hitting the fan, but I've managed to miss the spray.

One guy was shooting at my ambush last night. I reported it as heavy contact and got eight barrels of artillery to shoot white phosphorus and high explosives in the wood line. We found a body this morning so the colonel was happy.

A company ambushed my platoon, and I only lost one man. A rocket ricocheted off my truck, and the VC charged it. Your prayers must have been talking up a storm to God then. No kidding. I believe!

You'd be surprised how similar killing is to hunting. I know I'm after souls, but I get all excited when I see a VC, just like when I see a deer. I go ape firing at him. It isn't that I'm so crazy. I think a man who freezes killing a man would freeze killing a deer. I'm not perverted, crazy, or anything else. Civilians think such thinking is crazy, but it's no big deal. He runs, you fire. You hunt so I think you'd feel the same way. It isn't all that horrifying.

When you see a man laughing about it, remember he talks the same about killing a deer. Of course, revenge has a part in wanting him just like you want a deer for a trophy and meat. I know I'm not nuts. If I killed a man in the U.S., everyone would stare. Last night I killed and everyone has been patting me on the back, including the battalion commander. What do you think?

A friend got killed on an ambush last week. [The colonel] told him to move in the middle of the night. As he drew in all his claymores, Charlie hit. Last night they told me to move twice. It'll be a cold day in hell when I move. Thirty minutes later I reported "Moved." The colonel isn't about to come out to see where I am. I'm chicken but not stupid!

It isn't all that horrifying. It's rough living in the field, but big deal. They sell mohair tailored sports coats for $35 here and sharkskin suits for $60. I'll buy a few before I leave. What a deal! . . .

Hi Vern,

Got your letters today. It was great hearing from you. Actually, I can't summarize my feelings of my trip to Australia [for R&R]. I don't know if I had a fabulous time or not. It was weird. Getting back to a completely English-looking and -speaking country made me feel kind of ashamed of the way I've thought and acted over here. I realize that I've actually enjoyed some of the things I've done which would be repulsive to a healthy mind. This place does make you sick in the head. When one starts to enjoy the sickness of war, he is sick. . . .

Hello Vern,

I got your letter and really enjoyed the news. I got a company of my own now, and I'm King Shit. A mess hall, about 50 vehicles, recon platoon, 4.2-mm mortar platoon, all the staffs, maintenance section, 198 men, a desk and office, two jeeps and drivers. I'm running my butt off trying to care for everything. I'm sticking my nose in everything—from complimenting the chef to sicking my first sergeant on somebody. I love it. However if a captain comes in I'll get bounced, being the only first lieutenant as company commander.

Vern, we ran into some problems here with our new battalion commander. He wanted to take Charlie on with his M-16s and trucks and forgot that he had artillery and jets to help him. Nine men were killed and about 30 hurt (no VC killed). He wanted to be a hero like our old battalion CO and goofed. What a bungle—he was relieved.

At the same time I got your letter dated 4 July asking about ambushes and booby traps. I was chicken and I'm proud of it because I got no one even hurt. For ambushes, I'd call artillery around me at night, and the VC couldn't tell where I was but they'd stay away. I killed eight known VC that way. As for booby traps, I'd always have civilians walk point for me. They ranged from 14-year-olds to men with canes, but they never hit a booby trap whereas all the other platoons [got] men hurt and killed. We did disarm four booby traps. . . .

Our new battalion CO said, "Maybe we'll run into some VC soon and get a good body count and the morale will go up again."

I'm becoming quite conservative in my ideas and tastes here. When you see men suffer and die for principles, and take it so great, it's hard to forgive liberals and free thinkers crying over nothing.

Your brother,
Jim

1Lt. James Simmen, from Danville, California, was a platoon leader with the 5th Battalion, 60th Infantry (Mechanized), 9th Infantry Division in the area south of Saigon during 1968. His battalion later transferred to the 1st Infantry Division, operating in the Parrot's Beak near the Cambodian border. He now works as a carpenter in Alaska and has written three unpublished novels. These letters were written to his brother, assistant pastor at St. Catherine's parish in Martinez, California.

--- ☆ ---

Tiger Patrol

Some teethless,
some dropouts,
coral beads on burnished necks,
sweat bands of silk,
tiger-striped pants,
Camels bit between parched lips,
a callus inside the index finger
matches the
distance from stock to trigger
of a machine gun,

they laugh,
speed down roads hanging like goblins to
their low slung carriages,
tough guys spitting on oriental sand
they wait as patiently as Buddha
under black charred clouds,
commuter trains of screaming
banshee-like tracers,
the whistling fury of flechettes from
a recoilless rifle,
quiet,
moans of the dying,
then death,
they kick and count the bodies,
a lieutenant colonel is promoted,
the Tiger Patrol sports NVA belts,
laughs in the daylight's hard grin,
each night they come,
I show them
sites,
hunting grounds,
soon they'll vote,
youth in delirious revolt,
in command of
John Wayne's mystique,
to them an amulet,
to them
a way home.

—George E. Samerjan
1970

Capt. George Samerjan wrote this poem while serving as a Mobile Advisory Team leader in III Corps between March 1970 and March 1971. He is president of Ocelot, a generic video-software company, in Sudbury, Massachusetts.

— ☆ —

23 Nov '69

Red,

We've been going pretty strong over here lately, and we're starting to pay the price. We lost a man on one of our teams operating out of Duc Pho two days ago when he pulled a one-man assault on a line of NVA who had half his team pinned down. He beat off the NVA but was killed doing it, and has been nominated for the CMH [Congressional Medal of Honor], which along with the Purple Heart is one medal I've no use for. We went out on one mission up here which made the papers, even if they didn't get the whole story right. We knocked [off] two base camps, killed one NVA, who could've been taken prisoner if our ARVNs hadn't cut him down out of hate and general principle, and took one VC prisoner.

It was a real textbook operation, but the one we went on yesterday turned out to be the shortest on record and was almost Charlie's big inning. We were to have been inserted with another team for a one-day operation against an arms repair factory with an estimated battalion camped in the general area. I think that estimate too conservative. We went in with two choppers, a chase ship and two [gunships]. When we were about 10 feet off the LZ and our interpreter and I were halfway out on the landing skid, about two seconds from the ground, the feces really hit the fan. On the other chopper the man on the skid was about to jump [to the ground] when a .30-cal machine gun opened up directly under him —he had almost jumped onto [an enemy] bunker. The pilot saw another bunker directly in front of him, and the woodline for 360° was a string of blinking tree lights. What I could personally see out of my door were spider holes opening up and green tracers coming in. One hole opened up less than 50 meters away, and I watched its occupant shoulder an AK [and] point it right at me. Then all I could see was muzzle flashes, and we had our own little duel right there as he tried for me and I did my best to walk my tracers up on him and hose him out of existence. How he ever missed not only me but a target the size of a Huey at that range I'll never know, but I can still see that rifle winking at me. Just as my tracers got up to him I ran out of ammo, which is about the most frustrating thing that's happened to me yet.

The whole thing was morbidly fascinating, and during the whole exchange I was never scared, which scares me now. I think the whole thing was that for once you could actually see your enemy, which doesn't happen too often in this war, and the only thought in my mind was to nail him before he nailed me. There was simply no room for fear. We came back with one chopper losing fuel and oil, with an underbelly in pieces but—miraculously—no one was hurt. The Cobras who worked the area over as we left took fire from .51 cal MGs [machine guns], yet the major who asked for the operation insisted we still go in—11 men to assault a battalion!! If I get the opportunity, I'll tell you honestly that I will kill that son-of-a-bitch. I have more hatred and contempt for him than I ever thought I could possibly feel for any human being. If there's one thing I can't abide, it's an armchair leader who sends his men off to die on hopeless, meaningless operations. To be killed is one thing, to die senselessly another. The major piloting the lead ship refused to reinsert us and put us all in for air medals with "V" for valor for the way we helped out his door gunners in their hour of need. I'd put him in for sainthood for having the guts to tell his superior to go to hell, that he didn't want 11 men on his conscience, and under no circumstances was he going to put us on the ground. I would definitely give credit for all of us coming out of that in one piece to Almighty God. We definitely had an extra, unseen passenger riding with us that day. If they had opened up 10 seconds later, we'd all still be out there. It's as close as I've been yet to hell, and I hope it's as close as I'll ever be.

George

Sp/4 George Olsen, Co. G, 75th In. (Ranger), Americal Div., Chu Lai, 1969–1970, KIA 3 March 1970.

— ☆ —

Dear Doug,

. . .The monsoon had been late up to now, but this day it rained in torrents. The jungle and the rice paddy we'd been wading around in wasn't affected much, but waist-deep streams we had waded [through] coming out were now impassable swamps 300 yards wide. I was put in the point now, with instructions to hurry toward what was a likely crossing on the map in hopes that it hadn't risen too much.

Almost immediately we discovered tracks, obviously too small to have been Occidentals. The scout read them as a mixture of VC and NVA. There was no way I could make any time and check every possible ambush, so I sent a double point as far ahead as practicable and kept everyone widely dispersed. We all expected to be hit any minute as fresh tracks were discovered. There was sniper fire at the rear of the column, and this heightened the tension. But we reached the river without incident. It was now impassable. We were cut off from our base and requested a helicopter evacuation with priority for 30 cases of immersion foot, many of which had begun to bleed because of the constant water. We were all in sad shape now. I know that at one point, my feet about to crack open, my stomach knotted by hunger and diarrhea, my back feeling like a mirror made of nerves shattered in a million pieces by my flak jacket, pack, and extra mortars and machine-gun ammo, my hands a mass of hamburger from thorn cuts, and my face a mass of welts from mosquitoes, I desired greatly to throw down everything, slump into the water of the paddy, and sob. I remember a captain, an aviator, who, observing a group of grunts toasting the infantry in a bar, said, "You damned infantry think you're the only people who exist." You're damned right we do.

Love,
David

1Lt. Victor David Westphall III, who arrived in Vietnam in October 1967, a platoon leader with Company B, 1st Battalion, 4th Regiment, 3rd Marine Division, was killed on 22 May 1968 in an ambush at Con Thien. He was 28 years old. In his memory, his father built the Vietnam Veterans Peace and Brotherhood Chapel in Eagle Nest, New Mexico. Doug is his brother.

— ☆ —

3
Beyond the Body Count

"In Vietnam, the only measure of victory was one of the most hideous, morally corrupting ideas ever conceived by the military mind—the body count," Philip Caputo, author of A Rumor of War, *a memoir of his tour in Vietnam, wrote in an article in* Playboy *magazine. "[We] fought over the same ground again and again, month after month, [our] only object to kill more of them than they did of [us]." When we did, the official logic went, that week at least we had won the war—even if the contested area was still controlled by the enemy, even if we hadn't won any "hearts or minds" in the countryside. Commanders liked good body counts, even when they were fudged, which was not uncommon. They liked high kill ratios; it meant they were doing something right.*

Many soldiers, however, did not equate kills and ordnance expended and caches recovered with "success." The issues of the war for them were the consequences of combat. "I've seen some things happen here that have moved me so much that I've changed my whole outlook on life," wrote Private First Class George Robinson, who was wounded in action while on an operation with the 1st Infantry Division. "I feel different now after seeing some horrible things, and I'll never forget them. I can't say what I mean, but some of the things you see here can really change a man or turn a boy into a man. Any combat GI that comes here doesn't leave the same."

In their correspondence, soldiers reflected on these "horrible things," on combat and its carnage, on their fears about getting hit, on the destruction they saw and caused, on the people they fought and the country they fought to "save," on being, as Lieutenant Brian Sullivan wrote, "mostly proud, sad, tired and relieved" after endless days and nights in the bush.

[April 1967]

Dear Ma,

How are things back in the World? I hope all is well! Things are pretty much the same. Vietnam has my feelings on a seesaw.

This country is so beautiful, when the sun is shining on the mountains, farmers in their rice paddies, with their water buffalo, palm trees, monkeys, birds and even the strange insects. For a fleeting moment I wasn't in a war zone at all, just on vacation, but still missing you and the family.

There are a few kids who hang around, some with no parents. I feel so sorry for them. I do things to make them laugh. And they call me "dinky dow" (crazy). But it makes me feel good. I hope that's one reason why we're here, to secure a future for them. It seems to be the only justification I can think of for the things that I have done!

Love to all.

Your son,
George

PFC George Williams served with Company B, 1st Battalion, 16th Infantry (Rangers), 1st Infantry Division, operating in III Corps, from February 1967 to February 1968. He is now a firefighter in Brooklyn, New York.

— ☆ —

12 July '70

Dear John,

I'm sitting here on CQ [Charge of Quarters] duty (I have to stay up all night in the orderly room), waiting for the rockets to come in (it's 0100 hrs. now—they usually come around 0300 hrs.) and wishing like hell that I was somewhere else. I don't know if I have fully described what it's like over here, John. I was not fortunate enough to get one of those luxurious MI [military intelligence] jobs in Saigon—unfortunately I've been assigned to the 101st Airborne Division near Hue, which seems to be the hottest spot outside of Cambodia. It's one of the most gung-ho units in this Army. The place can only be described in terms of a medieval or early German Renaissance vision of hell, with flying monsters in the air (the helicopters) preying on the huddled sinner masses (all the combatants in this senseless war!).

Really, the physical and human damage done over the last few years is much greater than I realized—especially the human damage. There are the usual scars of war all over—the bomb and artillery craters, the ruined villages and the like. These things you can understand as the by-product of war—but I can't accept the fact of the human damage. Not just the dead, but the GIs who can't talk in coherent sentences any more, or the ones who have found they love to kill, or the Vietnamese, who must have been a very gentle, graceful people before the war turned them into thieves, black marketeers and prostitutes—a good fuck costs only one carton of cigarettes. I feel like I'm at the bottom of a great sewer. . . .

Well, I'm falling asleep here. Do write. I hope all is well. . . .

> Yours as always,
> Tom

Sp/5 Thomas Pellaton worked in intelligence with the 101st Aviation Group, 101st Airborne Division, based at Phu Bai, from June 1970 to May 1971. He is an opera singer, and maître d' at the Carlyle Hotel in New York City. This letter was written to John Niles, his college roommate and best friend.

— ☆ —

18 May 66

Dear Mom & Dad & Everyone,

Praise the Lord, I'm finally writing. I realize that isn't the nicest way to start a letter home after so long, but what would you have me write, "I'm sorry?" Right now the word (sorry) doesn't seem to be able to convey my feelings about my negligence.

Today marks my 79th day in Saigon, and I feel as though a "5" should be placed in front of that figure. I can't begin to explain how long a day (of work) lasts or seems to last around here. I guess it's the constant thought of still another 22½ months to go!! Doesn't two years seem so unbelievable at times to you, Mom & Dad? I mean, what a difference it will be, in '68. The trees will be a little bigger (and bearing some eatable fruit, I hope) and the crab grass will be a little wiser to your plan of attack,

Dad. Mom, your poor hands will show two more years of "dish water" and I imagine the interior of the house will have changed a little by then.

What's it like in Saigon, Matt? A question I know you're all dying to get an answer to! Well, I've got mixed feelings about Saigon and as a foreigner, I will probably lean toward the bad on this. I could never live in Saigon with a family or by myself because there is such a difference in conditions, as I'm sure you realize. Sure, they're at war, but the filth, for example, is beyond anyone's wildest dreams. The way they go about doing things at times really amazes me. Oh, and don't believe in this old saying about how wise the old folk are from the Far East either! Sure, they have a knack for using "ear-catching" sayings and ways to express or bring about what they want to say, but no more than the American salesman, Dad & Dick. I'm sure you've got a few tricky sayings in your line of business.

The American serviceman has changed Saigon so much in the past year that it would shock you. They are mostly money-hungry anti-American, and that is straight from a horse's mouth. You see, it's hard to really judge the Vietnamese people because I've only come in contact with the ones in Saigon. They've got a taste of the foolishness in the way the Americans throw [their] money around and they want more. They even cheat each other and you can't trust them. Not in my book! Maybe after two years I'll be able to give you a better understanding of what is what over here. . . .

Oh, and I've had my baptizing with "Saigon Tea." This is the usual approach of a bar-hog! You walk in and sit down at the bar. Before you get to order a drink, a girl will be sitting next to you and she'll begin with, "Hello. What is your name?" Then she'll say, "Would you like a drink?" You order one. "I have not seen you here before. You are very handsome," or "You look young. How old are you?" They usually like you to be 21–23. But I tell them 19. Then they say, "You Baby-San?" Which means, "Have you ever been to bed with a woman?" A "baby-san" is a virgin. Ha!

Well, then she asks you after a laugh-filled conversation, "You buy me Saigon Tea?" or "You buy me drink?" which is the same thing. Colored and scented water for 180 piasters, about $1.50. And if you're a "fish," she'll end up having you spend maybe an easy 1500 or 2000 P's, about $18, in the bar. If you want her and you're a fish, it's 2000 P's to buy her out of the bar. I have my regular places I go to and laugh at the fools who throw away their money on different bars all the time.

The rainy season started officially on the 15th of May and I'll go along with that. It now rains in torrents every day, sometimes all day! This makes it a little cooler out and at night there is usually a real nice breeze blowing the storm out to sea.

Riding the "cyclos" [motorized rickshaws] and taxis and illegal scooters is a lot of fun—at times. I plan on asking for my movie camera in a couple of months to capture Saigon on the go. They are something else driving over here. I can't help but laugh half of the time. . . .

I hope all of you are well at home. I *will* write again soon, folks. God Bless You All.

> Your Pen Pal,
> Matt

Matthew Henn, a Marine lance corporal, was assigned as an embassy guard in Saigon from March 1966 through March 1967. He now works as a cook in a hotel in southern California.

— ☆ —

15 April 70

Wid:

I just got back from burning the classified trash and happened to think about you. It's a beautiful day. Probably about 90°—but since Long Binh has [a] constant breeze, you never feel it. I was thinking how I've never written to anyone about how much I like this country. The weather is great. Usually sunny during the day, and at night it's just cool enough that you need a blanket. Because it is hardly ever humid, you get used to the heat and don't find 100° temperatures tough to take. From what people tell me, it sounds like Hawaii.

And I like the people too. At first I hated them all because I thought everyone was a VC sympathizer, a whore or just after my money. Not that a lot of them aren't, but it just doesn't bother me much anymore. They are a great ballbusting people. And I've always held ballbusters in high regard. Our barracks has four girls who make our beds, clean our laundry and polish our shoes. And we have a fuckin' ball with them. No end of good screwing around. Even the older women are always laughing and talking and shitting around. I hardly ever see young men so I don't know how they are. The young girls are sometimes so beautiful that you don't think they're real. There are more good looking women in Saigon than any city I've ever been in. Peasant girls with perfect complexions, black eyes, long shiny black hair and incredible figures. The wealthy ones wear Western clothes. They can be teases, but more often than not, they're attractively shy, soft and extremely feminine. They're easily the cream of Southeast Asia. . . .

Fitz

Tom Fitzharris, a sergeant assigned to the General Staff Company, USARV-G2, Intelligence, was based at Long Binh from July 1969 until July 1970. He is now associate director of the Home Box Office program guide in New York City. This letter was written to his friend, Peter Widulski.

—— ☆ ——

July 15, 1969

Dear Mom,

We went out again with the 17th Armored Cavalry. We drove all over this area. We went to some villages and searched the hooches for VC or weapons. All we found were some tools. We took them from the dinks.

I still can't believe how these people live. They're just like animals. They live way out in the middle of nowhere. There isn't even a road for miles. It's all just unused rice paddies. Their homes are made of grass and mud. They crouch down to eat their little bowl of rice and I don't know what else but it smells like dead dog. They don't mind the flies all over their food.

When they go to the bathroom they just do it wherever they may be. They don't do it in the house.

When we come roaring in on our armored personal carriers, the men take off (probably VC). The women and kids stay behind and beg stuff off the GIs.

They have holes in the ground that are amazing. Some of them run for miles and some are big enough to stand up in. Some are very large living quarters and usually run into the smaller ones. We just throw a few grenades in or blast the hole with a large charge of TNT. These people are like moles. They can dig miles of tunnel but there is no dirt to be found anywhere. They must eat it.

Some of these people are treacherous. They say "GI number one" when we're in their village, but at night the dirty little rats are VC.

Well, we haven't seen anything exciting lately, just routine patrolling. It is boring.

I'll keep you informed.

Tell Francis and George to write once in a while. Patricia and you write a lot. Thanks.

Love,
Paul

Paul Kelly was a sergeant with the 1st Battalion, 52nd Infantry, 198th Light Infantry Brigade, Americal Division, operating in I Corps, from March 1969 through March 1970. He is a grade-school science teacher in Garden City, New York.

— ☆ —

Tuesday, Sept. 6, 1966

Dear Mom,

. . . You'll probably be hearing about us again. Yesterday my platoon had six injured and one killed. We had a fire fight that lasted nine hours. We killed a lot of VC on this operation we're on now, but we also have had a lot killed.

I wrote Sue and told her to give you back my ring. It's still a good ring although it doesn't work too good. I can always give it to some other chump, I mean girl.

Well, Mom, I don't have much time, and I just wanted you to know I'm all right.

When you go to church, I want you to give all the people you see this address and tell them to send anything they can, like old clothes and anything.

I went down to this orphanage the other day, and these little kids are pitiful. They sleep on plain floors and don't get hardly anything to eat.

The reason I want you to tell everyone to help them is because I feel I may have killed some of their parents and it makes me feel sick to know they have to go on with nothing. Address: Mang-Lang Orphanage, Le-Loi Street, Tuy Hoa, Vietnam.

Love, Your son,
Dan

PFC Daniel Bailey was assigned to A Troop, 2nd Battalion, 17th Cavalry, 101st Airborne Division, from May 1966 through June 1967, operating in II Corps. He is unemployed and receives disability compensation from the Veterans Administration for post-traumatic stress disorder. He lives in Clarington, Pennsylvania.

— ☆ —

20 July 1969

Dear Mom,

I've become involved recently in a situation that I had heard about but was never fully aware of before. I thought, as a child, that growing up in a single-parent family was rough. Now I know that I was very well off compared to those with no parents at all, no home life to build a healthy young life on. I think of something in the Bible, "I cried because I had no shoes, and then I saw a man who had no feet."

Let me start from the beginning. When I first arrived in Vietnam, and was assigned here in Ban Me Thuot, I was astonished at the poor, seemingly unimprovable conditions that the majority of Vietnamese live under. True, over the last three decades new conveniences [and] new ideas have been introduced by us and the French before us. [But] I had to talk with the people before I realized that the sole hope of this nation lies in its youth. The elders, the parents, are tired. They've lived with war, and the hardships involved, for too long. They no longer believe another kind of life is possible. The children do, though. They want to learn. They want to do things the way we do, have things like we have. They have hope for their future.

One day when I wasn't scheduled to fly, my platoon leader, Capt. Roy Ferguson, asked me if I wanted to go to the orphanage in town with him. We picked up some things some friends had sent him and went down to the Vinh-Son Orphanage and School, run by eight sisters of the Daughters of Charity of St. Vincent de Paul.

Sister Beatrice, in charge of the school, greeted us at the gate. As we walked through the grounds, we were followed by scores of children who wanted to touch us, talk to us, or just smile at us. We left the books and pencils we had brought with Sister Beatrice and walked to the building which is the orphanage itself.

We were welcomed by Sister Helen and a group of kids that had been playing in front of the building. They just went wild when they saw us. And no wonder—for the past five months, Capt. Ferguson, who comes from Wyalusing, Pennsylvania, has been practically their only link with the life of clothing, toys and personal American friendship. They've adopted him, in their own way, as a sort of godfather.

I was at once ashamed and proud. Proud because we in America have so much, and ashamed because we take our good fortune for granted, wasting so much that these people, especially the children in this orphanage, so desperately need. Things like blankets and sheets, clothes for little boys and girls, even shoes. How many times have you or I made a rag out of something because it had a little hole in it? Mom, these children need those things desperately. Capt. Ferguson will be leaving soon, and I will sort of assume the privilege of being the go-between for these children and the assistance that comes in from their friends in the United States. . . . The most beneficial thing we can do is donate our time by going down to the school to teach English to the more than 1,200 students that receive an education there.

I'm amazed that eight nuns can oversee so large an effort. In addition to the orphanage and school, they run a dispensary, giving aid to the local Vietnamese and Montagnard families in the area. They have so little for themselves, and yet they give away what they do have.

The shame of it all is that these children had nothing to do with bringing all this on themselves. It's hard to sympathize with someone who causes his own misfortune. These children, though, are the victims not of their generation, but of yours and mine. Many are orphans because their parents have been killed. They haven't died of old age or heart attacks . . . they've been killed by terrorism while defending their homes, their country, their freedom. Others are orphans as a result of the assistance we have given to their country. We have fathered many children, unable to take them home, their mothers unable to care for them. You and I must do something for these children, for this orphanage, [so it] can expand its work and care for children who now walk the streets with no one, no one at all.

The children need things that are part of our everyday lives. Toothpaste, soap, a pencil, a pen, a notebook to write in as they go through school. A picture book that says, "See the dog. His name is Spot. Watch the dog run. Run, Spot, run." These kids aren't underprivileged—they're nonprivileged, and they're running. Running towards a way of life where they can better themselves on their own. But they're so young, we have to help them to walk before we let them run.

Plates on which to put their food, silverware to eat it with, even the food itself—they need it all. They raise chickens and pigs, and all of their vegetables. The only way they can buy even rice is to sell one of their pigs.

[The children] are taught by a staff of 30 teachers who work for nothing or are paid in produce. There's no law here requiring children to attend school. They go because they are hungry for knowledge and because their stomachs are hungry. An education can change that, and we must help them get that education.

I could write a book about these children, about the look of fear in their eyes, their cries of joy upon seeing an American, someone who can help them change their circumstances. Some are too young to fully realize what it's like to have nothing. You and I and our friends must prevent them from finding out. We speak different languages, but we're all the same kind of people. They need, and we have. We must help them.

I'll stop here, because the sooner this letter gets to you, the sooner our friends at the orphanage will get some help. Send *anything* that might be useful to Vinh-Son Orphanage care of myself. I'll see that it gets there. And don't be surprised if the next piece of mail you get from Vietnam is a thank-you note from some very, very grateful Vietnamese youngster.

Run, Spot, run.

With love and thanks,
Your Son

Bruce McInnes was a chief warrant officer with the 155th Assault Helicopter Company, 10th Combat Assault Battalion, 1st Aviation Brigade, from May 1969 to December 1970, based at Ban Me Thuot. He works as a tree doctor in New York City.

— ☆ —

12 August 1966

Dear Almoo:

Thank you very much for your letter. We have fallen into a sort of breathe-easy period here and have not had to go out on any very long patrols lately. So I'm sitting here writing letters like mad and letting my feet breathe again.

We have been doing a lot of work in the villages lately, of the community-development type, so it looks as though I will never get away from my Peace Corps days. We must be really messing up these people's minds. By day we treat their ills and fix up their children and deliver their babies; and by night, if we receive fire from the general direction of their hamlet, fire generally will reach them, albeit not intentionally. They must really be going around in circles. But I guess that just points up the strangeness of this war. We have two hands, both of which know what the other is doing but does the opposite anyway. And in the same obscure and not too reasonable manner, it all makes sense, I hope.

I am sorry this is so short, but it is going to rain and I must make sure my men have their gear stored correctly.

Love,
Sandy

2Lt. Marion Lee Kempner wrote this letter to his grandmother, Mrs. Marion Levy, one month after he arrived in Vietnam, where he served as a platoon leader with Company M, 3rd Battalion, 7th Regiment, 1st Marine Division, operating out of Chu Lai. He was killed on 11 November 1966.

— ☆ —

7 Jan 69
Hello Folks,

. . . [J]ustice can be such a vague and damning thing. A girl was brought in here yesterday—she was about 16—with her mother, a wizened creature who rather numbly waited outside the treatment room awaiting, I suppose, the inevitable results. They had been walking along the Ben Cat road when her daughter was struck by an American vehicle, probably one of these huge earth movers with an eight-foot plow on front, and which appear out of the perpetual dust like a bat out of hell. We had an ambulance struck by one recently—that's how secretive the dust can be—and an entire side was sheered off—and the ambulance was tough army equipment. Tracing military vehicles along the road would be an almost impossible task.

The girl fortunately died, but the grief of the mother was the like of which I had not witnessed here—the Vietnamese generally tend to be reticent about their display of emotion. Shock could have been part of it this time, for it would have been an inutterably terrible thing to see happen, as the results showed us. One of her sons worked here on base and came over. The look on his face mirrored all the frustrations and failures of foreign intervention. It was an anger and undoubtedly hate—hate at what he already knew to be true (as did I) that though there would be an "investigation," there would be no blame fixed and no justice rendered by us. (How could there be when the one man who might possibly have done it denied any knowledge of the incident—though if he did it, he has himself to live with.) Are we to try ourselves?

All this which I convey in words flashed through his face in an instant. . . . As one of the men in the treatment room remarked, who had also noticed the look on the son's face, "There's a new Viet Cong for you. . . ." We seem still cursed by a generalized inability to view these people whom we "came to save" as equals. First, they must have clean towns, nice cars, TV sets, and Western clothes before we will accept them as being almost our peers. I say general curse, because there are always exceptions, but they, from my experience, are exceedingly rare. A Vietnamese remains a "gook" no matter whose side he's on.

Well, these are thoughts—I rarely acknowledge the emotions attached anymore. At such a frequent and confusing pace, it might be bad for the health.

On the other side of things—Lucy, our company's dog (one of two—Charley Brown's the other), has given birth to seven pups. It brings back fond memories, and there is really nothing nicer than a puppy. So it goes. . . .

Love,
Rob

Sp/4 John R. ("Rob") Riggan was assigned to Company D, 1st Medical Battalion, 1st Infantry Division, based at Lai Khe, from September 1968 through September 1969. He is the author of Free Fire Zone, *a novel about Vietnam. He lives in Rowe, Massachusetts.*

— ☆ —

The Victors

What will become of us?
There is no answer;
Only the sound of the wind
Moving through dead trees.
And choking dust rising

Beneath our feet.
The furnace burns throughout
The day;
We suffer in agony, as women
In labor.
But we die with the birth, for
Our child is war.
Now we fathers move forward
To meet our fate
In open fields and jungle paths
Strewn with death;
And call on the name of
Our God,
Who will not hear our pleas.
We pile high the dead
Into a pale, bleached mountain,
And swing our bloody bayonets
Skyward to honor the victor,
Who looks through red-rimmed eyes.
And, in time of pain, we die,
And, somewhere other than home,
Our names and faces are one.
Under steel helmets, fear equalizes.
One is one.
What will become of us?
In the end, Valhalla is our hell,
And Heaven is obscured
In our agony of pain.
Homeward-bound in aluminum tubes.
We know that in victory
There lies a promise of defeat.

This poem, anonymously written, circulated through Sp/4 Barry Reeves's units. He spent two tours in Vietnam: from August 1966 to August 1967 with the II Field Force at Phan Thiet, and from March 1968 to March 1969 with the I Field Force at Nha Trang. He works as an electronics technician and lives in Maple Shade, New Jersey.

— ☆ —

31 Aug '69

Dear Red,

I am living in a green world with a green canvas roof over me, green sandbags all around me, dressed in green camouflage fatigues and sitting on a green cot that once was white, but now is mildewed while all around me an act of God is blowing this little radio station apart. We're getting the tail end of a tropical storm that has moved in down by Da Nang and is moving up north towards us. The monsoons are almost upon us. It's raining fairly hard, fog has cut visibility to 70 feet at high noon, and 0 at night, and a 30-mile-an-hour wind is gusting over our little relay station playing hell with my tent, blowing down our radio antennas and slowly, but surely, uprooting the cyclone fence around our little knoll that is supposed to protect us from incoming RPGs (rocket-propelled grenades). Yesterday some dunce threw a white phosphorus grenade down the windward side of the hill, and the resulting fire almost burned down our little post. Burning embers made a screen out of my tent, so now I'm sitting in here cold, wet, unbelievably dirty after eight days up here, fairly miserable—yet strangely content. My team was supposed to be relieved today but the weather has grounded the choppers and cut off all resupply, so not only are we stuck up here till this blows over but are low on food and almost out of water. Ammo is plentiful, however, and that's the important thing. A cold, hungry and thirsty man can fight, but a warm, well-fed and satiated man can't without ammunition. Yesterday our little garrison was cut by a third with one entire team being airlifted out and no replacements coming in. We are consolidated into two positions about 100 meters apart, with no one manning the hill between us and the fog keeping us from observing the ground. This makes for a very nervous situation, especially since air support will be erratic at best and nonexistent at worst in this weather if Victor comes up the hill. The merry life of a Ranger in the Orient.

I don't really know the reason I'm writing this. . . . Actually I'm writing because I have to write or go out of my mind, and you're "it," so to speak. Things happen over here that you just can't keep to yourself —if you do, you brood on them, slowly go "flak happy," get careless, and eventually get zapped when your mind has strayed from the job at hand. Sometimes, especially when inactivity has you going crazy and staring at the walls, you've got to talk things out, and it helps a lot if the other person is either a buddy over here who's been through the fire too and can understand, or a member of the opposite sex who can't and you hope is never able to. Even if I don't mail this, at least I'll have written it out, which will make me feel better.

Last Monday I went on my first hunter-killer operation and saw Mars close up for the first time. We had two teams—12 men—inserted at dawn about two miles inland and slightly north of Chu Lai about an hour off the choppers. We set up around a trail, and a lone NVA officer walked into the middle of us. We tried for a POW, but he panicked and took off in a blizzard of shells. I had him in my sights, threw three slugs at him and he just disappeared. No Hollywood theatrics—one minute he's a living, running human being, the next second he's down, just a red lump of clay. At first, I thought it was I that got him, but it was a shotgun blast that brought him down. After that everyone in hearing distance knew we were in the area, but on hunter-killer operations we stay to fight rather than extract upon breaking contact. We found some huts the NVA had been working on, then moved out across a dried-up paddy when all hell broke loose. We were strung out on open ground with the point man less than 10 feet from the NVA when we were ambushed with grenades and automatic weapons. If they'd had a heavy MG or a mortar, we'd all be dead, but as it was, we were unbelievably lucky and not a man was killed. Two men took shrapnel in the face, and I took some in the shoulder, and then our NCO and point assaulted the ambushing force, the wounded man rushed the NVA after them and Victor broke contact and ran. We ran into the woodline, beat the NVA back twice without taking any more casualties, then after being pinned down for about two hours were extracted under air support. Only one of us was really wounded—my wound and one other man's being insignificant—but we really lucked out that time.

The frightening thing about it all is that it is so very easy to kill in war. There's no remorse, no theatrical "washing of the hands" to get rid of nonexistent blood, not even any regrets. When it happens, you are more afraid [than] you've ever been in your life—my hands shook so much I had trouble reloading and it took a visible effort to perform each motion and control what would normally be called panic but which, somehow, isn't. You're scared, really scared, and there's no thinking about it. You kill because that little SOB is doing his best to kill you and you desperately want to live, to go home, to get drunk or walk down the street on a date again. And suddenly the grenades aren't going off any more, the weapons stop and, unbelievably fast it seems, it's all over and you're alive because someone else is either dead or so anxious to stay alive that he's run away and you are the victor—if there is such a thing in war. You don't think about it.

I have truly come to envy the honest pacifist who honestly believes that no killing is permissible and can, with a clear conscience, stay home and not take part in these conflicts. I wish I could do the same, but I can't see letting another take my place and my risks over here, and the pacifist ideal cannot drive one burning objection to it from my mind: the fact that the only reason pacifists such as the Amish can even live in an orderly society is because someone—be they police or soldiers—is taking risks to keep the wolves away. To be a sheep in a world of sheep is one thing; to be a sheep in a world of predators something else, and if someone hides behind the label of sheep due to cowardice while another has to take his place, holding the predators at bay . . . somehow I just can't see it, or do it—not when I can't believe in it. I guess that's why I'm over here, why I fought so hard to come here, and why, even though I'm scared most of the time, I'm content to be here. At least I'm doing my part according to what I believe. The only thing keeping the wolves from the flock are the hounds. But I tell you that, allegorically speaking, it is a hard and scary task to be a wolfhound.

I've run on here for quite a bit and am sorry if I bore you, but it helps to talk some things out and there aren't too many good conversationalists to write to. I hope you don't mind my ranting on like this, but it looks like I'm going to be stopped now as the winds are up to 50 mph and my tent is slowly being demolished and I've got to head for the trenches. This is shaping up to a full-scale hurricane which is expected to develop 80-mph winds up this high. It looks like a cold, wet, rough night, which will be made more so by the fact that all our clothes are tropical gear. I hope somebody somewhere is having fun tonight.

George

Sp/4 George Olsen, Co. G, 75th Inf. (Ranger), Americal Div., Chu Lai, 1969–1970, KIA 3 March 1970.

— ☆ —

Dear Bob,

Peace.

Well, I don't know a lot to tell you.

I got back here and two guys from my platoon got killed and seven guys wounded all from the same squad. My squad helped get them out. It seems they were pulling ambushes and got hit with an RPG. This happened while I was home. Now they've sent our company back into the hills—Payday Ridge. Last year seven guys got killed there. How many will get killed this year?

I feel as though I'll never come home. I told Chris, too. It seems too weird that I'll get to see the World again and then come back. I think it was my kiss good-by. I'll never talk about this to anyone else—just you and Chris—and I'll never say it again to you or her. But I love you both, and I'll always feel for you as a great Buddy and a No. 1 brother. Thanks for everything, kid, and don't forget to double clutch!

Billy
(Da Kid)

Sgt. William Nelson, who grew up in the Bronx, spent July 1969 through September 1970 with Company A, 2nd Battalion, 502nd Infantry, 101st Airborne Division, operating out of Phu Bai. He is an accountant and lives in Putnam, New York.

— ☆ —

24 Apr 70

Hi Kid,

I've got some bad news. I've lost three friends this week at Dak Seang. They were going in for a pick-up and got shot down. That didn't kill them. But when they were on the ground, they got mortared. Only one was alive when we got them out two days later, and he's in bad shape.

I also lost my ship. I think I told you about the overspeed we had on the engine. Well, it broke my drive shaft and cut the tail boom in half. This all happened on the ground. It's kind of like losing a real close friend. I felt real bad when they told me it had to go back to the States. I'm getting real sentimental in my old age. I put more work into her, I knew her from skids to blades, and now I have to break in a new one. I'm pissed.

283rd Dust-off at Pleiku has lost all of its ships this week—six of them—and we lost two, all at Dak Seang. Maybe you have heard about it in the news. Well, I have to go there in two days because of the shortage of ships. We have three up there now, but they are flying about 10 to 12 hours a day each, so I'm going to relieve the pressure. It gives me a chance to break in my new ship (I hope not the wrong way). This is the first time since I've been here that I've been worried. I can see if we lost only two or three ships, but eight is too much. No sweat. I've still got my charmed life.

I have to go, love. Write you soon, and you do the same.

Love,
Pete

Sp/5 Peter Torrano was a crew chief for a dust-off helicopter, assigned to the 498th Medevac Company. He was based at Lane Army Airfield, 12 miles north of Qui Nhon, from January 1969 through October 1970. He is a police lieutenant in Norwalk, Connecticut. This letter was written to his mother.

— ☆ —

14 November 1967

Dear Sue—

Got my birthday presents on time. Thank you for the wingtips. They're very nice. Only one question: Where do I wear them in Vietnam?

But thank you for thinking of me on 13 November 1967. I know how you love to make a fuss over me on birthdays and anniversaries, and I wish I were there to do it up right. . . .

Thank your folks for the food. It's going to be a welcome change of diet from Meatballs and Beans in Tomato Sauce, With Juices. I never want to see another one of those damn little cans.

I felt pretty bad the other day. One of the men who was on my patrol in 533 was wounded in an ambush. He was struck twice in the arm by machine-gun fire, and one round went through his helmet and didn't penetrate his skull, but left a quarter-inch-deep crease across his head from ear to ear. He always did have a thick skull, though. They were up in a canal again. I keep thinking that if I were there, he wouldn't have been wounded. I know what to look for (or should I say, look *out* for) in those canals, and I shudder when I think of some of these inexperienced men leading these boats indiscriminately up into one of them. Most patrol officers never keep book on the patrol areas. They don't get involved as deeply in the game as I do. It's a genuine battle of wits during the prelude leading up to the moment when the first shot is fired. I've trained myself so that I can sense when I'm being watched, and when someone has his sights on me.

The CO of 522 is in many ways ignorant of this patrol business. A Southerner of some social standing in Alabama, he adheres to a strict code of ethics as set down in the rules of engagement. He has no confidence in my ability, probably because I'm a brand-spanking-new Lt. J.G. with no fleet experience. Still he doesn't have half the experience I have in the Vietnam War. Success in fighting this war doesn't come from years of naval service, or age, or intelligence. It comes from a sense of survival and the ability to profit from one's experience. The more experiences you accumulate, the better able you are to handle the next situation that develops, for no two incidents are exactly the same, and you have to play it by ear. I'm treated like a man who's just arrived in country and doesn't know a damn thing about war. It's ridiculous. He doesn't want to do anything that would cause the VC to shoot at us, apparently making believe that there isn't a war going on.

At this rate, the war will last another 15 years. When will we get leaders who take an interest in the war, and who play to win? I want to beat the enemy. . . .

Love,
Dick

Lt. J.G. Richard Strandberg, River Patrol Sections 533 and 522, 1967–1968, Mekong Delta.

—— ☆ ——

Dear, Soldier Friend

Hi, my name is Roger Barber. I belong to Den 2 Pack 79.

I'm sorry you had to fight in the war. I don't like to fite do you? Please watch out.

I'm sending some gifts and I hope you like them. Please have fun.

Your Friend,
Roger Barber

Have a nice crismis.

Sp/4 Frank Russo, serving with D Battery, 71st Air Defense Artillery, II Field Force, Phan Thiet, from February to December 1971, received this letter from an eight-year-old pen pal, Roger Barber, from Conesus, New

York. Russo now lives in Staten Island, New York, and works as a computer applications engineer.

— ☆ —

Last Will & Testament
of PFC Richard E. Marks
December 12, 1965

Dear Mom,

I am writing this in the event that I am killed during my remaining tour of duty in Vietnam.

First of all I want to say that I am here as a result of my own desire—I was offered the chance to go to 2nd Marine Division when I was first assigned to the 4th Marines, but I turned it down. I am here because I have always wanted to be a Marine and because I always wanted to see combat.

I don't like being over here, but I am doing a job that must be done —I am fighting an *inevitable* enemy that must be fought—now or later.

I am fighting to protect and maintain what I believe in and what I want to live in—a democratic society. If I am killed while carrying out this mission, I want no one to cry or mourn for me. I want people to hold their heads high and be proud of me for the job I did.

There are some details I want taken care of. First of all, any money that you receive as a result of my death I want distributed in the following fashion.

If you are single, I want you and Sue to split it down the middle. But if you are married and your husband can support you, I want Sue and Lennie to get 75% of the money, and I want you to keep only 25%— I feel Sue and Lennie will need the money a lot more.

I also want to be buried in my Marine Corps uniform with all the decorations, medals, and badges I rate. I also want Rabbi Hirschberg to officiate, and I want to be buried in the same cemetery as Dad and Gramps, but I do not want to be buried in the plot next to Dad that I bought in mind of you.

That is about all, except I hope I never have to use this letter—

I love you, Mom, and Sue, and Nan, and I want you all to carry on and be very happy, and above all be proud—

Love & much more love,
Rick

PFC Richard E. Marks, who grew up in New York City, served in Vietnam with Company C, 1st Battalion, 3rd Regiment, 3rd Marine Division, which operated in I Corps. On 14 February 1966, two months after he wrote this letter, he was killed. He was 19 years old.

— ☆ —

2/18/68

Dear Brother Kyrin,

   . . . Right now I am with the 9th Infantry Divison in the Mekong Delta region. We live with the Navy on their ships, but when we go out on an operation we are out in rice paddies and jungles. I have been here for over a month and a half now, and I really wish I was back in my teens again getting on that bus at 69th Street.

   It seems that every time we go out on an operation we make contact. And each morning I say a little prayer thanking God for another day on earth. With bullets, artillery, mortars and air strikes going off all around you, it gets quite scary.

   I don't dare tell my parents or girl about how it is because they are worrying enough. I have been looking at it this way. If the Lord wills it, I will be back on the other side of the world ten months from now. Then I will do what I should have done two years ago—go to college. At least now I can use the GI Bill and won't have to worry about being drafted. I would like to thank you for all your kindness in the past when I was a "little troublesome," shall we say. I can remember that day as if it happened yesterday, sitting in your office with my mother and father there. I wish I knew then what I know now—two and a half years can do a lot to a person in the way of growing up.

   One again, if it is the Lord's will that I come back to the "World," as we say over here, I will make it a must to stop down at the school and see you. So until then, it is good-by for now. I will drop you a line whenever I get time so as to let you know I am in one piece.

                                   Paul Di Caprio

Cpl. Paul J. Di Caprio, from Brooklyn, New York, served with Company A, 3rd Battalion, 47th Infantry (Riverine), 9th Infantry Division, IV Corps, from December 1967 until he was killed in action on

17 May 1968. Brother Kyrin Powers was one of his teachers in high school.

— ☆ —

4 September 1966

Dear Mr. Mammolitti,

I am the Catholic Chaplain with the 1st Brigade. I had first met your son in Hawaii. I remember how pleased he was to have the opportunity to work in civic affairs. He felt that he would be doing something positive to help the Vietnamese. He certainly did not begrudge his time in the service. Quite the contrary he had high ideals and tried to carry them out.

While in Cu Chi, your son attended daily mass and received Holy Communion. While on this operation I had a daily mass at 6:30 P.M. Whenever his duties permitted it, he would be at mass. On the Friday before his death, two days prior, he went to confession, attended mass and received Holy Communion.

I was very close by when he was shot. I reached his side almost immediately. Although he was not able to talk, I gave him absolution and the Sacrament of Extreme Unction. He died about five minutes later. He was unable to speak any words before passing away.

Perhaps you say "Why?" Because it was the will of God. Be proud of your son. He died doing something he believed in. And I'm sure his death has not been for naught. We are all trying to help these people live freely. He gave his life for this.

I know all this does not bring back your son. But you have the consolation to know that he did his job and did it very well, that he remained a good Catholic young man, strong in religious conviction, that he received the sacraments regularly and that he had a priest by his side when he died. I am certain that Our Lord received him with open arms.

If I can be of any help, please write to me. I said mass for your son the very night he was killed. God bless you. Please pray for me.

Sincerely in Christ,
Father Armand N. Jalbert

Capt. Armand Jalbert served as a chaplain in Vietnam from April 1966 to March 1967. He now lives in Arlington, Virginia, having retired from the Army in 1984 as a colonel. PFC Joseph A. Mammolitti, who grew up in the Bronx, was assigned to Headquarters and Headquarters Company, 25th Infantry Division, based at Cu Chi. He was killed on 28 August 1966, five months after he arrived in country. He was 22 years old.

— ☆ —

LZ Hard Core
4:00 P.M., June 23, 1968

Dearest Bev,

Last night we had the VC all around us. [We] had some trapped near the water hole, but I guess they got away. Bev, don't ever tell Mother this, but at times I feel I will never come home. The VC are getting much stronger, so I think this war is going to get worse before it gets better. . . .

The days are fairly peaceful, but the nights are pure hell! I look up at the stars, and it's so hard to believe that the same stars shine over you and such a different world as you live in. I look at this war in the sense that it is an experience that can never be equaled and that someday I can make something [out of it]. I guess if I had it to do over, I would do it again!

I try and take great pride in my unit and the men I work with. A lot of the men have been in a lot of trouble and have no education or money. But I feel honored to have them call me a friend. In my heart I know these are the men that build America, not the rich or the well educated. I hope to spend my life in their behalf and try to help them all I can. I have been so very lucky to have had the chances I have had, so I hope I can put these chances to work in a good cause! Bev, I hope you decide to join me in my plans for the future, but if you choose not to, there is nothing I can do! But I promise you this. I will complete my plans one way or the other. If something does happen, my family can always say that I died for a good cause and that I did accomplish just a little in my lifetime. . . .

All my love,
Al

Sgt. Allen Paul served with Company D, 2nd Battalion, 5th Cavalry, 1st Cavalry Division (Airmobile), from April 1968 to April 1969. He wrote this letter to his girlfriend, Bev. They were married in 1972. He now works as information coordinator for a college in Richmond, Indiana.

— ☆ —

Sept. 7th [1969]

We're all scared. One can easily see this emotion in the eyes of each individual. One might hide it with his mouth, while another might hide it with his actions, but there is no way around it—we are all scared.

They say when fear is in a man, he is prepared for anything. When fear possesses the man, he is prepared for nothing.

As of now, fear is in me. I hope I can keep it from possessing me.

This journal entry was written by PFC William A. Maguire, Jr., of Short Hills, New Jersey, who died on 28 September 1969, two days after contracting a fever while on patrol near the DMZ with the 2nd Battalion, 5th Regiment, 1st Marine Division. He was 20 years old. He had been in Vietnam only four weeks.

— ☆ —

Dear Madeline,

Hello my dear sister.

Boy, I sure feel close to you. Since your last letter, I almost feel as if you are my sister. It's good to have someone to tell your troubles to. I can't tell them to my parents or Darlene because they worry too much, but I tell you truthfully I doubt if I'll come out of this alive.

In my original squad I'm the only one left unharmed. In my platoon there's only 13 of us. It seems every day another young guy 18 and 19 years old like myself is killed in action. Please help me, Mad. I don't know if I should stop writing my parents and Darlene or what.

I'm going on an operation next month where there is nothing but VC and VC sympathizers. The area is also very heavily mined. All of us are scared cause we know a lot of us won't make it. I would like to hear what you have to say about it, Madeline, before I make any decisions.

Oh, and one more favor. I'd like the truth now. Has Darlene been faithful to me? I know she's been dating guys, but does she still love me best? Thanks for understanding. See ya if it's God's will. I have to make it out of Vietnam though, cause I'm lucky. I hope. Ha ha.

Miss ya,

Love,
Ray

PFC Raymond C. Griffiths went to Vietnam just after Christmas in 1965 and was assigned to Company A, 1st Battalion, 9th Marines, 3rd Marine Division. He wrote this letter to Madeline Velasco, a friend from high school in San Francisco, California, in June 1966. He was killed a few weeks later, on the Fourth of July. He was 19 years old.

— ☆ —

Dec. 18, 1971

Hi, Frank

Do you still remember me? Well I'm Roger, the one who sent the Christmas stuff to you. Well now you know me I'll finish the rest of my letter.

I liked your letter but Frank why did you join the war? I'm sorry about your friends who died. And I hope they let you get out this Christmas.

And Frank I will pray for you and your friends.

I might get to send you another present if my mother lets me. Have a nice Christmas to and I hope you get some presents.

And have a nice time to won't you.

Have you had snow yet? Well we have and we got three snowmobiles. Last year me and my little brother rode the snowmobiles and every time I turned the corner real fast I tipped the snowmobile and then I looked back and he was laying on the ground.

Well, by and have fun
Roger David Barber

Sp/4 Frank Russo received this second letter from his pen pal, eight-year-old Roger Barber, a week before he left Vietnam.

— ☆ —

6 Dec. '69
1230 hr.

Dear Gail:

Hi, doll. How's my girl today? I hope you are not feeling too blue. Well, we are on the move again. We got the word to pack our stuff, and we are going to Ban Me Thuot. We are not going to the village itself, but to the airfield. I think we are going to guard the airfield for a while. From what we have heard, we can get showers there and we can even get sodas or beer. Boy, we have not had anything cold to drink in a long time. It does get us mad that we have to move again. We just got our bunkers built—it took us about 1,000 sandbags to build [them]—and now some other company is coming in and using them. That's the way it seems to be all the time. We do all the hard work and then we have to move. Well, that's the Army for you.

I remember in one of your letters you said you were surprised that I said I don't mind being here. Well in a way, that's true. Sure I want to be home with you and have all the things we dream about. But yet being here makes a man feel proud of himself—it shows him that he is a man. Do you understand? Anyone can go in the Army and sit behind a desk, but it takes a lot to do the fighting and to go through what we have to. When we go home, we can say, "Yes, I was in Vietnam. Yes, I was a line dog." To us it means you have gone to hell and have come back. This is why I don't mind being here, because we are men. . . .

Love,
Pete

Sp/4 Peter H. Roepcke, from Glendale, New York, served as a "line dog" —an infantryman—with Company A, 3rd Battalion, 506th Infantry, 101st Airborne Division, from September 1969 until April 1970, operating in I Corps, when he broke his leg while jumping from a helicopter. He died of a heart attack in October 1981.

— ☆ —

Lament

Mother
I am cursed.
I was chosen
trained to kill
asked to die
I could not vote
I can't ask why

Mother
I am cursed
spit on
and shunned
by long-haired doves

Mother
I am cursed.
I'm a soldier
in an age
when soldiers aren't in fashion.

—Tom Oathout

Sgt. Thomas Oathout served with the 172nd Military Intelligence Detachment, assigned to the 173rd Airborne Brigade, operating in II Corps, from August 1970 through July 1971. He lives in Bear, Delaware, and works in Philadelphia as a salesman for a publishing company.

— ☆ —

Feb 14th 66

Dear Mom,
   . . . I've seen some things happen here lately that have moved me so much that I've changed my whole outlook on life. I'll be the same in actions I guess, but inside I'll be changed. I feel different now after seeing some horrible things, and I'll never forget them. It makes you glad you're just existing. I can't say what I mean, but some of the things you see here can really change a man or turn a boy into a man. Any combat GI that

comes here doesn't leave the same. I don't mean the cooks, clerks or special service workers, but the fighting man. I doubt if anybody realizes what combat is really like. I *thought* I knew until a few days ago when I started facing harsh realities and forgetting TV and movie interpretations. I never had much respect for GIs even after I was in for a while, but since I've seen what his real job is, I have more respect for him than any man on earth. To shoot and kill somebody, turn your head and walk away isn't hard, it's watching him die that's hard, harder than you could imagine and even harder when it's one of your own men.

I've said enough about it. Don't ask any questions. When I come home, if I feel like talking about it I will, but otherwise don't ask. It may sound dramatic, and I'll tell you it is. It's just something you don't feel like discussing and can't begin to write about.

Well, Mom, I'll sign off. Be careful driving.

Love,
George

PFC George Robinson was assigned to the Recon Platoon, Headquarters and Headquarters Company, 2nd Battalion, 28th Infantry, 1st Infantry Division, based at Di An, when he was wounded on 11 June 1966. He lives in North Massapequa, New York, and teaches history at Roslyn Junior High School.

— ☆ —

March 2 [1969]

Darling,

I love you so very, very much. Finally it's over for a while and I can write. I don't know where to begin or what to say or how. I guess I'll just try to tell you how I feel, which is mostly proud, sad, tired and relieved. After all these endless days and nights, they gave me and the platoon 36 hours off. I spent today going to memorial services for my people, doing wash, catching up on work in my office and writing up people for medals.

Oh, Darling, it's been so unreal. I'm not going to go into detail—it would only scare, depress or worry you. Just be convinced I'm fine, it's over and all I have to complain of now is a bad cold and a lot of fatigue. These last days were just so filled with fighting, marching, thinking, all the time thinking, "Am I doing it right? Is this what they said at Quantico? How can I be sure I haven't led us into a trap and the NVA are waiting?" etc., etc., until I became so exhausted just by worrying. I'm just so grateful (to whom?). I "only" lost six men (I *know* how awful that sounds)! I had a seventh guy fall off a cliff and get a bad cut and concussion, but he'll be OK.

I'm so confused. At the services today they were talking about God protecting people and eternal life and I felt so desolate, so despairing. I know there is no reward waiting for them or any hope. I began crying I felt so awful and hopeless, but somehow held it back and it just looked like I was sniffling from my cold. (See! How awful my ego and pride that I couldn't even let myself weep for those poor, poor kids!) All I can say is that considering how awful it was, I'm so lucky I didn't lose more.

I said I was proud. Mostly of them. I'm putting 10 of them in for decorations. Enclosed are some of the rough drafts of citations. Don't read them if you don't want to. Just save them for me. I guess I should be honest. I've been nominated, I hear, for the Silver Star, the third highest medal. Please don't get upset. I didn't try to win it—I was just trying to keep my people alive and doing the best I could. I may not even get it, 'cause the reviewing board might knock it down to a Bronze Star. You know me so well, you know I'm lying if I say I'm not pleased. I am, I'm proud, but only the worst part of me. My better part is just so sad and unhappy this whole business started.

Again, though it may be foolish, I'll keep my word and be honest. The post-Tet offensive isn't over. All intelligence points to a return bout. However, my platoon is 1,000% better than it was, we have so much support now—like a family, really. We'll all watch out for each other. Also, we don't believe they'll hit again near here, so whatever happens, I'll be OK. That's the truth too, honey. I have fantastic good luck, as strange as that may sound, and what's US is too good and too strong for any badness.

Love,
Brian

Brian Sullivan, a lieutenant assigned to the 4th Battalion, 11th Regiment, 1st Marine Division, was a field artillery officer and infantry platoon commander in the area around Da Nang from June 1968 to June 1969. He is now an associate professor of history at Yale University and lives in New York City. This letter was written to his then-wife Tobie.

— ☆ —

Saturday
14 Oct 67

Dear Mom and Dad,

Well, the day after tomorrow we go on Operation Golden Fleece. All we do is go out and make sure that no one steals the rice from the harvest. All it is is a lot of walking and cold nights and hot days. I'm writing in the dark with only a candle for light, so please forgive the handwriting.

Well, I've got the 3rd Platoon—44 different, completely different, men. Some small, some big, some only 18 and some 24. Each one has his own problems, and what I've become is a mother hen watching over her brood all the time, day and night. I'm the first up, the last down at night.

It seems like a long time until I get home, but the days go by quickly. I have a platoon sergeant who keeps my head down for me. He says he doesn't want to lose me so I let him have his way. They haven't had any enemy contact here since June, and the men become hard to handle, too cocky and sure of themselves. There sure is a lot to think about here, and so much to do, really. Tonight I had a 19-year-old come to me for help and advice. He is married to an 18-year-old, and he was having problems. If he knew I was only 20, I wonder if he would have come. I think I helped him—he seemed happy.

Well, how are you both and Jeanene, Bob and Billy and Vallette and Sam and the kids? I do hope they're all doing well. I hope to get some mail from all of you soon.

Well, not much more. It is raining again. *Mud!*

Love,
Don

2Lt. Don Jacques, Co. B, 1/26th Reg., 3rd Mar. Div., Khe Sanh, 1967–1968, KIA 25 February 1968.

— ☆ —

18 October 1967

Dear Sue—

Well, I've been transferred to another section. River Section 522. I didn't really want to leave 533. I'd grown attached to the men in the section. My crews found it pretty hard to say good-by. I did, too. After all, we'd seen a lot of action together. When you've been under fire with the same people enough times, you don't even have to think about what they're going to do or wonder if what they do will be right. You work as a team. Torres, before he went home to Hawaii, told me he could tell by the look in my eyes what I wanted them to do. I didn't have to say a thing.

I got that letter from my mother. I'm trying to think of the best way to answer it. I know she only wants me to come back home alive and without battle scars—as you and everyone else [do]. But I can't be anything less than I am out there. You know that. I suppose it's because I'm a perfectionist in everything I do, including waging war. If I have a chance to shoot it out with the enemy, I'm not going to turn tail and run. I'm not [the] fool she thinks I am. I gambled and won. I killed at least one of the enemy and didn't lose a man, whether because of blind luck, or God, or ability to handle myself in a tight situation. There are too many armchair quarterbacks in this war, whether they're sitting in the States or a safe chair here in Vietnam. You have to be in the war to understand it and be able to make judgments on the actions of men in war. My ex-CO in 533 never went out on the river, except for an occasional special operation. Yet he had the balls to stand up before commanders, etc., and tell them which were the bad canals and what kind of weapons this or that VC company used—all of it based on information I'd brought back or actions I'd been in. I could tell you the name of the man who lives in the last house on the east bank near the broken bridge where I've been ambushed twice and give you a description of the man I've seen him meeting on the other side of the bridge. I keep book on my patrol areas. He couldn't even tell you the name of the sector the canal is located in. All he's thinking about are his promotion to lieutenant commander and the medals he's going to put himself in for. And he—like the commanders and captains above him—are afraid some obscure ensign is going to upset all of that. . . .

28 October 1967

Dear Susan—

The war is getting worse. The bastards are getting more and better weapons, and are making use of them. For the first week I was down here on the Ham Luong, the monotonous quiet of the river lulled us into a false sense of contentment that we had the Viet Cong on the run. The only way we could get him to fight was by going into his backyard. However, we went into his backyard once too often. During the previous night, a VC platoon (as near as I can figure) overran an outpost next to the riverbank almost directly across from the heart of the city of Ben Tre and set up an ambush for our PBRs. The battle was terrible. They hit the boats with recoilless rifles (like bazookas from WW II), wounding every man and completely destroying one of the boats. Fortunately the patrol officer had the sense to have his men bail out after the first two rounds hit the lead boat. No sooner had they jumped over the side than five more rounds hit. The men swam for it, and as they scrambled ashore, helping one another through the barbed wire, the VC fired the rockets after them. One man, having lost three fingers and much blood from numerous wounds, was about to collapse on the shoreline. The patrol officer was screaming at him to keep going and trying to haul the man (who was twice his size) over the fence, when a round exploded ten yards from them. The wounded man leaped completely over the barbed wire without any help —that was all the incentive he needed. All Americans are now well on their way to recovery.

Sue, I thought about keeping this whole thing secret until I got home. But I can't. I have to tell you people back home what this war is like. It's worse than any war the U.S. has fought to date. I know most people back home are wondering why we're even bothering to stick it out. I'm no superpatriot, as you know. And I'm no Navy stooge. It's just that for the hundred garbage-pickers you meet over here who have no belly for fighting the VC, I meet a couple of people I like and respect, who are my friends and who stick up for their rights, and I don't want to see them get killed by the VC. I've come to evaluate things as a soldier. I'm closer to life and death every day than the majority of men are on their last day on earth. And I tend to form my values about one simple axiom: Life.

Love,
Dick

Lt. J.G. Dick Strandberg, River Patrol Sections 533 and 522, Mekong Delta, 1967–1968.

— ☆ —

Hue–Phu Bai
29 June 68

Mom,

Today I received your letter in reply to my extension letter. You replied as I knew you would—always the mother who tries to put her son's wishes before her own, even when she is not sure it is best for his welfare. It made me sad. I want so much to make you proud. I want so much to make you happy. At the same time I have my life to lead with my own dreams, goals, and outlook. And I know all these things cannot be compatible—particularly over the short run.

But understand I love my family more than anyone or anything in the world. March 1969 is not really so very far away. I have been in Vietnam more than 11 months. I have only eight more months in the country. My chances of coming away unhurt improve every month because I know so much more than I did as a beginner. I know much better when to take a chance and when not to. Please trust my judgment. Try to understand that you raised a son who likes the excitement and challenge he finds here, and these qualities will see him through the opportunities he will face in the 1970s.

Know that I dream of that day when I return home to you and Dad, and hold you in my arms again. Sometimes I get lonely. Sometimes I want nothing more than to sit down at the dinner table, see before me roast beef, corn on the cob, mashed potatoes, bow my head for the blessing, and look up and see my mother—pretty and smiling—searching for any way she can [to] make her son more comfortable. Know that it is hard to turn your back on these things.

It is not easy to say I opt for six more months of heat, sand, and shooting. I know there will [be] the nights that I suffer the loss of another friend. And nothing can make a man feel so alien or alone as [a] walk by the seashore as he tries to adjust to the loss of another friend in this godforsaken country. But that is part of the draw, the attraction, the challenge. Here there is a job to be done. There are moral decisions made almost every day. My experience is invaluable. This job requires a man of conscience. The group of men that do this job *must* have a leader with a conscience. In the last three weeks we killed more than 1,500 men on a single operation. That reflects a lot of responsibility. I am needed here, Mom. Not that I am essential or indispensable. But my degree of proficiency is now undisputed as the best in 1st Marine Division. The young men coming in need the leadership of an older hand. I am that hand. I am the man. I relish the opportunity.

I am sorry I have hurt you. But if I thought I was needed at home more than here, I would come home. Things are going well at home. So where do I belong? This is an unusual time in our nation's history. The unrest around the world is paralleled only a handful of times in history. Young men are asking questions—hard questions. Much of the focus of the entire world is on Vietnam. The incompetency and the wrongs committed in Vietnam are staggering. But through it all I see a little light. Some men choose to fight on the streets. Some choose to fight in the universities. Some choose to fight in the parliaments. My choice is between two options—fight in Vietnam or shut up. I choose Vietnam. If I am to contribute, it must be Vietnam. And when I get home, you too will see that little light.

> Your son,
> Rod

Capt. Rodney R. Chastant, from Mobile, Alabama, served with Marine Air Group 13, 1st Marine Air Wing, based at Da Nang. Although his 13-month tour in Vietnam was up in September 1968, he extended for an additional six months. He was killed on 22 October 1968. He was 25 years old.

— ☆ —

> October 20, 1966

Dear Aunt Fannie,

This morning, my platoon and I were finishing up a three-day patrol. Struggling over steep hills covered with hedgerows, trees, and generally impenetrable jungle, one of my men turned to me and pointed a hand, filled with cuts and scratches, at a rather distinguished-looking plant with soft red flowers waving gaily in the downpour (which had been going on ever since the patrol began) and said, "That is the first plant I have seen today which didn't have thorns on it." I immediately thought of you.

The plant, and the hill upon which it grew, was also representative of Vietnam. It is a country of thorns and cuts, of guns and marauding, of little hope and of great failure. Yet in the midst of it all, a beautiful thought, gesture, and even person can arise among it waving bravely at the death that pours down upon it. Some day this hill will be burned by napalm, and the red flower will crackle up and die among the thorns. So what was the use of it living and being a beauty among the beasts, if it must, in the end, die because of them, and with them? This is a question which is answered by Gertrude Stein's "A rose is a rose is a rose." You are what you are what you are. Whether you believe in God, fate, or the crumbling cookie, elements are so mixed in a being that make him what he is; his salvation from the thorns around him lies in the fact that he existed at all, in his very own personality. There once was a time when the Jewish idea of heaven and hell was the thoughts and opinions people had of you after you died. But what if the plant was on an isolated hill and was never seen by anyone? That is like the question of whether the falling tree makes a sound in the forest primeval when no one is there to hear it. It makes a sound, and the plant was beautiful and the thought was kind, and the person was humane, and distinguished and brave, not merely because other people recognized it as such, but because it is, and it is, and it is.

The flower will always live in the memory of a tired, wet Marine, and has thus achieved a sort of immortality. But even if we had never gone on that hill, it would still be a distinguished, soft, red, thornless flower growing among the cutting, scratching plants, and that in itself is its own reward.

Love,
Sandy

On 11 November 1966, less than three weeks after he wrote this letter to his great-aunt Mrs. Louis Adoue, Marine 2Lt. Marion Lee Kempner, from Galveston, Texas, was killed by a mine explosion near Tien Phu. After he disarmed one mine, another was tripped by one of his men. Although wounded by shrapnel, Lt. Kempner ordered the corpsman to take care of the other wounded man first. He died aboard a medevac en route to the hospital. He was 24 years old.

— ☆ —

4
Base Camp: War at the Rear

In Vietnam, not everybody humped. Most GIs, in fact, worked in rear areas as support personnel. They were a significant part of the American presence in Southeast Asia. In the bloated military bureaucracy, some did jobs that were as wasteful as they were frivolous. Others performed necessary and vital tasks, as doctors and nurses, postal clerks and paymasters, intelligence analysts and graves-registration personnel.

Some lived in relative comfort, even plushness, with air-conditioned offices and hot meals; they lived, especially in the latter stages of the war, in comparative safety in such secure complexes as Long Binh and Cam Ranh Bay. Others occupied fire bases, camps, and fire support bases, where they risked nightly mortar and rocket attacks, and faced the ever-present threat of ground assault.

During the day, many support personnel ventured into the field to perform their assignments, subject to the dangers posed by snipers, mortars, and mines that others in the boonies dealt with every day. But for the "rear-echelon types," the possibility of swift and violent death was real, if not constant. As Sergeant Tom Fitzharris wrote about a mortar attack on his base, "The little men struck again last night. Just as [the movie] was ending, boom, boom. Everyone hit the concrete. Picture stopped. The lights were put out. And then a hundred people tried to get into the one bunker nearby. It holds about 30 people normally. This is really insane. . . . Somebody might get hurt."

25 November 1968
Tay Ninh

Dear Mom and Dad,

"Happy birthday to me. Happy birthday to me!" Thanks for your pretty card. The girls gave me a "surprise" party at the club—they got one of the cooks on the American side to bake a birthday cake. It was fun. The officers fixed me an "American" breakfast the next day. Instead of the usual cold rice and dried fish heads, they gave me corn flakes with chocolate milk! Oh, well—it's the thought that counts, right?

1st Cav moved in here a few weeks ago, and what a rowdy bunch. They came here from the DMZ and apparently these guys have been out in the mud and the boonies for months. They've caused lots of trouble on post. We weren't sure we could handle it. But they were no trouble at the club! For the first 20 minutes or so, they just wandered around staring at everything, trying out all the chairs, flushing the toilets, etc. It was funny to watch. But I guess when you've had to do without clean clothes, good food, and shelter for as long as they have, you might not believe your eyes either. They kept telling us they didn't believe anything like the club existed in Vietnam. It must be awful for them out there. . . .

So "Tricky Dick" will really make a difference, huh? Do you think the war will be over soon? I doubt it, but even if it does happen, the troops won't be pulled out that fast. I'd be willing to bet we'll be here for quite some time yet.

Last night we got a special treat. One of the officers was in Saigon and brought back a movie projector. We showed an old John Wayne movie on a sheet stapled to the side of the building (very primitive, huh?). Actually, it's not really a building—more like a carport, open air but with a roof. It was *weird* to sit and watch an old WW II movie, surrounded by GIs, in a war zone!

This is all for now. Did Grandma and Grandpa get my letter? I'm well. Hope both of you are too.

Love always,
"Me"

"Me" is Cathleen Cordova, who worked for Army Special Services from October 1968 to October 1969 as a club director in Tay Ninh, Di An,

*Vinh Long, and Can Tho. She is a former banquet manager living in
Redondo Beach, California.*

— ☆ —

April 20, 1969

TO: THE PRESIDENT OF THE UNITED STATES, COMMANDER-
IN-CHIEF OF THE UNITED STATES ARMED FORCES:

We are members of Delta Company 3/21, 196th Light Infantry
Brigade of the American Division currently serving our tours in Vietnam.
We are a group of dedicated individuals who have done our best to serve
our country in this conflict. We have been here long enough to know how
things should be done, and are deeply disturbed at operations on the
company and battalion level because of their unfair treatment of the
combat infantryman. We feel that these shortcomings in the higher levels
of our command should be brought to the attention of someone who is
capable of trying to correct this situation. This is our purpose in writing
you.

Our first and major complaint is that we are spending more than we
feel is our fair share of time in the field. From the time we entered
Advanced Infantry Training, we realized that we, as infantrymen, were
destined to have it harder than most. We have accepted our responsibilities and have fulfilled our duties to the best of our ability. We feel that
after spending a reasonable amount of time in the field, we should be
given the opportunity to work in the rear or secure area for the remainder
of our tour. This is a standard procedure in most units here in Vietnam.

In order to clarify the matter, I think it is necessary to explain to you
that basically there are two different wars here in Vietnam. While we are
out in the field living like animals, putting our lives on the line 24 hours
a day, seven days a week, the guy in the rear's biggest problem is that he
can receive only one television station. There is no comparison between
the two. The combat infantryman would rather take permanent KP or
burn human waste on a fire support base than spend another night in the
field. The man in the rear doesn't know what it is like to burn a leech off
his body with a cigarette; to go unbathed for months at a time; to sleep
without an air mattress, let alone in a fox hole; to walk all day on feet raw
from immersion foot; or to wake up to the sound of incoming mortar

rounds and the cry of your buddy screaming "Medic!" In short, he does not realize the tremendous emotional and physical strain that the men in the field are forced to endure.

We feel that there should be a system set up that allows men to obtain jobs in rear areas for the last three or four months of their tour. Officers and medics only spend half of their tour in the field. We have men with 11 months and days in the field who have seen five platoon leaders come and go. Why can't we get the breaks that officers do? After all, we are all men. There are both ample jobs in the rear and capable replacements in the field to allow deserving men to get out of the field. You cannot imagine how disturbing it is to have a friend with just days left before he goes home lose his life. As a man nears the end of his tour, he becomes tense and nervous and cannot properly function in the field. He hesitates to act in situations where he once would have acted instinctively. He becomes so concerned about his own welfare that he neglects the well-being of others. It is at this point that a man becomes more of a hindrance than a help to his unit. This is why we want, in the best interests of the individual and his unit, to get men out of the field when they near the end of their tour.

Another factor which concerns us is that the morale and incentive of the new men is being affected by the way the old timers are getting the raw end of the deal.

We have sought help from the lower levels of the chain of command, but have had negative results. Being our commander-in-chief, we would appreciate anything you might be able to do for us to resolve our problem. We anxiously await your reply.

Your fighting men in Vietnam:

Sgt. Edward F. Noonan

Sgt. Alfred D. Seaman

Sp/4 Fredrick R. Bagwell

Sp/4 Steve Ivey

Sp/4 William H. Tross

Sp/4 Bruce Joel Dunham

Sp/4 Charles P. Harang

PFC Raymond L. Williams

PFC James J. Lindsay

Sgt. Phillip J. Boyenga

Sp/4 David W. Campbell

PFC Andrew Norton

PFC Charles W. Fletcher

PFC Jay William Rech

PFC Gary L. Stull

PFC David F. Ney

PFC Clark Williams

PFC David B. Anderson

PFC Bruce M. Applegate

PFC Clyde Beckham, Jr.

PFC Daniel T. Erickson

PFC Thomas J. Hatte

PFC Thomas J. Jordan

PFC Glenn E. Holland

PFC William I. Purnell, Jr.   PFC Gary C. Schneider
PFC David A. Bild   Sgt. Robert R. Rudesill
PFC Gary H. Thole   PFC Dennis G. Foell

According to Sgt. Edward Noonan, the members of Company D, 3rd Battalion, 21st Infantry, 196th Light Infantry Brigade, operating in I Corps, never received a reply from President Nixon. They did get some responses from congressmen. They were not transferred out of the field. Ed Noonan, who lives in Tom's River, New Jersey, is now a special-education teacher in high school.

— ☆ —

Hi Babe,

Boy, am I ever pissed off! This damned place is getting completely unbearable. We have had our hours increased—now we work from 6:45 A.M–5:00 P.M. and come back to work from 6:00 P.M. till 8:00 P.M. I'd sure as hell write to my congressman if I thought it would do any good.

Things are getting so bad that I almost wish that I was back in basic training. If I had any more time left than I do, I know that I wouldn't be able to make it. As things stand, it's going to be an awful close race to get home with my sanity intact. . . .

As you can see, babe, things aren't going too smoothly in this part of the world. The lifers keep fucking with us, and taking away our few privileges until we're ready to react in a disastrous way. Tensions are on the breaking point. . . .

Oh, hon, how I wish time would fly and I was sailing home to you. I've been alone much too long, and it's really getting me down. It's sad to be away from loved ones for even one day, and a whole year of this is totally devastating. . . .

Things aren't really that bad over here except [for] the agony of waiting and living without you. If I wasn't so much in love, life would be much easier—but also empty. I love you, Ingrid.

            Ron

Sp/4 Ronald Buehrer, of Vallejo, California, was assigned to the person-nel office at Headquarters and Headquarters Company, II Field Force,

Bien Hoa, from November 1969 through November 1970. He now works as a data processor in his county's welfare office.

— ☆ —

12 March 69
Wednesday
2005 hrs
Nui Ba Den

Dear Mom, Dad & Tom,

. . . There are a lot of inconsistencies about this war—a lot of things seem unreal. At times you wouldn't even think a war is on. You're watching movies on television. Or [you're listening] to the radio, and getting the same disc jockeys and the same predominantly rock 'n' roll music [that] you'd get on an American station. However, instead of commercials or public-service announcements, you get reminded to drive carefully or to keep your weapon clean or to be constantly vigilant, etc., and then back to the music. Yet at other times, you are aware that a war *is* on. This is a war of contrasts in a land of contrasts. . . .

I hope you all are well.

Love,
Bobby

1Lt. Robert Salerni wrote this early in his tour with the 554th Engineer Battalion, 79th Engineer Group, 20th Engineer Brigade. He was in Vietnam from February 1969 through February 1970, based at Cu Chi and Nui Ba Den. He is now an architect and lawyer in New York City.

— ☆ —

5 June 1968

Dear Tom,

No, Dak To is not the place to be. I didn't mean to paint a picture of the Garden of Eden. Although you may hear of Dak To now, it was much worse awhile back. We suffered one of our worst losses here, but there wasn't much said about it. We have expected an attack for a long time, but for some reason it never came off. Pleiku suffered badly during Tet, but right now it is amazingly quiet.

We live in an enormous base camp and are protected by helicopters 24 hours a day. We hear artillery fire most nights and once in a while see the helicopters shooting their guns at night. I ride back and forth to town to talk to people and make liaison meetings with other agencies. We are always back on the camp before six o'clock. After that the roads are not safe. During the day there are so many soldiers on the road and they are all armed, that any ambush would be suicidal. The fighting is done away from the base camp because there is so much firepower available at a minute's notice. People here live a very relaxed life except when rockets are shot into the camp. This is done seldom, and the aim is poor.

About morale: The morale is very high, as the generals will tell you. The mistake is believing the reasons they give. Americans do have many things to be proud of. Among these is the ability to create a means of survival in an absurd situation. Because the tour here is one-year long, you are able to count the days till DEROS, Date Eligible to Return from Overseas. You are able to say, "This time next year I will be home."

We have movies five times a week. There is radio and television, when the situation permits. After being out in the field for a while, men return to base camp and relax for a few days. Everyone knows there are helicopters within minutes of them. There is a hospital on the other side of Pleiku, and the copters pick up the wounded and have them in the operating room within minutes. Everyone knows that the "heroes," the helicopter pilots, will come through the most dangerous combat situations to pick up a wounded man.

What all this means is [that] there is a feeling of being American and taking care of other Americans. The people here see the money being spent and see the uselessness of it. There are more trucks, buildings, airplanes, and one civilian contractor who is robbing the American people blind. [The contractor has] mostly retired military people who don't know much about their job but do know military jargon and have connections in Washington, D.C. A civil engineer who works for the company told me a lot about it. He mentioned a dock on the Saigon River at a place called Camp David. The pilings were slipping and, as it was his job, he told his superiors. They told him to forget it. When it collapsed, it cost the government another million dollars to reconstruct it. He mentioned some $2 million in materiel and cash being unaccounted for, but who cares? I asked him if he thought the company's presence here had been beneficial to the Vietnamese. His answer was hell, no—if anything, it was detrimental. He said the employees do not receive a fair shake. We worry more about how much money we put into the country and too little about the people and their culture.

It is a shame to see educated people making the mistakes they are taught to avoid. Remember the *Kulturkampf?* We are doing the same thing here. Remember the Germans in Paris? When everyone was starving, the whores had all they needed. During Tet, when most of the people were starving and clean water was scarce, the GIs were driving up to their girlfriends' houses with trucks [of] food and clothes. These girls would flaunt their goods around town. This was bad in Europe, but think of the Asian mind and the delicate culture of these people. We speak of the black market and the corruption of the people in Saigon. The goods sold on the black market don't come from the Vietnamese, but from the Americans. We buy a Coke for 10 cents, sell it for 25 cents and it is in turn sold for 50 cents. The black marketeers have to be supplied, and the GI loves to supply him. The same GI will speak of defending his country and tell war stories when he comes home. . . .

Vietnam is one of our mistakes, and our generation will unfortunately be linked with this mistake unless we use the means available to rectify this situation. In our country there are many ways to make ourselves heard. I hope that the legitimate means afforded us through the democratic process will be used. If the swifter and more dramatic means of violence are used, then history will have that much more reason to condemn us. . . .

I heard about the shooting of Robert Kennedy, and although no comment is necessary, I am sorry for a country where such things become a national habit.

Ed

Edward Murphy was a sergeant with the 4th Military Intelligence Detachment, 4th Infantry Divison, based at Pleiku, from May 1968 to May 1969. He now serves as special assistant to the director of the New York State Division of Veterans' Affairs in Albany, New York. Tom is his brother.

— ☆ —

6 September '70

Dear John,

. . . Saigon [is] completely different from I Corps—almost luxurious. The MACV [Military Assistance Command/Vietnam] complex, where so many of my friends work, has a golf course, Olympic-size swimming pool, etc. But with all the surface glitter and bustle of Saigon, I came away with a very gloomy feeling. The people are frantically trying to make every last cent they can from the Americans before [the soldiers] leave. The war has brought out all the venality imaginable in these people. . . .

My friends are somewhat depressed. It now seems they have to rewrite all their reports because the truth they are putting out is too pessimistic. The higher echelons, for their career's sake and the plans of Nixon's Vietnamization, will not allow a bad situation to exist—no matter how true it may be! I saw myself some of the different drafts of some reports that were to go to [General Creighton] Abrams [commander of American forces in Vietnam]—and how they had to be changed to get to him. What a disgrace—and still people are dying every day!

To top this all off, we got hit again last week—twice in one night. The second phase was while we were all watching a Korean floor show. It was mass hysteria when those rockets started coming in! Chairs flying, people running to bunkers! Boy, do I hate those things. I'm going to be a nervous wreck when I get out of here! Then, there has begun a witch hunt for pot smokers. We have a group of self-appointed vigilantes (most of whom are Southern beer-drinking, obnoxious alcoholics! You can see my prejudices in that statement!) who go around spreading untrue rumors about those they do not like. It's at such a point that open warfare might break out in the company. I'm so worked up now because one of the vigilantes is my own boss. It just makes me sick! My own impressions are that the supposed "pot heads" are much easier to work with, more pleasant, never bothersome, and more intelligent than the redneck faction of boozers! Yet that counts for nothing in the Army. . . .

John, Peace—my warmest regards—and thanks for letting me ramble on and take out my frustrations.

Tom

Sp/5 Thomas Pellaton, 101st Avn. Gp., 101st Abn. Div., Phu Bai, 1970–1971.

— ☆ —

23 Nov 1970

Dear Mom,

I need your blouse and pants measurements and Barbara's also. Also, each of you must tell me your favorite color. Send me the info soon, and I will soon send you a lovely surprise.

Last week I spent two days attending a conference for generals, colonels and high-ranking government bureaucrats at the U.S. Embassy in downtown Saigon. I was the only junior officer there and was the youngest by 10–15 years. Worlds apart are the attitudes and approaches toward life of those running the show here and those impelled to do the fighting. Heard Ambassador [Ellsworth] Bunker and General Abrams, both very imposing, speak a lot of simplistic bullshit. But, then again, they probably would spurn my views. . . .

Have fallen spectacularly in love with Kim, my little Vietnamese whore. She is very beautiful in that tight-skinned, exotic, Oriental way. She very quick, cheerful and affectionate. She say things like:

"I go pee—I come back."

"Never hoppen GI."

And she sing singsong in my ear:

"I love you beaucoup—you love me titi." It's a page out of Hemingway or Henry Miller. . . .

20 Dec 70

Dear Mom,

Typing the date I realized a New Year has almost overtaken [us]. Time is timeless here. . . .

Outside of MACV, life continues to be a polluted merry-go-round of the unusual. Have been meeting more Vietnamese (mostly female). These chicks find something very appealing in me. I think it's my submissiveness. I get pummeled, pinched, bitten, ignored, screamed at—they definitely are not indifferent. My friends don't understand the magic. As for me, I just smile and cry a lot, bewildered by the universe one discovers in little-known and uncherished places.

Playing the beneficent American, I've been visiting an orphanage in Saigon. Me and Sgt. Goode have arranged a Christmas party. Brought a tree and decorated it. There we were, Buddhist, Catholic, Episcopalian and Jew. But as a Vietnamese said: "They're really all the same."

Finally started getting a day off, this week. Me and Dick, my roommate, went to Cholon (the Chinese section of Saigon) for a party given by a girl I know for her little boy (a GI baby). Grand meal. After eating the chicken, French bread, salad and something else, we sat back to relax. Oh my, she said, there more. And there was: shrimp, beef, pastry, sausage, and the birthday cake. Traditional Vietnamese meal—Christ, they put together a fine spread!

Latest pearl from Kim: "I love you beaucoup, you love me titi, I give you VD."

And another, said last night: "Mer Chikmit," which diagnosed for several hours turned out to be, of course, "Merry Christmas."

3 Jan 71

Dear Mom,

. . . Have been having the usual (for me) sour and aggravating exchanges with senior officers at MACV. It is surprising, even to me, how little Army discipline and decorum have influenced me. If anything, I am more sensitive about my freedom and individuality. As discharge nears, I am less prone to adhere to silly convention and arbitrary command. I know I am a bit abnormal about this freedom thing, but I have to accept it, live with it and humor myself about it. In the past six weeks I've told two majors that if they didn't like my attitude that was too bad. "I'm paid to work, not to say 'Yes, sir,' 'No, sir,'" I tell them. They responded furiously, a great deal of shouting, etc.—most ungentlemanly, I think. Were it not for the Army (and the war, of course), Vietnam would be an ideal place to work and play.

Love,
Jim

Capt. James Gabbe served as command historian for Military Assistance Command/Vietnam (MACV), stationed at Long Binh, from July 1970 through June 1971. He is now a business and financial writer in New York City.

— ☆ —

February 8, 1967

Hi-you-all,

Dad asked about the laundry. Mama-san does all cleaning, every-thing for $10.00 a month. Sheets are picked up and taken to some place on the Mekong River, rinsed in muddy whatever water, and pressed slightly.

Dress by the Vietnamese is interesting. Men and women wear silk or silken-like pants, usually dark, shiny and paper thin. Tops are of cotton. Woven reed hat and sandals or bare feet complete the costume, depend-ing on how rich one is at the moment.

The beach formed by the bay in town is a real stinker, resulting from all sorts of debris, fish heads, vegetable garbage, urine and God knows what. The coastal beach is clean and excellent for swimming, although currents can be treacherous.

The guys in the barracks have their radios on all day long, whether they are in or not. They're foolin' around with a tape recorder now. Some are high on marijuana—it is widespread here. I haven't touched it and don't consider it essential for a blast.

Starting tomorrow, the Vietnamese celebrate their big holiday of "Tet"—we are not allowed downtown for three days as Viet Cong activi-ties could be nasty. Guards will have their hands full.

I'm pulling guard duty now. Every 7 to 14 days I get to stay awake for 2 hours, sleep 4 hours, guard for 2 hours—for 24 hours straight, at various military posts in and around Vung Tau. These could be either battalion headquarters, the airfield barracks, a beach-based artillery unit or that cozy spot known as the "Pink Pussycat," a combo bachelor officer quarters and social club.

One gets to know what night is really like at 3 A.M. The only noise you hear is a faraway droning of electrical generators and an occasional dog bark. Once in a while a two-wheeled cart drawn by some sort of cow comes creaking along heaped with pineapple or vegetables for the next day's market. Otherwise all you smell is a musty worn-out stink, and all you see is shadow.

Sleeping or drunkenness on duty is death for anybody caught, and most everybody takes it seriously, surprisingly.

That's all for now.

Regards,
Rick

Sp/4 Richard Loffler was a draftsman and supply clerk with the 36th Signal Battalion, 2nd Signal Group, in Long Binh and Bear Cat, between November 1966 and October 1967. He is now an architectural draftsman and lives in Little Neck, New York.

—— ☆ ——

Wednesday
27 April 69

Darling,

It is 9:30 P.M., and I am beat. Today was one of those days when you get out of bed at a flat run and don't stop until you collapse back into it. This morning started with the usual rush-rush of getting the A.M. reports out by 0900. This seems to be a daily race which you can never get ahead of. The information for the reports doesn't make it into the office until 8:00 or 8:30. Then it has to be compiled and typed (hunt-and-peck method) up by 0900.

After 0900, we usually have a cup of coffee or juice and get on with doing our other work. Today the other work consisted of doing our monthly reports, updating our training records and putting together a completion report for one of our projects. This pretty well occupied our time until the 1530–1730 rush came up. This is the period when all the P.M. reports are compiled. At 1530 the platoon sergeants come in to report the day's progress. By 1600 we have the CO's daily SITREP (situation report) out so he knows exactly what the company accomplished today. From 1600 to 1730 we have to get the mail sorted out [and] put out our progress reports for each individual project. Again at 1730 we breathe a sigh of relief. The usual nonsense is over with, and we break for supper.

After supper there is always something to catch up on. Tonight we were just about ready to take a night off since we were fairly well caught up, when one of our juvenile-delinquent types went wild. He refused to change a flat tire on a truck. This was plain childishness because this kind of stuff has to be taken care of at night, or in the morning we will find ourselves with half our vehicles down for things they could have had repaired. What followed was a series of arguments between this guy and his platoon sergeant and platoon leader. Finally he was ordered to his quarters—he refused and disappeared for a while. This resulted in his being put under guard and held for a court-martial.

I don't really understand why he got so hot and bothered about changing a flat. I think he was up on pot, but I'm not about to say anything. He is really just a kid who hasn't learned to adjust to his surroundings and play the game by a set of rules that the bad guy (Uncle Sam) set up. I really feel sorry for him, but on the more practical side he has caused me about three hours' work taking statements and preparing charges. From the sound of it he will probably get six months in LBJ (Long Binh Jail) and get a dishonorable discharge. I hope this doesn't start a rash of such outbursts since morale in the unit is pretty down.

Well, that's my day. I didn't receive any mail today—damn—damn. I's a lonely critter. I need to be held and cuddled and in general gotten away from this place into my baby's arms. I love you.

Eddie

Sp/4 Edmund Fanning served in Vietnam from March 1969 to March 1970 with Company D, 168th Combat Engineer Battalion, 20th Engineer Brigade, based at Lai Khe and Cu Chi. His "darling" is Janet, who is now his wife. He lives in Brooklyn and is manager for technical policy development for NYNEX Service Company in New York City.

— ☆ —

Sunday, 1850 hrs
23 Mar 69
Nui Ba Den
"Camp Straight Ahead"

Dear Mom, Dad, & Tom,

It's Sunday evening here at Camp Straight Ahead, Nui Ba Den quarry. I've been here two weeks, and I just found out the unofficial name of this camp. . . .

Sometimes people complain about conditions here. There's no hot water, and it's dusty. The only time you have white anything is when it's new. The Vietnamese laundry "cleans" your stuff, but they obviously haven't heard of bleach. People complain about the food.

The last week we've had a company of infantry to secure this place at night. They're in the field all the time—sweeps in the day and patrols at night. For them a week's stay here is like R&R. My heart really goes out for those guys. It is they who have it worst here. I guess everything's relative. . . .

2015 hrs.

Monday, 19 May 69

Dear Mom, Dad & Tom,

Last night was another one of those unreal times I've spoken about before. We had a picnic-style barbecue supper.

I used some sandbags as a bench. You know, all buildings where people congregate (meaning almost every building) is sandbagged a few feet to guard against shrapnel from mortars and rockets. After the supper, we went on "yellow alert," an intermediate state between white (normal) and red. But it proved to be a quiet night, as are the vast majority of nights. One minute you're picnicking, the next minute preparing for a possible attack. Well, that's life.

I hope all is well at home. See you in about 39 weeks.

Love,

Bobby

1Lt. Robert Salerni, platoon leader, 554th Engr. Bn., 79th Engr. Gp., 20th Engr. Bde., Cu Chi, Nui Ba Den, 1969–1970.

— ☆ —

March 26, 1967

Dear Folks,

New place, new faces, a few old. I've been transferred to a region near Bien Hoa, almost 20 miles southeast of Saigon. Our base is about one mile square. Scraped out of the jungle, with the name of Bear Cat; it's the code name for the home base of the Big Red "One" (First Infantry Division).

We came by chopper. Ride was all vibration—hot, noisy, kerosene smell, door open wide, man at machine-gun–ready. This camp has dust over everything. A beige landscape. It's a fine powder that blows at the slightest breeze. Clouds of it blow into the mess hall while you're eating and get in your food, mouth—gritty, gritty.

I'm with a signal company again and still have my draftsman's job —doing charts, etc.

I've heard the camp has been shelled in the past. This means a red alert is in progress. You have to grab your flak jacket, rifle and ammo, and go stand at a post for a half hour or so until the "danger" is over. 105-millimeter cannons surround the perimeter of the camp and go off any time and rumble the tents, and the middle of your stomach. It's not bad, though. 242 days to go.

April 15, 1967

[Dear Folks,]

This is your "on the spot" correspondent in the BIG NAM reporting. . . .

Answers to pertinent questions first. Yes, we sleep on cots. One can buy mattresses and pillows at a Vietnamese store outside our base. I have a towel for a pillow and roll myself in the blanket. Just not energetic enough to get sheets and pillow.

On a trip to Vung Tau, I noticed red flowers abundant. Small, white, bell-shaped type are shaped by kids into garlands for the neck. They sell for five piasters. Trees are scrubby junk or a banana type. Soil is really hard as rock for about three feet down, then becomes sandy.

Well, guard duty is a drag. We go to a command post (a solitary telephone sitting on a bench) at 2:30 P.M. for instructions, then are driven out to the bunkers—sandbag shelters with broken cots inside. There are peepholes for observation. Chow is brought out to us at dusk. Three guys to a bunker. Two stay awake at all times. We eat, and sit, and sit, and sit. Then the cannons start.

Here are the noises of the ritual of firing one round: Whhiirrrrrrrr-klick. SSkkllaannkkk. WWhhiiiirrr-kkllaannk. That was the charge and shell being loaded into the breech. More whirring follows; asimuth and elevation controls are set. Then a guy gives a short "yell" and then an instant's silence. Then a BAM-BOOM-TTHHAATT sound combination that bounces the ground, the cot, and you. Maybe a half hour of this is followed by an hour and a half of silence. Then BBAAMM, BAAAMM for another half hour. This goes on all night. Flares can be seen nearby, fired off when somebody sees "sumthin out dare." There [are] the whining choppers slipping by, landing lights glowing red. Mice and rats squeak, and the night goes on.

Well, the routine goes on. We're just "paper soldiers," that is, the people doing administration, although somebody has got to do it. The "roughness" we endure is only the water rationing, being hot, and the somewhat dreary atmosphere of it all. Dirty Boy Scouts moved up a notch.

Hope all are in good health. Me, I just puff, don't inhale.

May 6, 1967
8:A.M. Hot

Dear Folks (car, bird, house, etc.),

New jungle fatigues, boots, cooling fans, typewriters trickle into supply and are dispersed as needed. Also, napkins, silverware, grass seed!? Jeeze.

As a draftsman, I do little odd jobs like painting captain "bars" on helmets.

We are working four to five hours extra in the supply room trying to straighten out the foul-up in our records.

Yh'know this is an "in" war, one of the hippest things in this crazy world. I've read where officers were quoted as saying: "This is the only war we've got. Don't knock it."

August 27, 1967

Dear all,

Surprise! Charlton Heston visited our company for a few minutes, and I shook hands with him! He looked like an old farmer the way he was dressed in old drab green jungle fatigues. He said "almost everybody is backing us over here" and "I'd like a beer."

Can't think of anything else to say. The new library opened up— air-conditioned and quiet.

Well, cheerio
Rick

Sp/4 Richard Loffler, 36th Sig. Bn., 2nd Sig. Gp., Long Binh, Bear Cat, 1966–1967.

21 May 1970

Peter:

I would never ask anyone to contemplate the insanity of the 20th century if I didn't think he was good at it.

. . . Long Binh, USA. I'm not really in Vietnam. An occasional rocket. The helicopters during the day and artillery at night, but that's it. I'm living in a moderate-size town which combines the worst features of the Midwest and the South—i.e., midwesterners and southerners. The only Oriental food I've had is at a bad Chinese restaurant on post. I've never seen a Vietnamese village, been in a local hut or talked to someone who raises rice for a living. It's weird how we get the news. It goes from correspondents here back to the States and then back to us. All the news reports I read have "(AP)" tacked on to them.

Like I say, I have not lived in Vietnam for 10 months. I have had a shit existence on a bad army post in a deserted area. If I had really been living in Vietnam, I might have seen some of the country, talked to its farmers, eaten its food, played with its children or killed some of its men. Rather, like you, I get reports, statistics and photographs. I don't know how clear I'm being, but this whole thing fucks up your sense of time and place.

It's not like the war is over here, and you and the campus riots are back there. No, not at all. Everything—the war, the riots, New York, the Rangers, the DMZ, cars, Saigon—is back there. It's not here anyway. Nothing is, except the office, the mess hall, my room and my books. At the moment, it doesn't seem to me too absurd to say that if the Army wanted to go to the trouble, this might all be a charade. I might be on an island in the Pacific being fed news, radio and television reports about what is supposedly happening around me and back home.

No one actually *does* anything here. When I get back, everyone is going to ask me about the war and how bad it is and what are my feelings toward Nixon, etc., all supposedly backed up by my experience of a year in Vietnam. And they're going to be disappointed. I have opinions about [Nguyen Van] Thieu [South Vietnam's president], the war and Vietnamization, sure. But based on almost the same information that any informed reader/listener has. Not much more. I sometimes realize that a week has passed, and I've only had my eyes open halfway. It is not quite, but it is a little dreamlike. And being in it makes it difficult to write about but, I hope, not impossible. When I come back from Australia [R&R] after six days, I'm going to be able to tell you much more about Sydney than about Saigon or Bien Hoa. This didn't really hit me until around February. And I've been off balance ever since. . . .

    Only 66 more days. Now that's nice.

Fitz

Sgt. Tom Fitzharris, USARV-G2, Long Binh, 1969–1970. This letter was sent to his friend Peter Widulski.

— ☆ —

Tightening the Noose

Months ago
metal mortar fingers
jabbed through our door
months ago a small probe sensed our
northern wire,
they've registered on our house,
sounded out the depth of our
defense
and the quickness
of our reaction,
we wait
each night,
last night we set
an extra place
for dinner.

—George E. Samerjan
1970

Capt. George Samerjan was a Mobile Advisory Team leader in III Corps during 1970–1971, when he wrote this poem. He is president of Ocelot, a generic video-software company, in Sudbury, Massachusetts.

— ☆ —

01 Oct 68, Tues
Chu Lai

Dear Mom,

I haven't had a chance to write to you in the past two days or so because I've been very busy, as I told you I would be. Tomorrow things should slacken off, and maybe I'll be able to take it easy.

I finally received a good deal of mail today. It's been pretty slow in getting here. I still haven't received the banana bread yet or the second jar of peaches.

The weather has been pretty crummy lately, but today it began to get a little better. There was a typhoon several hundred miles off shore, and the winds have been very high.

The last time I wrote you I said we might get hit, but we didn't. I hardly slept at all that night. The winds and rain made all kinds of noises, and I kept waking up. Then, during the middle of the night, my buddy woke up and [thought] he saw someone looking in at him. We both sleep here at Commo [communications], which is a secure area—so secure no one is supposed to be in here. We didn't find anyone, so we're still not sure if he was dreaming or if someone was really in here.

We both spent the rest of the night with our rifles practically in bed with us. We were really scared. What made it even worse was that only last week Charlie got into one of our batteries in the hills, and they didn't know until he started running through the hooches and blowing things up.

Today our new commo chief asked me to write to this kid in a hospital in Boston. A story in the American news sheet said he was dying and wanted to receive as much mail from around the world as possible. It took me an hour to write one postcard. What do you write to a 14-year-old boy who hasn't got long to live?

I'm getting sleepy, so I'll close for now. Take care.

Love and XXXXX,
Ray

Sgt. Raymond Wahl was a radio teletype operator for Headquarters Battery, Americal Division Artillery, stationed at Chu Lai, from March 1968 until April 1969. He lives in Glendale, New York, and is a vice-president of an insurance company.

— ☆ —

Hello Yolanda,

I hope that when you receive this letter, you and Jessie are in the best of health.

I'm doing all right. I'm working straight nights. I work with what is known as "Devil Flight." There are about 150 men to Devil. We're responsible for protecting the base in case of an attack. We're pretty well protected. There is a line of fire fences around the base. We have 5 tanks, 30 German shepherd sentry dogs, Vietnamese Air Force ambush patrols, helicopters and planes.

But guess what? There is no known protection against mortars except a bunker built with sandbags and steel. Mortars do a lot of damage. The VC fire them from about five miles out, and they do it at night when they can't be seen. On the 23rd of February, my first night here, we got hit with 14 mortars about 3:30 A.M. Nobody was hurt—one helicopter was hit. I wasn't working that night. I was asleep when they hit. I think I broke a record in the time it took me to get to the bunker outside the barracks —I almost ran over one guy. We always joke about when we're supposed to get hit, but nobody knows—there's no way of knowing, so we just wait. I'm glad I work at night. Nobody likes sleeping in the barracks—some guys even sleep in the bunkers at night. I don't mind [it]. There's something [here] that appeals to me. I don't know—it's not a very popular place to be.

All my love
Chicky

Hector Ramos was a sergeant with the Air Force's 632nd Security Police Section at the airbase at Binh Tuy from January 1969 through February 1970. He is an electrical designer with an architectural firm in New York City. Yolanda, then his girlfriend, is now his wife.

—— ☆ ——

July 28, 1967

Dear Mom,

I don't know how to tell you this, but like I have said before, there's no sense in holding anything back from you. Last night about 2:30 A.M.

we got rocketed by the VC. I am fine. Nothing came directly near our hut, thank God.

By the time you get this letter, you will probably have found out about it. Like I said, don't get all upset because I'm fine. All I got was two scraped-up legs and a few cuts and bruises from scrambling into the bunker.

Here's how it started. All of a sudden I woke up to the sound of a loud whoosh! Then all hell broke loose. The explosion from the first one demolished one hut and killed three guys instantly. That happened about half a block away. So those poor guys never felt any pain. There's so much to say, so I'll try and do as good as I can. If I keep mixing things up or repeating, please forgive me because I haven't had any sleep for two days. I'm so tired, but I thought before anything, I should write and let you know.

Then before I knew it, everyone ran out of the hut, and when I got to the door I looked up and saw flames across the runway. Later on, we heard that two of the helicopters got direct hits and were all ablaze. Then we all got into the bunker, and one guy had a gash from one side of his forehead to the other and all the way to the bone. It seems he ran into one of the window shutters that raise up and out like awnings. Anyway, we sat in the bunker shaking, and listening to the 31 (140-mm) rockets we received.

Then I realized Murray was bleeding like crazy, so I took some guy's T-shirt and wrapped it around his head. Then I said I had to go back out and get my Unit 1 and my glasses. So out I ran, and just as I go inside the hut, another one went off, and I dropped to the ground. It's a good thing I did because I heard metal hitting metal all over the place. I found out later that one landed over on the next street and sent shrapnel flying all over.

Then I got up and went back outside, and some other guys knew I was around there so they came over because they were hit and had minor cuts. Before a truck came I had them all patched up, and then we loaded all of them into it and they went to sick bay. Then I ran back to the hut and got my Unit 1 and started running around looking for more casualties. I couldn't find any and ran to sick bay, and when I got there I couldn't believe my eyes. There were guys all over the place half dazed and bleeding. So I started to treat a few and we had things going pretty good, and by 4 A.M. we had every patient treated and released or sent over to the hospital. There were quite a few seriously wounded people. Later on one guy died from shrapnel wounds over at the hospital. Altogether there were about 120 wounded as of this afternoon.

Sick bay took almost two direct hits. The dental department got it the worst. The rocket hit about five yards from the part where the dental techs sleep. Three of them got hit pretty bad. Shrapnel from that one blast went through medical supply and smashed all kinds of bottles of pills and stuff. Then some went through the OR [operating room], and a piece bounced off the ceiling and came two feet from the duty corpsman and smashed the resuscitator to bits. Plus our water tank got full of holes, and we had no water after a while. Then another rocket landed on the other side of sick bay and smashed the doctors' offices to smithereens and also broke the other water tank and also sent a round through the x-ray machine putting that out of commission.

A rocket also landed by the E-5 Club and smashed all the liquor bottles on the shelf of the bar. Then one landed out behind our club, but it didn't do too much damage. Then one landed right on top of the Vietnamese laundry, and there's nothing left of that either. Then one landed but didn't go off, so they worked on it all morning and finally disarmed it.

One amazing thing happened today. The Seabee's moved in, and they have almost all the damage repaired already.

There must be something fishy going on because all the waitresses left the base at 8 P.M. last night. Also, there were no fishing boats out in the harbor. I tell you, Mom, all these so-called friendly forces and civilians are all in cahoots with the VC. If I had my way, I'd shoot all of them and put them out of their misery.

Today also Dong Ha got hit, but I just heard that they are getting it right now. I know something is up because there were all kinds of ground action all over today.

Mom, please do me and all of us guys a favor and ask the president to do something. Things aren't getting any better here. Well, please don't be worried too much. Also please call up Claire and tell her to read this letter because I won't be able to write her for a few days. So in a way this is to both of you. Okay? . . .

You asked me about the Air Medal? Well that gold star is in lieu of a second award.

I'll close for now because I'm tired, and I'm almost falling asleep.

All my love,
Gary

Gary Panko, a Navy hospital corpsman from Yonkers, New York, was wounded early in his tour with Marine Air Group 16, 1st Marine Air

Wing, which flew medevacs out of Da Nang. A nurse for 12 years after he was discharged from the service, he died in Houston, Texas, on 8 February 1983.

— ☆ —

17 June 69

Well, old man,

. . . The combat-artist slot? I lost. I wanted that badly. I was tired of being a bloody clerk. I wanted to do something which I could feel and in which I could learn, not grow further confused. I wanted out from under the hands of stupid NCOs for [whom] I'd been doing an unprecedented amount of work. And I wanted to find out, with lots of time and freedom to do it in, if I could express what I was feeling. . . .

For once in my life I did not jump into the "new" experience, here in Vietnam. A buddy, who volunteered for the field after five months, showed up the other day and took me aside tonight, and, through his own waverings (from his very real heroism to his false excuse to let himself out of the field), I tasted both those things that nag me: the experience I avoided and in some backwards way still desired, and the act of self-justification which plagues every man over here. For without that blessing of dedication and cause, everyone seems to have to justify his own being, his own failures, and excuse himself, which is a very unpleasant business. . . .

Donny, the friend, tells with obvious mixed feelings of the hunt and killing and staying alive. And I tell with mixed feelings that I don't know the hunt and the kill, and know too well the results. [Then] someone [else] tells with mixed feelings that he doesn't know the results, but knows too well what a piss-hole being in Vietnam itself is. And so on. I wonder, [if] I really needed to fight, would I, and at the same time hope to God the situation never arises. [Yet I] still wish the comfort [of knowing] I am brave. Am I a fool? We will know no further comfort back home, because nobody back there really knows about this place anyhow. . . .

Donny can go back home and tell what it is that he has done and seen, but never why. And I can go back feeling that I've both seen a war, and not been in one, so maybe I'd best keep my mouth shut, not even trying to answer why. And so on, down to the man that goes to prison to protest Vietnam, or the guy who, through hook and crook, avoids the situation entirely. And who is right or wrong? . . .

Here, now, in the context of Vietnam, I am torn, but I wonder in what depth being "home" will heal my new self-doubts. Only I will ever really know what it was that I did or didn't do, or how important it will seem 10 years from now, if it isn't totally pushed out of the mind.

It seems at times that we are gilded leaves feeling the first chill winds of winter that will blow us away. Or maybe down there on the ground we will find substance again. I have never felt more human in my life, nor more a part of a sea of fumbling mutants born of gods.

There you have it—the deepest level of my concern, both self and otherwise, and I can't even begin to fathom the full meaning and import of what I've said. Everything else that has happened to me here [is] only eruptions of this basic thing, little poutings both good and bad. It is not nice to find out that you can't always be a hero. . . .

Take care all,

Love,
Rob

Sp/4 Rob Riggan, Co. D, 1st Med. Bn., 1st Inf. Div., Lai Khe, 1968– 1969. He is a writer living in Rowe, Massachusetts.

5
"World of Hurt"

"World of hurt" is one of the idiomatic expressions that gained currency among troops in Vietnam.

When a grunt screamed "Medic!," blood spurting from a perforation in his anatomy, he was in a world of hurt. When he collected the bodies of slain comrades, when he learned that the blackened body in the body bag was that of his best friend, he was in a world of hurt. When he got the letter telling him that his girl had gone, that she didn't care if he ever came home, he was in a world of hurt.

For troops in Vietnam, spiritual desolation and emotional despair could be as scarring as physical injuries. And for many, their world of hurt—spiritual, emotional, physical—has lingered long after their return to "the World."

7 Nov. 67

Hello Darling,

. . . My RTO, who has 28 days to go, cracked up. He was shaking and crying, not loud, but the tears were running down his face.

I told him to come out and get in my hole. A little companionship never hurt anyone. I put my arm around his shoulders until he settled down. [In] the last couple of letters he has received from home, his wife has said she didn't care whether he came back or not. He is real proud of his son, whom he hasn't seen yet, and his wife. The bitch doesn't know what she is doing to him. It is bad enough over here. But when your wife writes shit like that, it completely destroys a man. . . .

Last night I was comforting everyone, but there was no one to comfort me. When it got bad, I thought of you and the kids and I felt better.

I love you, Linda.

> Your husband,
> Fred

This is a segment of a letter from 2Lt. Fred Downs, platoon leader with Company D, 1st Battalion, 14th Infantry, 4th Infantry Division, operating out of Duc Pho, to his wife Linda. They have since divorced.

— ☆ —

3/23/67

Dear Mom & Pop:

Guess what! They nailed me yesterday. I guess that Marine recruiter from Fifth Avenue came down to see you. He probably scared the ass off you but there's nothing to worry about. I got scratched by a piece of shrapnel by my left ear. It's a little swollen now, but it'll go down fast. The docs say it looks like I got the mumps. It hardly even hurts me! In a couple of weeks I'll be able to give it another go. What surprised me the most is I wasn't nervous. I was nervous a little, but I wasn't scared. If I had to, I could have stayed and fought some more. . . .

Well, I have to finish now. I'll write again soon, and do me a favor and just don't worry.

                                        3/27/67
Dear Mom & Pop,
    I'm still at the hospital here at Da Nang, and I'm doing fine. They
have terrific chow here. The milk is real, and they even have chocolate
just like the base at Le Jeune. Don't worry too much about me because
I'm really doing great. I've been doing good since the guy in the hole with
me put the bandage on after I got hit.
    General [Lewis] Walt came in the ward the other day and passed out
the Purple Hearts. Boy, it really looks good. I guess I'm a genuine veteran
now, getting wounded and everything else. Well, that's the fifth ribbon
I rate now. Seven more months and I'll be rotating. It's still a long time,
but it sounds a hell of a lot shorter than 13!
    If a couple of yas could get together at any one time, I'd sure
appreciate a picture. . . .

                                        Love,
                                        Mike

*Cpl. Michael Boston, who grew up on Staten Island, New York, was a
squad leader with Company B, 1st Battalion, 4th Regiment, 3rd Marine
Division, operating in I Corps from October 1966 through November
1967. Hospitalized twice since Vietnam, he receives disability compensation from the Veterans Administration for post-traumatic stress disorder. He works as an independent auto repairman in Brandon, Ver-
mont.*

—— ☆ ——

                                        July 5, 1968
Hi Family,
    Well, Aunt Rose and Uncle Leo, I guess you know by now that I
was wounded. Well, I'm doing OK. Right now I'm in Japan. I'm at [the]
249th General Hospital. I'll be here for about two weeks, then I'll be on
my way home.
    I can't walk yet, but as soon as they sew me up I'll probably start
walking. I received my wounds in both my legs, in my side, in my back,
and in my butt, the right cheek. I'm going to have some pretty nice-

looking scars. The worst ones will be in my right leg. All my other scars are fairly small compared to my right leg. All together I think I have 13 wounds. Sounds like a lot, doesn't it? But I'm gonna be OK, so don't worry. If I know you, Aunt Rose, you'll be worried about me until you see me, but don't worry. I promise you I'm OK.

Well, Aunt Rose, how are you and Uncle Leo coming along? Gee, I hope everything is fine, and everyone is in good health. How's the kids? I hope they both are feeling well. Aunt Rose, just think, in two weeks I'll be home. Wow. Can't wait to see you and Uncle Leo. I miss you both very much.

Well, family, I guess I'll be cutting out for now. Be good and take good care. See you soon.

Joey

P.S. Uncle Leo, Baby, I hope you're ready to go out and get drunk.

Sp/4 Joseph Parisi was serving with H Troop, 17th Cavalry, 198th Light Infantry Brigade, Americal Division, in I Corps when he was wounded in action on the Fourth of July, 1968, six months after arriving in country. He lives in Elmont, New York, and works as a bread deliveryman.

— ☆ —

Tuesday, April 4 [1967]

Dear Family,

Hello! How is everything? I'm doing pretty well. I guess you can tell that I'm writing with my left hand, so please excuse the appearance of the letter.

Let me give you the extent of my injuries. I got a shrapnel wound in my shoulder and one in my knee. The one in my shoulder caused some nerve damage. The wound itself is not bad, but the nerve damage will take quite a while to return to normal. . . .

I'm really getting lazy. All I do all day is lay around and heal. It's quite hard work. I wish I knew a little more about what's in store so I could let you know, but I don't. I'll try to write again soon.

Love,
Bobby

PFC Robert Ptachik, assigned to Company B, 1st Battalion, 27th Infantry, 25th Infantry Division, was in Vietnam three months when he was wounded by a booby trap near Cu Chi on 27 March 1967. He is an administrator for the City University of New York and lives in Brooklyn.

— ☆ —

Letters from Pleiku

each of us
is a can of tomato paste
and though we may not
all have the same label
as we spin thru the air,
when we land too hard
or get torn,
from the outside or within,
we spill out and
stain the hands of everyone
who knew us.

—Michael O'Donnell

Michael O'Donnell, then a captain with the 52nd Aviation Battalion, 17th Aviation Group, 1st Aviation Brigade, was declared missing in action when the helicopter he was piloting was shot down near Ben Het on 24 March 1970. His status was changed to killed in action in 1978, a year after he was promoted to major.

— ☆ —

Mon, March 18, '68

Dear Tom,

Hi! I got [the] letter you wrote on 28 Feb. Saturday, and on Sunday I got your package. Thanks a lot. I go for that Shake-a-Puddin.

As for my condition, I'm in fine shape. I've been going to physical-therapy sessions twice daily, and my left hand is OK, meaning I got most of the strength back but I still can't bend my wrist in certain directions, which means I have to keep on with this PT until I can. It is going to take a while—how long I can't say—maybe two more weeks. All the tendons and nerves are intact and working fine. To look at the two scars, which [are] all that remain of the wound, you'd think that some tendons would have been cut. The fragment went through the center of my wrist. I didn't bleed much so no main arteries were cut. I was lucky. The fragment did nothing but cut meat. . . .

When I get to Chu Lai, I will look into the "college early-out" and fill out the forms necessary. . . . It will be worth it to get out of this garbage pit. I put up with these assholes long enough. When I get out, I want it to be permanent.

As for the details of what happened when I got wounded—me and the guys in my team and a couple of guys from the first squad where sitting around our position. At about a half hour after dark we heard grenade handles popping off, and then four grenades landed all around us. We only had four seconds to clear out, so we didn't bother to grab for weapons— at least I didn't as one grenade landed inside my tent where my weapon was lying. I was sitting about eight feet behind my tent. So I tried to put as much distance between me and the grenades as I could in four seconds, which was about 30 feet, before the first one went off. That was the one that got me because when it went off I had stumbled and felt the fragment hit my wrist.

Hell started then. I didn't see no VC, but I heard people running around throwing grenades and shooting so I guessed they were trying to overrun our position. I had seen my tent blow away, so I kissed my rifle and gear good-by. Man, what a feeling I had out there with no weapon. I sat there in the grass with my knife in my right hand and waited for a gook to come and finish me off. None did, so when the lead slowed down, I crawled to the platoon CP and there they sent me down to the company CP, where they were sending the wounded.

When the medevac chopper came in, things started getting hot again and artillery started coming in. As our chopper started lifting off, Charlie was shooting at it. I thought for sure we were going to get blown out of the air. When we got to Chu Lai, there was just the three of us and what was left of Doug. They tried to save him but he stopped too much shrapnel. I figured he was dead before he was loaded on the chopper but they kept giving him respiration and heart massage. I guess they thought they could bring him back to life. Well that's it. No heroes like on TV. Everybody is just trying to stay alive. . . .

After I was in Chu Lai a couple of days, more guys were brought in that were in bad shape—missing legs and feet, etc. They were from our hard-luck company, Company B. Them and my company ran into some NVA mines and were then hit by the NVA, but none of the guys in my company were brought into the hospital. They brought in a pile of NVA that were really torn up. I think a lot of them didn't live long as they were looking like Swiss cheese with all the holes in them. In my opinion they should just let them bleed to death, but sometimes they don't.

Take care.

Dennis

Cpl. Dennis W. Lane, from Brooklyn, New York, was wounded by a grenade fragment in February 1968, two months after he arrived in country with Company A, 4th Battalion, 3rd Infantry, 11th Infantry Brigade, Americal Division. He was killed by fragments from a mine explosion on 21 May 1968. He was 21 years old. Tom is his brother.

— ☆ —

8 May '68

Dear Vern,

I was in Saigon. My CO attached me to the 4/39th. I was King Shit working straight for Battalion. Some ARVN outpost was surrounded by 150 VC, so I (my four tracks) went to support about 100 ARVN. They got pinned down in about five minutes. There was a major there who [also] got pinned down, so I ran the show. I controlled two observation helicopters, four gunship helicopters, two jets, and put in over 1,000 rounds of artillery.

After four hours of fighting, we got the ARVNs pulled back and medevac'd the injured. Finally they sent a company to help us. A captain took over then. I didn't agree with his attack plan and told him so, but my track went in first. An RPG hit it, and I got some pepper frags in the side and forearms. No sweat—just skinned up. My RTO sitting next to me was killed. My [machine gunner] lost his leg. I was lucky. I always preached to my men about the day I get hit. I wanted my platoon to be able to function without me. They did. Before my track blew they rescued all the injured under heavy fire and worked courageously.

I talked to [Danny], the man who lost his leg, this morning. Some ass made a wisecrack about the 9th Division, [Danny] said, referring to me. He's from California and used to lead the Hell's Angels. Now he's leading us. [Sam] here was a cop. He's a mean bastard. We got killers in our platoon, and if they'd let us fight like we want we'd take 'em all on. I've never seen such bravery and guts before, and I'm stunned by it. Half my company is here. Our CO was supposed to be replaced, but his replacement panicked and started crying. Lt. Sharpe took five hits but still kept controlling his company! (He was in another fight.)

Really, I'm fine. I was frightened at the blood, but all the wounds were skin deep. I just hope they'll send me back to my 2nd Platoon. Don't tell Mom. Tell her I'm going on my R&R to Vung Tau and probably won't write. Be real subtle. I'd hate like hell to send her any of this stationery. And don't you worry. I got hurt yesterday at 4:30 P.M., and I showered, shaved, and am as good as new. They just gave me a local to remove the metal. I'm not scared any more. The 5th/60th is the talk of the hospital again. We're always raising hell.

You should have seen my men fight. They were going after wounded men shot right in front of my track whom no one else would go after. I went too. . . .

"Do you want me to go get him, sir?" I remember that. When I got blown out of the track, three of my men were right there helping me. My platoon sergeant came running up. [Sam] was temporarily blinded, but he still dragged [Danny] off the track and dragged him off the road. A blind man consoling a man with a lost leg. Paynor got blown off the track. Before I got dusted off he came up and said, "I'm sorry, sir. I didn't want to get off the track, but I was thrown off."

When I came in here, they cut my pants off. I caused a small panic here—they had a line of men carrying with both hands the frag grenades, incendiary grenades, white phosphorus and flares I had in my pants. I was so damn lucky—no big holes. Somebody up there likes me. This is my fourth close call. Just a stroke of luck.

You should have seen my brave men. It'd give you goose pimples.

10 May '68

Hi Vern,

Did I luck out. They sent me to Japan to recuperate. The hospitals in Vietnam were overflowing. I say again, I'm fine. I don't know why they sent me so far away. You're the only one who knows I got hurt, by the way. I'm going to tell Mom I took a leave to Tokyo. Did you read about my division south of Saigon? We kicked ass but pretty well got wiped out doing it.

I got off the bus here tonight, looked at that full moon, and said, "What a night for an ambush." Mentally I'm still in Vietnam. I can give you a pretty good idea of Vietnam by telling you my first impressions of Tokyo. First of all I noticed no barbed wire, which is everywhere in Vietnam. I also noticed that car windows weren't shot up, and no curfew. Weird. Also they don't carry weapons here. I'm naked.

Just talked to a doctor. I sure hope they send me back to my old unit. I feel like a crudball leaving my men. They got kind of scared when they found out I got hit. The leaders I trained performed, but when the man who has commo with battalion, FAC [Forward Air Control], artillery, medevac, and gunships is hit, there's bound to be concern. The poor guys.

What'll I tell Mom? I think I'll send her a picture of myself because I look fine and explain I got scratched up a bit and am in Tokyo. Five weeks without mail would be too long. Got a Purple Heart. No sweat! I wish I was back with my men. They're good.

Your brother,
Jim

1Lt. James Simmen, a mechanized infantry platoon leader, was wounded in May 1968 in action south of Saigon. After recuperating in Japan, he returned to Vietnam to complete his tour with the 5th Battalion, 60th Infantry. These letters were written to his brother, Vern. He is now a carpenter working for the Coast Guard in Alaska.

—— ☆ ——

5 Sept. 1967

Dearest Mom & all,

By the time you receive this letter, you will probably have known already that I got hit last night while flying medevac. I don't know how they notify you about these things, but I'm really not hit bad. I'll only stay in the hospital for 10 days, and then I should get out.

I don't know where to start, but here goes. We were flying emergency medevac to a call from 13 Marines seriously wounded. As we got over the zone, there was so much firing going on down below that the pilot decided not to go down. So we went back to refuel and take some ammunition with us to give to the troops because they were low.

Anyway, on the way back, we had to pick up a heat casualty. As we dropped down, I guess the pilot must have misjudged the height, and we landed with a plop on the sand. When we landed at the base, the pilot decided that it was a good idea to "down" the bird and get a new one, so we did. So off we went [a] second time to try and get out the wounded and dump the ammo. As soon as we got about 30 feet from the ground, we took sniper fire from the right. So the crew chief and I both opened up with our weapons. He had a machine gun and I [had] an M-16. It's like that new one Mattel toy makers put out. But it's the real thing. We made it out and went up quickly out of range. Because the bird took rounds, we had to down it also and get a new one.

The third time, we landed in the zone and didn't take any fire at all. So the crew chief and I dumped off the ammo, and then the five wounded came on. As soon as we took off, though, at about 30 feet, again we took fire, but from both sides and quite a bit too. Four out of the five got hit. Plus I think the gunner got some shrapnel.

Anyway, as I got hit, I fell over, and the crew chief realized I got hit, so he dressed my wound and said to stay there and he would see about the others. I said bull-------!, that I wasn't hurt that bad and he had to stay at his gun. I was in a lot [of] pain, but I managed to look all of them over and dress their wounds. Then I sat back down as I couldn't believe it.

We finally got to [base], and they took us all to the emergency room. Then they showed me my pistol and holster. Evidently a round must have hit it, and it tore the holster and messed up the gun. So guns are also good for saving lives instead of killing.

Well, so much for all the bad stuff. The hospital is very nice. They treat us real good here. The Catholic chaplain came up to me this morning and gave me this stationery and some shower shoes to wear.

Also about 10:30 this morning, the commanding general of all forces in Vietnam came in and pinned Purple Hearts on us. Me and four of the five medevacs we had are together on the ward. It's a very pretty medal, but I still wish I hadn't earned it. But that's life.

Well, Mom, I'll close for now because I'm very sleepy. I haven't had a good night's sleep in about a week with all the stepped-up fighting and mortaring the VC are doing now. As you have probably heard, they leveled the base at Dong Ha and almost—well they did destroy a whole squadron of helicopters. . . .

Bye for now.

All my love,
Gary

HM/3 Gary Panko, Mar. Air Gp. 16, 1st Mar. Air Wing, Da Nang, 1967–1968, died 8 February 1983.

— ☆ —

Dear Mom and Dad,

Well, I've had my baptism by fire, and it's changed me I think. Two days ago my platoon was on a mission to clear three suspected minefields. We were working with a mechanized platoon with four tracks, and our tactic was to put the tracks on line and just roar through the minefields, hoping to blow them. Since the majority of the VC mines are antipersonnel, the tracks could absorb the explosions with no damage done to them or the people inside. My platoon rode along just as security in case we were attacked. We spent the whole day clearing the three fields and came up with a big zero.

The tracks were then returning us to where we would stay overnight. When we reached our spot we jumped off the tracks, and one of my men jumped right onto a mine. Both his feet were blown off, both legs were torn to shreds—his entire groin area was completely blown away. It was the most horrible sight I've ever seen. Fortunately he never knew what hit him. I tried to revive him with mouth-to-mouth resuscitation, but it was hopeless to begin with.

In addition, the explosion wounded seven other people (four seriously) who were dusted off by medevac, and three others lightly, who were not dusted off. Of the four seriously wounded, one received a piece of shrapnel in the heart and may not survive. The other three were almost completely riddled with shrapnel, and while they will be completely all right, it will be a slow and painful recovery.

I was one of the slightly wounded. I got three pieces in my left arm, one in my right knee, and about twenty in both legs. I am completely all right. In fact I thought I had only gotten one in the arm and one in the knee. It was not until last night when I took off my clothes to take a shower that I noticed the other spots where I had been hit.

I came back to Chu Lai yesterday because my knee is now quite stiff and swollen, and will probably be here a couple of days, what with x-rays and what not. Believe it or not, I am extremely anxious to get back to platoon. Having been through this, I am now a bonafide member of the platoon. They have always followed my orders, but I was an outsider. Now I'm a member of the team, and it feels good.

I want to assure you that I am perfectly all right. You will probably get some sort of notification that I was lightly wounded, and I just don't want you to worry about it at all. I will receive a Purple Heart for it. People over here talk about the Million-Dollar Wound. It is one which is serious enough to warrant evacuation to the States but which will heal entirely. Therefore, you might call mine a Half-Million-Dollar Wound. My RTO, who was on my track sitting right next to me, caught a piece of shrapnel in his tail, and since he had caught a piece in his arm about two months ago, he'll get out of the field with wounds about as serious as a couple of mosquito bites.

I said earlier that the incident changed me. I am now filled with both respect and hate for the VC and the Vietnamese. Respect because the enemy knows that he can't stand up to us in a fire fight due to our superior training, equipment and our vast arsenal of weapons. Yet he is able. Via his mines and booby traps, he can whittle our ranks down piecemeal until we cannot muster an effective fighting force.

In the month that I have been with the company, we have lost 4 killed and about 30 wounded. We have not seen a single verified dink the whole time, nor have we even shot a single round at anything. I've developed hate for the Vietnamese because they come around selling Cokes and beer to us and then run back and tell the VC how many we are, where our positions are, and where the leaders position themselves. In the place where we got hit, we discovered four other mines, all of them placed in the spots where I, my platoon sergeant, and two squad leaders had been sitting. I talked to the mechanized platoon leader who is with us and he said that as he left the area to return to his fire base, the people in the village he went through were laughing at him because they knew we had been hit. I felt like turning my machine guns on the village to kill every man, woman and child in it.

Sorry this has been an unpleasant letter, but I'm in a rather unpleasant mood.

All love,
Mike

2Lt. Robert C. ("Mike") Ransom, Jr., raised in Bronxville, New York, a platoon commander with Company A, 4th Battalion, 3rd Infantry, 11th Light Infantry Brigade, was wounded for the first time in early April 1968, one month into his tour. Then on 3 May, he was wounded by a mine during a night ambush near Quang Ngai. His death on 11 May was officially attributed to peritonitis and pneumonia resulting from his wounds. He was 23 years old.

— ☆ —

September 16, 1966

Dear Mom and Dad, doting father-to-be, Peach and Fuzzy:

As I suppose you can see by my new stationery, this is not my normal letter. While walking down the road one day, in the merry, merry month of September, my squad got into a heluva fray, and lost (momentarily) one member.

ME!

I am all right, I am all right, I am all right, etc.

A carbine round hit me where it would do the most good, right in the butt, the left buttock to be exact, exiting from the upper thigh. It hit no bones, blood vessels, nerves, or anything else of importance except my pride. It was, however, a little bit closer to my pecker than was comfortable. But that is as good as ever, although it is now going through a year's hibernation.

I am writing this letter in the hospital less than one hour after I got hit, so please don't worry—by the time you get this letter and can answer it, I will probably be back on my hill.

Please, now, I am all right. The only thing that bothers me is the "indignity" of it, as Jose would say and Dad would feel, and disappointment that the wound ain't serious enough to warrant taking me out on the Repose where it is air-conditioned and there are nurses.

P.S. I am all right!!

September 19, 1966

Dear Mom, Dad, Shrub, Peach, and the Future President:

I was walking along a trail and turned to my left to tell one of my men to get his *tocus* up to the head of the column when I heard a loud noise below me and felt like some one had kicked me right in the butt. So the mighty oak fell to the ground, [after] having urged his men on to greater heights of glory with the resounding battle cry of "Oh, shit!" I thought I had been hit by a booby trap, and it wasn't until three to five seconds had passed that I realized that people were shooting at us in general and me in particular since I was still lying on the road. This also occurred to my unalert band of cutthroats, and one of them dragged me off the road and down an embankment, which felt oh, so good.

By this time I regained my form and was screaming at my men to return fire and charge the ambush—which they did to no avail—while my corpsman was explaining to me that they had never taught him how to bandage up a wounded butt. I explained to him in graphic detail what the consequences to his personage would be if he didn't think up a way, and quickly. He invented a way, using my penis as an anchor or something—anyway, as an integral part of the mummifying act. The helicopter finally came, and I was thrown aboard and taken to the hospital in Chu Lai. . . .

So, I am lying in bed here, and it comes time for that most thrilling event: "When the General Gives Out the Purple Hearts." The general in this case is a two-star general, a big, gruff, hearty type whose first words to me were, "Aren't you the one who wrote on that form that supplies weren't getting to the troops? Do you have any specific examples?"

So, what the hell, I gave him a few, and he, predictably enough, cut me off, explaining how the folks back home were having to be forced to make utilities. And in a very small voice I pointed out that a great deal of the problem was right here in River City. He ignored that and never stopped smiling, although it got a little forced after a while and his entourage stood around with little grins etched into their empty faces, which occasionally laughed heartily whenever the general made a funny, which was signaled by his own chuckling. All in all, it was a dreadful performance by everyone but, in a way, a classic of stereotype, one of a large number of stereotype characters and situations I have watched acted out, much to my growing concern. They finally left me sicker than I was before and with a medal I never wanted anyway. . . .

Love,
Sandy

2Lt. Marion Lee Kempner, platoon leader, Co. M, 3rd Bn., 7th Reg., 1st Mar. Div., recovered from these wounds. Two months later, he was killed by shrapnel from a mine explosion near Tien Phu.

—— ☆ ——

Feb. 23rd [1967]
2:30 P.M.

Dear Mom & Dad,

I was just about giving up on mail when I received your letter. It sure did a lot to cheer me up.

To be honest, I'm getting sick and tired of being in a hospital. It seems like yesterday when I was in for malaria.

I'm constantly on my back. The only time that I have been up is when they put me in a wheelchair and wheeled me to the x-ray room. I'm not able to walk as yet, and it will probably be a few months before I'm even able to try. I was on a stretcher when they flew me here.

This morning they took the cast off, and the doctor changed my dressing. I felt brave enough to peek at my wound for the first time, and what I saw didn't make me feel too good. The doctor said the wound is clean and there should be no problem when I got to surgery. What the doctor is most concerned with now is the possible blood clot in my chest. I have been taking pills and getting shots in the stomach to "thin my blood," besides getting streptomycin shots in my cheeks (smile again) to keep the wound sterile. The wound doesn't give me any more pain, but I get a tremendous shock of pain at the sole of my foot and toes. The doctor said it is caused by the damaged nerve tissue and there is nothing they can give me to relieve it. So all I do is just scream—day and night. Everyone in the ward knows about it because I yell at the top of my lungs to relieve the pressure. Don't worry, I'll just "scream and bear it" (smile).

Every other day a nurse comes around for physical therapy. I get a little exercise for my toes. It is difficult for me to move them. But with great effort I can manage to wiggle them a wee bit, and this is all she asks of me.

I haven't received any back mail yet, so I haven't received the pictures. Those pictures of Uncle Jimmy and the family were nice. Say, that was a cute little tree you had at Christmas.

I don't know what will happen to my personal things. Imagine they will ship them to me some way.

I suspect there's a letter from Richard on the way. I don't think it will be a disgrace [for him] to go to jail for something he truly believes in. I wrote a letter to his company commander requesting that his status be changed to a noncombatant, and I hope it did some good.

. . . I guess I'll try to read a few pages or listen to the radio. My leg (rather foot) is acting up again.

So long for now.

Love,
Kenny

Sp/4 Kenneth Peeples, Jr., Company A, 2nd Battalion, 18th Infantry, 1st Infantry Division, arrived in Vietnam in June 1966. He wrote this letter to his parents two weeks after he was wounded in action in III Corps. He now lives in South Orange, New Jersey, and is a librarian at LaGuardia Community College in New York City.

—— ☆ ——

February 21, 1967
St. Eleutherus
7:30 P.M.

Hello Son,

How are you feeling today? Hope this letter will find you successfully recovering. Today we received your Purple Heart medal. I looked at it with mixed emotions. Happy, because you are out of Vietnam; sad, because of the price you had to pay to get away from there. However, I do hope that you won't have any serious complications and that you will fully recover and be restored to health. I also realize the thousands of boys who will never return home, and the parents who have received the Purple Heart because of their son's death. When I think of these things, I know that I shouldn't feel too bad about your condition. Our main concern now is your recovery!

Let me say here and now that I'm extremely proud of you, son. Not because you were awarded the Heart, but because you did an honorable thing. I know that you were bitterly against going into the service and rejected our reasons for being in Vietnam. I also knew of your feelings about the U.S. and its treatment of Negroes. I also imagine that you were contemplating going AWOL. Yet, in spite of these conditions, you did everything that was asked of you. Whether it was to please your mother or your grandmother I do not know.

But I do know that you made a prudent and honorable decision. It may not matter at all to you, but you are coming home a hero to us. Not a war hero, because you had to fight and get shot, but more so because you made a man's decision and stuck it out. You should feel proud of yourself! You are now in a position to take every advantage that is offered to a GI (and there are many). You can hold your head high everywhere you go, and you can go anywhere you wish. Had you chosen the alternative, these things would not be so. I hope Richard will realize these things and take that "chip" off of his shoulders!

Everyone here is so concerned about you, all of our friends constantly ask about you. Your mother told one person about you on the telephone, and a few days later the whole parish knew. Certainly will be glad when you are sent stateside. Let us know as soon as you find out. . . .

You know, I was thinking that for a person who never traveled much, you are really seeing the world. Who would have thought that you would be writing from Japan, and your letters would arrive here in just two days. Hope ours reach you just as fast.

Rest good, and eat hearty. Relax, and don't worry about anything. Will write again soon. Until then, may God continue to bless you.

Love,
Mom & Pop

Sp/4 Kenneth Peeples received this letter from his parents.

— ☆ —

25 Jan 68

Dear Linda,

Some good news today. Doctor said that I wouldn't have to lose my right arm and will be able to regain almost full control. I've been moved to a hospital in Japan near Tokyo where I'll probably spend two or three weeks. Then they'll send me to a hospital in the States as near home as possible.

The other day my executive officer and a couple of my men stopped by and talked to me before I left for Japan. The day or so after I got hit, one of my men stepped on the same kind of mine I did and was killed. In the space of five days I lost 16 men in my platoon to mines. One KIA and the rest WIA—quite a few will lose their legs and maybe a couple their hands. My good friend, the third platoon leader Bill Ordway, was killed two days after my accident. So looks like I was pretty lucky after all.

Write to this address as I should be here if you answer right away. I'm anxious to find out how you feel and what's been going on this last month of January as no mail has caught up to me yet.

They pulled a few stitches out of my hind end yesterday, so only have about a thousand to go.

It's rather uncomfortable now but something I'll be able to look back on and laugh about. It always seems funny to tell someone you got shot in the butt.

I spent a night in the Philippines on my way to Japan in a new hospital which was fabulous. You can't imagine what a new military hospital can look and be like. TV in each room—two men to a room—radio for each bed—private bath with shower in each room—each room has a balcony—full glass window, one side of wall overlooking the country-side.

Everywhere I've been I've been treated real well by all the person-nel with whom I've had contact—nurses, doctors, Red Cross, chap-lains, wardboys, and guys who are healing but able to be of help all they can.

After seeing the patients around me, I consider myself very lucky. There are many who have lost legs, arms, eyes and other parts of their bodies, which leaves them in worse shape than I am. I'm really very anxious to know how you feel about me losing my arm because naturally I don't know how you will react when you see me. With my new arm they will give me, I'll be able to act like I normally did, which was always a little crazy. I haven't been depressed or anything like that, so [I] don't want you to feel bad either. I just paid the price that many soldiers pay defending our country, and I've accepted the fact that I can get along as well with an artificial arm as I did before. Some guys feel so sorry for themselves. They're miserable all the time. But our mind and soul don't come from our extremities. My personality is the same as it's always been and is not going to change because of a little setback.

Tell Tammy and Teri that I miss them and look forward to seeing [them] both very much.

You know how much I miss you and how very much I want to see you after so long an absence. It shouldn't take too much longer for me to come home—probably at least a month.

I love you and miss you very much.

Your husband,
Fred

[Dictated to a Red Cross volunteer.]

2Lt. Fred Downs suffered extensive wounds, including the loss of his left arm, when a land mine exploded near Chu Lai on 11 January 1968. He has incorporated his experiences in and after Vietnam in two books, The Killing Zone *and* Aftermath. *Today he is director of the Veterans Administration Prosthetic and Sensory Aids Center in Washington, D.C.*

——— ☆ ———

[written between June
and September 1967]

Dear Daryl,

You asked about Vietnam, so I'll tell you. I LOVE IT! I really am happy over here. The work is hard and all the time, but it keeps me on my toes. The men are grossly wonderful and fully appreciate a "round eye" in their midst. . . .

Several times a week we visit the hospitals and either chat with the troops or program them, depending on their condition. This is one of the most disheartening and yet morale-boosting jobs for me. Just this past Monday we went to the big [Navy] hospital, and what a sight we saw! Some of the guys had just been moved from the Intensive Care ward prior to being moved out [sent back to the States] within the hour. We see fellows with their arms and legs blown off, their heads smashed in and pieced together, eyes lost and hearts completely broken. Surprisingly enough, without sounding like a Clara Barton, the biggest lift we can give them is a human, female hand and some cheerful words. You know that they feel like hell and then some, but it's an American, a real, live, walking, talking girl! It's amazing to see them perk up, and from some it's a feeble attempt to move an arm or even talk.

Monday I chatted for almost ten minutes with a kid who had all his intestines lying in a plastic bag next to him and so many tubes and bottles that you could hardly get close. But he was happy to see me and smiled like a normal fellow would. Another tried to talk and tell me about all the pieces of shrapnel in him when he started to cough up blood and mucus through his larynx tube. He tried, and after they had cleaned him up, I went back and talked to him a little longer. Another was in a revolving bed. This kid was so proud to be alive that he had to show me all those wonderful wounds. [There's] nothing like a pieced-together leg! He felt pleased with the American Red Cross and just asked one favor—back issues of *Stars and Stripes* so he could find out if any of his unit or buddies were still alive.

But the one that really pleased me was a fellow I almost passed right by because he looked so completely out of it. He was lying with many bandages and his extremities all pieced together, his face all covered with gauze, and a towel-like cover [over] it all. On my way out they took the towel and the gauze off, and I could see why they had had it on. He was just one big mess of mush! His whole head was taped up. He had stitches all over, shrapnel all over, and tubes coming out of his nose and mouth. Along with all that mess he had scabs and the gooey crust left from the drainage. The only thing was he could see [just a little] out of his right eye, but that was all he needed. Apparently his mouth had been shattered along with everything else because when he started to talk you could see how much had been destroyed. Aside from the blood, guts and gore, he was alive, and when I teased him about his peep hole and looked him square in the face, he responded so beautifully that I wanted to hug him. He had gained enough of his senses to know who he was talking to, where he was, and what condition he was in. I spent over 15 minutes with him and even got him to give a feeble but painful laugh. It's men like that that make it all worthwhile. I would visit and talk with them every day if I could, and yet we're not in the business of giving sympathy but just honest, straight American girl talk. We have to treat them as if nothing were wrong at all, absolutely nothing. . . .

Jeanne

Jeanne Bokina Christie, a "Donut Dolly" with the American Red Cross, was based in Da Nang from January 1967 through February 1968. She now works part-time as a teacher in Milford, Connecticut.

— ☆ —

29 December 1969

Hi all,

    . . . I don't know where to start except to say I'm tired. It seems that's all I ever say anymore. Thank you both for your tapes and all the little goodies in the Christmas packages. Christmas came and went, marked only by tragedy. I've been working nights for a couple of weeks and have been spending a great deal of time in post-op. They've been unbelievably busy. I got wrapped up in several patients, one of whom I scrubbed on when we repaired an artery in his leg. It eventually clotted, and we did another procedure on him to clear out the artery—all this to save his leg. Well, in my free time I had been working in post-op and took care of him. I came in for duty Christmas Eve and was handed an OR slip—above-knee amputation. He had developed gas gangrene. The sad thing was that the artery was pumping away beautifully. Merry Christmas, kid, we have to cut your leg off to save your life. We also had three other GIs die that night. Kids, every one. The war disgusts me. I hate it! I'm beginning to feel like it's all a mistake.

    Christmas morning I got off duty and opened all my packages alone. I missed you all so much, I cried myself to sleep. I'm starting to cry again. It's ridiculous. I seem to be crying all the time lately. I hate this place. This is now the seventh month of death, destruction, and misery. I'm tired of going to sleep listening to outgoing and incoming rockets, mortars, and artillery. I'm sick of facing, every day, a new bunch of children ripped to pieces. They're just kids—eighteen, nineteen years old! It stinks! Whole lives ahead of them—cut off. I'm sick to death of it. I've got to get out of here. . . .

                                        Peace,
                                        Lynda

From June 1969 to June 1970, Lynda Van Devanter worked as an Army nurse with the 71st Evacuation Hospital in Pleiku and the 67th Evacuation Hospital in Qui Nhon. She has written a book about her Vietnam experiences, Home Before Morning. *She is now a teacher, counselor and freelance writer living outside Washington, D.C.*

— ☆ —

DEROS Day

It was early morning when they came and got you
And the litter bearers looked like they knew their job
Heavy, fat and sweating in the Asian heat
Hoisting each stretcher with the same emphatic jolt
As garbagemen or weightlifters with years of training
It was all so unreal
Flat back strapped down rolling along from the ward
Saying good-by to your ward buddies for the last time
Litter cart clack clacking on the rough concrete path.
The cart man was in a hurry, he hated being around
All those guys leaving Vietnam strapped back down
Tubes and bags dangling with all sorts of juices
Dripping into and thru them, besides he was short.

There was this guy already loaded
An Army sergeant going bald with red hair
And he didn't have any legs or a right arm
But it really didn't matter, they had him drugged up
and he just kind of snuffled
Every now and then while everyone watched
The glucose gurgle into him
And tried to keep from knocking into the catheter bag
That they had tied underneath him.
The nurse just kind of stood there by him
Draped like a southern belle around a front porch pile
Sniffing flowers, only she was not smiling and
Cradled an extra glucose bottle at her breast.
Every now and then she would turn around
And look at everybody else lying there and
She had such a bland nothing look like
People accustomed to eating hot dogs
In a hurry at lunch, standing up.

Each time a stretcher was loaded it was the same—
The gutteral strains as the man was lifted
Carried clump clumped up the wooden ramp
Past the one-armed man

And the faceless nurse
To be lodged into the metal racks.

Nobody waved good-by when the bus left for the flight line
Not that anybody was looking for that
But it would have been nice if some dude
Had flipped a "V" sign and smiled
Maybe saying keep on trucking man,
If not for me then for the others who really needed it,
Only everybody kind of didn't look
They had other places to go.
Nobody said a word.

Being on that bus was like
Riding home from the stadium with the losing team
Only there wasn't any coach
Just nurses hard as nails with dried up hurts.

They took the one-armed man into a special sealed
Containerized van inside the plane
And nobody saw him again.
Being lashed inside a Starlifter on a stretcher
Is kind of like being shelved in a pipe warehouse
on the East River
All sorts of banging and whirring gizmos
Weird noises and nothing to look at
But exposed dripped pipes.

The Air Force method of taking off is to
go screaming flapping into the blue
Hellbound for higher stars.
And it was over I was gone
Derosed.
Gone.
Never again, and I did not look back.

—Graham S. McFarlane
26 May 71

Graham McFarlane, born in Bronxville, New York, was a lieutenant with
the 8th Battalion, 4th Psychological Operations Group, based at Ninh

Hoa, from April 1970 to May 1971, when he was evacuated from Vietnam with hepatitis. He is now a certified public accountant working as financial manager for an independent oil company in Dallas, Texas.

—— ☆ ——

26 Aug. '70

Dear Mike,

I've been trying to write you for about a month it seems and for one reason or another never got down to it. You know how it is being in the field—you can't plan a damn thing.

So how are you doing? I really hope you'll be OK. You didn't look too good the last time I saw you, laying on that trail covered with blood. I really couldn't believe that damn thing went off. I heard the explosion and I hit the ground. There was shrapnel dropping all around me. I got up and saw Newcome about 10 to 12 meters farther down the trail rolling around. I went down there and he was bleeding. And I thought, where the hell is Cook? There was still dust and dirt flying around so I couldn't see you.

So I called for the medic (good old Kiminski). He came down there and saw me putting a dressing on Newcome and said, "How is he?" I said "He's got titi. Take care of Cook." So he went to you. When I finished with Newcome I went to see how you were. I had no idea you were hit that bad. Then the dust-off came and I put all your gear on the bird. I was going to keep Newcome's 79, but it was all bent to hell from the shrapnel. (If it hadn't hit the 79, it would be in his stomach. Lucky, huh?)

Then you were gone. I was messed up for two days, and I'm not even kiddin'. All I could think, what if you were dying or were dead when I was screwing around with Newcome's shoulder? I really felt bad about that. No one to talk to, make fabulous C-rat meals with, or pull guard with.

Newcome came back to the field the 23rd of August so he's A-OK. Can you believe our squad was down to two men? Suarez and myself. We were in bad shape.

The rest of that mission wasn't bad. Except for one day we were pinned down while humping out of a ville. They held us for about 30 minutes. We couldn't move. Salas was stuck in the middle of the trail and couldn't get up until Lester, Dadisman, Norton, Melisi, Griffin and myself put one burst of fire into that woodline that would have made King

Kong get his head down. No one was hurt, and I can't see how we made it. [Smitty] called in "arty" right on top of us. Lucky it was only a marker round, and even that was about 75 to 100 meters away. Good old [Smitty]. Still screw'n up by the numbers.

We moved into Dragon Valley and really hit some shit. Seven dinks with 47s opened up on our day fogger. The first burst hit Dadisman—five rounds in the chest. Melisi hit by two ricochets only titi. Barker titi in the leg. Eller titi in the fingers. Duford shot through the hand. Jerry Sholl got it in the hip—fractured it. They were all in one big cluster playing cards. They drew the fire. [Newman] shot himself with a short 79 round. It was really hell. It rained AK rounds like no one could imagine. Battels got hit. They couldn't even see him—they just shot up his hooch.

Battels is back in the World. We don't know how he's doing. He was pretty bad—shot right through the lung. Jerry and Duford are back in the World, too. Dadisman, God rest his soul, is dead. We really took it bad. Especially Eller. Dadisman was sitting right next to him when it happened.

The day before this happened the 1st Platoon walked into a booby trap of claymores and hand frags hooked up to a trip wire that was attached to a branch hanging in the middle of the trail. Someone hit it, and it went off. A new E-5 and two new soul brothers were killed. The lieutenant got it in the head. He's a vegetable now. Can't even talk. Moose got it almost in his eye. He's permanent OP now.

Charlie Company had 22 men dusted off in two days. We were operating with 41 men in the field. We came on the hill and got 27 replacements out there in Happy Valley now. And haven't seen or hit anything. Unusual, isn't it?

I'm sham'in now. I've been having a lot of trouble with my left arm. My ruck sack keeps pinching the nerves in my shoulder (remember when that started happening?), so I got a 30-day with no ruck sack and I have to go back to Da Nang hospital for a recheck. I was in the hospital for four days. I'm hoping for a permanent profile for not being able to carry a ruck sack.

I think you got out just at the right time. Consider yourself lucky you're not Dadisman or one of the other three who didn't make it. I'm keeping my fingers crossed for this profile.

I tried to cover the most important things that have happened since you left. I hope you can read and understand this letter without too much trouble. I can't possibly write all the details—it would take forever. I'm not trying to get you depressed by telling you about Dadisman and the rest of the men, but knowing you I thought you would be wondering what's happened here.

It's not very pretty, is it. It's happened before, happened then, and it will happen again. I just keep my fingers crossed. Stay out of clusters, and keep my distance while humping.

So be cool. Stay A-Head and Keep Peace.

Oh, yeah, there was one thing I wanted to tell you. Do you remember when we were out in the field and I couldn't get any "D" rings for my ruck sack? And you told me if someone goes in on a dust-off to take them off their ruck? *Well I did, thanks. They were on your ruck!* I laughed like hell when I thought about it later.

Write back and let me know how you are and what you're doing.

Always,
Mike Mancuso

Sgt. Michael Cook and Sp/4 Mike Mancuso served together in Company C, 1st Battalion, 52nd Infantry, 198th Light Infantry Brigade, Americal Division, operating in I Corps. Cook, who arrived in country in March 1970 and was wounded by a booby trap on 24 June 1970, is now an independent film producer in New York City. Mancuso, who served in Vietnam from June 1970 to August 1971, lives in Waterbury, Connecticut, where he is a postal worker.

—— ☆ ——

2130/13 March 1967

Dear Brian,

Received your letter today and was hoping you would write. Things here at Recon are fine, except for the fact that we've had more casualties in the last month and a half than we had in the previous six months. I think it all started with our platoon.

The part that hurts is the fact that I wasn't out with Rog when he got hit. Since that patrol, the 3rd Platoon has had many men medevac'd and they are not all here right now. But before they were wounded or left Vietnam, I got this much of what actually happened.

The platoon was inserted and hiked to the hill they were to observe from. Rog was told to set his squad into half of the perimeter. Then he [started to] set up an OP. From this point it's heresay and I'm not sure, but this is what I could ascertain among the many stories.

Rog moved out, with Frank in front and Tex behind, when he set off the mine (a bouncing betty). I think he realized he had set it off and fell back on it to try and save the others, but fragments still hit Tex and Frank, killing Tex instantly (he got hit in the head). Rog's buttocks and legs were torn to shreds, and he was bleeding quite a bit but still alive. Nick Vendetta, who tried to help him as best as he could (there was no corpsman, as theirs was medevac'd the night before with an acute sprained ankle), said Rog was saying over and over again "Thank you, God, thank you" I think because of the fact that he was still alive.

Nick and the man who had the corpsman's first-aid kit started packing dressings on Rog as fast as they could. Now and then he would stop breathing, and Nick gave him mouth-to-mouth resuscitation and he'd start breathing again. But then he just ran out of life and died. Frank had already died as he, like Tex, had a head wound and there was nothing they could do for him. All in all, Rog lived about 20 to 30 minutes after he was hit.

I was working in the battalion aid station in the rear. I got word that 3rd Platoon had 1 KIA and 2 WIA (serious), and this shook me up because this was the first patrol I'd missed in six months and I'd also lived with these guys for six months. I was told they were being medevac'd, so I got a jeep and drove down to where they come in, and waited.

I waited for an hour and a half, and by this time found out that the KIA was Tex but still didn't know who the WIAs were. The chopper finally came in, and I was there on the LZ to help carry them out of it. As I ran up to the chopper, the corpsman inside lifted his hand for me to slow down. But this I couldn't understand, because I had 2 WIAs on board and nothing was going to keep me from getting them up to the doctors faster. But when I looked inside, I realized that all three were dead. I helped put them in the ambulance, and when we got to where the casualties are taken care of and as I got out, I just seemed to break apart. I couldn't believe that they were dead, and I started shaking and I couldn't see through the tears.

Believe it or not, Rog and me were like brothers, and I don't think I'll ever really believe he's dead. We did so many things together in the few scant months that I knew him. We both got put up for Silver Stars for pulling a couple of pilots out of a burning chopper and everything else.

When Rog was hit, we tried to find some way to get ahold of you, but it wasn't possible—and besides, the CO wouldn't let us.

Well, Brian, I hope I've answered all your questions to the best of my ability. Take it easy and write again. I'd like to keep in touch.

Your friend & Rog's,
John

John Reed, a hospital corpsman assigned to the 1st Reconnaissance Battalion, 1st Marine Division, wrote this letter to Roger's identical twin, Brian, who was also in Vietnam, stationed at Pleiku. Roger C. V. Burke, who arrived in country in July 1966, was a corporal assigned to the 1st Recon. Battalion, operating in I Corps. When he died, on 6 February 1967, he was 23 years old..

— ☆ —

I swear I thought them asleep
Laying there stacked like dugout canoes
Waiting to be sailed.
I kept waiting for them to wake up
Smile
Ask for a cigarette
But they just lay there
You could hardly see the holes
It was all so strange, strange
These dead men freshly killed.

—Graham McFarlane
11 Mar 71
Nha Trang

1Lt. Graham McFarlane, 8th Bn., 4th Psyop Gp., Ninh Hoa, 1970–1971.

— ☆ —

16 November '70

I'll be home in *207* days

Dear John,

I had to write you tonight since I guess the inevitable has happened —someone who I knew was just killed yesterday. Partially to help me overcome my depression, I have to write you about it. It's all so meaningless, so horrible, that I'm having trouble coming to grips with the situation emotionally.

Believe it or not, I met Paul only a week and a half ago. He was visiting a close friend of his who lives in my hooch and is also a close friend of mine. He was part of the 3rd Brigade Recon Squad at Camp Evans, about 20 miles from here. We spent the night talking. Paul was just one of those people who you like immediately. He seemed to be a truly good person. He is a devout Mormon, married, opposed to the war, had worked against it, but got caught in the system—like so many of us—and now he's dead, blown up by a booby trap—he had no chance—one day before he was to come down to visit us on his way to visit his wife on R&R.

I just can't express how I feel. In writing, I'm crying. I called the Episcopal chaplain in Da Nang and had prayers offered for Paul. I felt it was at least something that I could do, consistent in a broad sense with Paul's life and my own beliefs. I put on the *Messiah* and immersed myself in the text—"The trumpet shall sound, and the dead shall be raised, and we shall be changed!" "Oh, death, where is thy sting, where thy victory?" "If God be for us, who can be against us?"

That's been a great help—but still, there was no need for Paul to die. Why did he have to die for the sake of the silly games the politicians and the Army play—why? My God, what do we do to ourselves? Why do we hate ourselves so much that we have to kill each other? What *are* we doing here! I'm losing control again—forgive me—but I seem to still be able to feel Paul's handshake—I had just gotten him a helicopter ride back to his unit. There are so few good, sensitive people. I feel the loss that he was my best friend. I just don't know.

John, I don't know how much more I can write. I will say I was overwhelmed with your good political work. Did he win? And, I almost forgot—Helen, your fiancée? You can't imagine how happy that makes me. John, I only wish you the greatest happiness. My love to the both of you!

Tom

Sp/5 Tom Pellaton, 101st Avn. Gp., 101st Abn. Div., Phu Bai, 1970–1971.

— ☆ —

25 Nov 66

Hello dear folks:

It's going to be hard for me to write this, but maybe it will make me feel better.

Yesterday after our big dinner my company was hit out in the field while looking for VC. We got the word that one boy was killed and six wounded. So the doctor, medics and the captain I work for went over to the hospital to see the boys when they came in and see how they were.

The first sergeant came in the tent and told me to go over to the hospital and tell the captain that six more KIAs were coming in. When I got there, they asked if anyone from A Company was there. I just happened to be there, so they told me that they needed someone to identify a boy they just brought in from my company. He was very bad, they said. So I went into the tent. There on the table was the boy. His face was all cut up and blood all over it. His mouth was open, his eyes were both open. He was a mess. I couldn't really identify him.

So I went outside while they went through his stuff. They found his ID card and dog tags. I went in, and they told me his name— Rankin. I cried, "No, God, it can't be." But sure enough, after looking at his bloody face again I could see it was him. It really hit me hard because he was one of the nicest guys around. He was one of my good friends. No other KIA or WIA hit me like that. I knew most of them, but his was the first body I ever saw and, being my friend, it was too much. After I left the place, I sat down and cried. I couldn't stop it. I don't think I ever cried so much in my life. I can still see his face now. I will never forget it.

Today the heavens cried for him. It started raining at noon today and has now finally just stopped after 10 hours of the hardest rain I have ever seen.

Love,
Richard

Sp/5 Richard Cantale, of Floral Park, New York, served with the 5th Battalion, 7th Cavalry, 1st Cavalry Division (Airmobile), based at An Khe, from August 1966 through August 1967. He is now a manager in a brokerage firm in New York City.

— ☆ —

Dear Mrs. Perko,

I'm sorry for not writing sooner. I received your letter when I was discharged from the hospital 29 April, then went straight to Saigon for a week or so.

What can I say to fill the void? I know flowers and letters are appropriate but it's hardly enough. I'm Johnny Boy, and I'm sick both physically and mentally. I smoke too much, am constantly coughing, never eat, always sit around in a daze. All of us are in this general condition. We are all afraid to die and all we can do is count the days till we go home.

We're all in desperate need of love. When we go to Saigon, we spend all our money on women and beer. Some nights I don't sleep. I can't stand being alone at night. The guns don't bother me—I can't hear them anymore. I want to hold my head between my hands and run screaming away from here. I cry too, not much, just when I touch the sore spots.

I'm hollow, Mrs. Perko. I'm a shell, and when I'm scared I rattle. I'm no one to tell you about your son. I can't. I'm sorry.

Johnny Boy

Cpl. John Houghton—"Johnny Boy"—was the friend of Terry J. Perko, a lance corporal from Maple Heights, Ohio, who was killed on 21 February 1967, five months after arriving in Vietnam. They were serving with the 1st Anglico Detachment, 1st Marine Division, operating out of Chu Lai. Terry's twin, Jerry, also served in Vietnam at the same time. John Houghton, in Vietnam from October 1966 to October 1967, now lives in Camden, New Jersey, and works as a deckhand on a tugboat.

— ☆ —

I Must Go On

We fought together, six months today,
As I rolled over, there he lay.
His eyes were open, his hands clenched tight,
The look of death, a look of fright.

I knew right then that he was dead,
And wondered why, not me instead.
His life was short, not many years,
Full of hope yet full of fears.

We'd talked and laughed of times gone by,
And never thought that we might die,
But here he lay, no breath of life,
No thought of home, or his young wife.

I turned my head and looked away,
I fought the words I could not say.
HE'S DEAD, He's Dead and gone,
But I am here and must go on.

I must go on.

—Timothy F. Schlink

1Lt. Timothy Schlink was assigned to Company C, 2nd Battalion, 1st Infantry, 196th Light Infantry Brigade, Americal Division, based at Tay Ninh and Chu Lai, from September 1966 through June 1967. After his best friend was killed by a land mine, Lt. Schlink wrote this poem to his father while trying to find words to express his feelings to the new widow. Today he is financial manager for Pacific Bell in San Jose, California.

— ☆ —

6
What Am I Doing Here?

*"Some GI's," wrote Cathleen Cordova, who worked as a club direc-
tor in Vietnam in 1968 and 1969, "say this war could have, and
should have, been won by now if it weren't for the politicians
meddling in military matters. Others are opposed to the war and
don't think we should be here. . . . Actually, the majority of the guys
aren't concerned with issues, moral judgments or politics. Most of
them are young guys who didn't want to come here, and they just
want to get out in one piece."*

*Any impression that those who fought in Vietnam were in
universal agreement with its justification or its conduct is false. In
the early stages of the war, many GIs were imbued with a sense of
mission, of purpose: to fight communism. For others, going off to
war was more a young man's adventure than any ideological crusade
trumpeted by a generation of our nation's leaders.*

*Just as the war had its phases—limited presence, build-up,
retrenchment, phased withdrawal—so, to a great extent, did the
opinions of those who fought in it. The chronological ordering of
the letters in this chapter reveal, with some exceptions, a similar
progression of sentiment. An initial let's-stop-communism-and-
make-the-world-safe-for-democracy naïveté was fueled by the cold
war and the idealism engendered by President John F. Kennedy:
"Ask not what your country can do for you. Ask what you can do
for your country." But as the proverbial "light at the end of the
tunnel" proved to be dim at best, this feeling gave way for many
to a sense of frustration and expressions of bitterness that maybe the*

war wasn't being handled correctly or was exacting too high a toll, and that maybe it shouldn't have been fought at all.

In many ways, the sentiments of troops in Vietnam mirrored the conflicts of conscience in the United States, where the same questions were being asked: What are we doing in Vietnam? Are we doing it well? Should we be doing it at all?

20 September, 1965

Dear Uncle and Aunt,

. . . Some people wonder why Americans are in Vietnam. The way I see the situation, I would rather fight to stop communism in South Vietnam than in Kincaid, Humbolt, Blue Mound, or Kansas City, and that is just about what it would end up being. Except for the fact that by that time I would be old and gray and my children would be fighting the war. The price for victory is high when life cannot be replaced, but I think it is far better to fight and die for freedom than to live under oppression and fear.

Living in a country where communism thrives on illiterate people, I look to the many teachers I have for relatives and I know in the long run that the victory will truly be theirs—for communism cannot thrive in a society of people who know the whole truth. This war is not going to be won in a day or even a year. This war and others like it will only be won when the children of that nation are educated and can grow in freedom to rule themselves. Last year alone 4,700 teachers and priests in South Vietnam were killed. This we are trying to *stop*—this is our objective.

Well, enough soothing my own conscience and guilt. . . .

Your nephew,
Jack

Jack S. Swender, a lance corporal from Kansas City, Kansas, was sent to Vietnam in July 1965. He was assigned to H & S Company, 2nd Battalion, 7th Regiment, 1st Marine Division, operating in I Corps. He was killed in action on 18 December 1965. He was 22 years old.

—— ☆ ——

21 May 66

Dear Class C-4,

South Vietnam is a very small country struggling to keep its freedom. Many of the little boys and girls in South Vietnam may never have the opportunities that you children will have. Nevertheless, the children of South Vietnam are very much like yourselves in the games they play and the things they do. I am enclosing some paper toys that the boys and girls of Vietnam play with. I hope that you enjoy the toys as much as they do. In Vietnam, the little things mean a lot more than the big things.

It is nice to know that you children are safe and sound in America. The reason that I and all the other soldiers are in Vietnam is so that you children will always be safe in our great country. Thank you all again for thinking of me in this strange land. I hope that all the soldiers in Vietnam have as many boys and girls thinking about [them] as I do.

Sincerely yours,
PFC Robert B. Jackman

PFC (later Sgt.) Robert Jackman was a truck driver with the Army's Headquarters Area Command, working out of Saigon and Long Binh, from April 1966 to August 1967. He is now a limited partner in the New York City brokerage firm of Bear Stearns & Company.

— ☆ —

August 9, 1966

Dear Mummum and Muggins:

. . . Muggins, I am told that, to put it mildly, you have some reservations about this war and its effect upon the American psychosis. You, of course, are not alone in these feelings, but a couple of points should be made.

Our claim to legality is that we were invited to come here by the Vietnam government and, however flimsy that legality is, such is the peg upon which we hang our hat, and it is a lot stronger than many we have hung it on before, such as the Spanish-American War, a host of expeditions against South American sovereignties or, for that matter, our declaration of war against Germany in World War I. But the legality or lack of it is really of no importance because our friends on the other side are not bothered by such trivialities and, if we are, then we can primly say that we have followed the legal and narrow trail and lose the battle to an opponent who is not playing by our rules. We are here because we think this is where we must fight to stop a communist threat. But not having gained momentum in conquering this country could bowl us out of Asia altogether—and perhaps out of existence. [If] this makes us the policemen of the world, then so be it. Surely this is no more of a burden than the British accepted from 1815 until 1915, and we have a good deal more reason to adopt it since at no time was Britain threatened during this period with total annihilation or subjection which, make no mistake about it, we are.

This is not the place we would prefer to make this stand. Thailand is a great deal more stable. We have backing in the Philippines, and Pakistan and India would be [a] better environment to utilize our standard armaments in which we have invested so much. But we were given no choice and we must fight where the confrontation is, despite its cost, infeasibility, and possible illegality, and physical and mental toll upon the participants. . . .

As to the effect of this war upon the people, who can tell? All of our wars have had some effect, usually for the better, increasing our sense of internationalism in [the] Korean War and World War II and showing us that war is not all glory as we discovered in World War I. While the war —for that matter the civil rights movement—may be responsible for pushing a few deranged minds over the brink of sanity, there is no guarantee that something else would not have done it later. Certainly our churches and laws are strong enough to withstand any feeling of the populace that murder and lawlessness are acceptable ways to deal with problems. I think that the human being has a stronger sense of right and wrong than that.

Love,
Sandy

2Lt. Marion Lee Kempner, platoon leader, Co. M, 3/7th Reg., 1st Mar. Div., I Corps, KIA 11 November 1966. He wrote this letter to his grand-parents, Mr. and Mrs. I. H. Kempner.

— ☆ —

[June 1967]

Dear Editor:

I'm writing this letter to you to help clarify some of the objectives of the United States' participation in the Vietnam War as I see them.

I was with the 9th Infantry Division in the Mekong Delta and we had many missions to accomplish. Search-and-destroy missions were carefully planned to avoid any loss of life to innocent Vietnamese.

Pamphlets were dropped by air in advance to warn the people of our attack. . . .

Every soldier in Vietnam is much more than a fighting man, for on many missions we passed among the villages information concerning the Chieu Hoi ("Open Arms") program which is set up for VC defectors. Defectors that turn themselves in are given the opportunity of starting a new life with the help of the United States and South Vietnam governments.

Many of us were engaged in our own civic action programs on our own time. It might be giving undernourished children C-rations, teaching a teenage boy a little English or helping an old man tie a bag of rice on his bicycle. Wherever we were, we had to win over the people if we wanted to accomplish our assigned mission. The Vietnamese are naturally wary of our presence for they have been taken advantage of before (by the French) and they don't want it to happen again.

The spirit of the men in Vietnam is overwhelming, for most every man believes that he is doing an important job and believe me, he is.

To see your buddy step on a VC antipersonnel mine is a hard thing to take, but the real scare is when you go back to your base camp and see the smiling villagers all around you and then start to wonder if one of them set it there.

Here also our job is twofold, for we must protect the farmers from the VC terrorism, taxation and pillaging of the hard-earned crops. Also, after doing this we have to gain the confidence of the people and make them understand that we don't intend to take over where the VC left off.

The men we have in the Republic of South Vietnam know why they are there and are willing to fight in this country where the people have really never known what a free society is like.

It is a weird feeling to prop yourself against a dike at night in a dry rice paddy and think about the Golden Gate and Telegraph Avenue and wonder if you'll ever see them again. Your short periods of sleep are uneasy, for you are constantly scared of the possibility of the deadly mortars that may come silently on your position at any time. Every sound is a potential danger, and a good night's sleep is an unreality for the American in South Vietnam. You wonder if the South Vietnamese ever sleep well. . . .

I am writing this letter from a hospital bed in Yokohama, Japan. I was wounded about six weeks ago by a Russian pineapple grenade which was boobytrapped by a VC who was most likely just a brainwashed farmer.

There are about 800 soldiers here at this hospital, and this is one of several in the country. Most every guy here realizes that he was wounded while doing an important job in South Vietnam. Most of the wounded here are, or were, in pretty bad shape. It's a hard sight to see an 18-year-old soldier with one leg shot off struggling with his first pair of crutches. The morale here is surprisingly high, and there are more laughs than tears, thank goodness.

Myself, with God's help, I'll be able to walk in 8 to 12 months.

In closing, I'd just like to say that every American should know by now that the war we're fighting in South Vietnam is a war against communist aggression, which is an ever-present threat to the free world today.

Take a minute now and think about the guys in South Vietnam and the guys that are going home on stretchers and in pine boxes. They are your countrymen, and, believe it or not, they have been fighting for you.

Sp/4 Rodney D. Baldra

Rodney Baldra had been in country 42 days, serving with the 5th Battalion, 60th Infantry (Mechanized), 9th Infantry Division, out of Bear Cat, when he was wounded by a booby trap on 1 April 1967. He lives in Walnut Creek, California, and is a self-employed restaurant consultant He wrote this letter to the Berkeley (California) Gazette.

— ☆ —

10 September '67

David,

. . . Here in Vietnam the war goes on. Morale is very high in spite of the fact that most men think the war is being run incorrectly. One of the staggering facts is that most men here believe we will *not* win the war. And yet they stick their necks out every day and carry on with their assigned tasks as if they were fighting for the continental security of the United States. Hard to believe but true.

The Marines are taking a fierce beating over here. They don't have enough men. We must have more men, at least twice as many, or we are going to get the piss kicked out of us this winter when the rains come. The Marines have been assigned a task too big for so few. We are fighting for our very lives in the north. In the last 15 weeks we've lost 47% of all helicopters in Vietnam. One of the basic problems is that [President] Johnson is trying to fight this war the way he fights his domestic wars—he chooses an almost unattainable goal with a scope so large it is virtually undefinable, and he attacks this goal with poorly allocated funds, minimum manpower, limited time, and few new ideas. The magnitude of what he is trying to accomplish here can only be realized when you firmly establish in your own mind that Johnson is trying to take 5,000 villages living on a rice economy with a 2,000-year-old Asian tradition of chieftain rule warped by 100 years of ugly colonialism and *build a nation* with an industrial base and a democratic tradition in the midst of a 20-year-old war.

We should have never committed ourselves to this goal, but now that we have, what should we do? We must destroy the will of Hanoi quickly and stop doling out American lives in that penny-ante effort. Then reallocate our resources of money and materiel and, with two or three times the present manpower, crush the guerrillas.

And how can we adopt this approach? By electing a president who will restate our objectives, restate our motives, and who will end this ill-thought-out approach to world peace; a man who rejects a status-quo world, who has the long view of history and nation-making, who does not overreact to the label communism, who can establish priorities whether they be at home or abroad, who can understand that a Ho Chi Minh Vietnam is better than a Vietnam of old men and women without the dedication and vision of its young men, and finally a man who will be content to influence history rather than make it. . . .

19 October 67

Mom and Dad—

Your oldest son is now a captain in the United States Marine Corps. I was promoted yesterday. Of all the men selected for captain, 1,640 men, only about 50 men have been promoted to date. I was one of the 50, to my surprise and pleasure. My effective date of rank is 1 July 1967, which means I have technically been a captain for 3½ months. I am thus due back pay for 3½ months. With this promotion, my annual income is $9,000.00 a year. I'm single, 24 years old, college-educated, a captain in the Marine Corps, and I have $11,000.00 worth of securities. That is not a bad start in life, is it?

As I understand, Dad, you were married about this point in life. There was a war going on then too. I really know very little about those years in my parents' lives. Sometime you will have to tell me about them

—what you were doing, what you were thinking, what you were planning, what you were hoping.

Mom, I appreciate all your letters. I appreciate your concern that some of the things you write about are trivial, but they aren't trivial to me. I'm eager to read anything about what you are doing or the family is doing. You can't understand the importance these "trivial" events take on out here. It helps keep me civilized. For a while, as I read your letters, I am a normal person. I'm not killing people, or worried about being killed. While I read your letters, I'm not carrying guns and grenades. Instead I am going ice skating with David or walking through a department store to exchange a lamp shade. It is great to know your family's safe, living in a secure country; a country made secure by thousands upon thousands of men who have died for that country.

In the Philippines I took a bus ride along the infamous route of the death march in Bataan. I passed graveyards that were marked with row after row after row of plain white crosses. Thousands upon thousands. These were American graves—American graves in the Philippines. And I thought about the American graves in Okinawa, Korea, France, England, North Africa—around the world. And I was proud to be an American, proud to be a Marine, proud to be fighting in Asia. I have a commitment to the men who have gone before me, American men who made the sacrifices that were required to make the world safe for ice skating, department stores and lamp shades.

No, Mom, these things aren't trivial to me. They are vitally important to me. Those are the truly important things, not what I'm doing. I hope you will continue to write about those "trivial" things because that is what I enjoy learning about the most.

Your son,
Rod

In September 1968, Capt. Rodney R. Chastant, from Mobile, Alabama, extended his 13-month tour of duty in Vietnam with Marine Air Group 13, 1st Marine Air Wing, Da Nang. He was killed on 22 October. He was 25 years old. David is his brother.

— ☆ —

Tuesday
November 14, 1967
7:00 P.M.

Dear Mom, Dad, Chris and Vicki,

We were well informed here about the demonstrations by both sides. Even though I'm here, I still have an open mind—realizing, of course, that an immediate pullout or anything of the sort is out of the question. It would degrade the heroic deaths of those who never returned because it would mean going back on everything that we have done. There are many here who feel as I do, but we will continue to fight for the country in which we believe.

Saul Alinsky, the social agitator, once said that no matter how much he criticizes his government, once he has left the United States he suddenly can't find a nasty thing to say about it.

I am sure that that is what the most sincere people feel, whether liberal or conservative. That is one of the very essences of our nation.

Take care of yourselves and keep writing. Vicki, thanks for the turkey. . . .

Love,
Your son and brother,
Stephen

PFC Stephen W. Pickett, from Jackson Heights, New York, served with Company C, 4th Battalion, 23rd Infantry (Mechanized), 25th Infantry Division, based in Cu Chi. He was killed on a search-and-destroy mission exactly one month after he wrote this letter, seven weeks after he arrived in Vietnam. He was 20 years old.

— ☆ —

[January 1968]

To Cub Scout Pack 508
Saratoga, California

I don't know how to thank you for the wonderful gifts you sent to me and my buddies.

We are located on top of a hill, and it is isolated. The only way in is by chopper, so you can see we don't get many treats such as you sent. After eating C-rations, the popcorn, cake and candy were like gold. The biggest hit was the plastic Christmas tree.

Last week I had a fever and had to spend three days in the medic tent. In the tent sleeping next to me was a 12-year-old Vietnamese boy who had shrapnel in his elbow and shoulder. He was hiding in a bunker with his parents when a grenade exploded, killing all his family. I became friends with him and tried to converse with him in our different languages. When I shared with him the present you sent, he smiled for the first time. He sure got a kick out of the game.

We all hear of protests and riots and get mad. When our buddies die, we wonder why, but we also think of the boys of Den I and Den V and know why this must be done, and we know how lucky we are to live in America.

I pray that none of you will ever have to put on a uniform for hostile reasons.

> Your friend,
> David Hockett

Sp/4 David Hockett, Company A, 13th Signal Battalion, 1st Cavalry Division (Airmobile), was wounded on 1 February 1968 near Hue during the Tet Offensive. He lives in Santa Rosa, California, and works as a regional sales manager for an electronic digital-scales corporation.

— ☆ —

> April 5 '68
> LZ Sally

Dear Dad—

I'm sick—very sick, bad stomach cramps, diarrhea and a fairly high temperature. I was evac'd from the field to recover. I've been listening to the Vietnam radio station. They just had a news report special on the assassination of Martin Luther King in Memphis. I realize how involved you are with the whole situation. I also realize how bad this makes Memphis look to the rest of the nation. I'm sorry that the people in

Memphis had to see all of this. I heard President Johnson's speech but now I've a story to tell.

On Friday, March 29, in our AO just south of Hue near the ocean, we received small-arms fire from a village. Two platoons went into the village. Our platoon maneuvered to the right, attempting to set up a blocking force so when the NVA were pushed out of the village we could cut them off. My job was carrying the platoon radio. My platoon leader, Gary Scott, 2nd lieutenant, Infantry, was in command. Lt. Scott, a Negro from Rochester, New York, graduated recently from the University of Syracuse.

As the platoon moved toward the rear of the village, automatic-weapons fire suddenly came from a near woodline. Lt. Scott and one other man were killed, another seriously wounded. I was very close to Lt. Scott. I was his radio operator. He was a fine man, a good leader, yet he could not understand the whys of this conflict which called him 10,000 miles from his home, to a land of insects, poverty and hostility—this conflict which killed him. Why?

Fighting for a people who have no concern for the war, people he did not understand, [who] knew where the enemy were, where the booby traps were hidden yet gave no support. People that he would give portions of his food to yet would try to sell him a Coke for $1.00. People who cared not who the winner was—yet they will say he died for his country, keeping it free. Negative. This country is no gain that I can see, Dad. We're fighting, dying, for a people who resent our being over here. The only firm reason I can find is paying with commie lives for U.S. lives, Dad.

Tonight the nation mourns the death of Martin Luther King. Not me. I mourn the deaths of the real leaders for peace, the people who give the real sacrifice, people like Lt. Scott. Tonight as the nation mourns Dr. King, they drink their cold beer, turn on their air conditioner and watch their TV. We who mourn the deaths over here will set up our ambushes, pull our guard and eat our C-rations.

I will probably get a Bronze Star for the fire fight. Lt. Scott will get a Silver Star. That will help me get a job someday and it is supposed to suffice for Lt. Scott's life. I guess I'm bitter now, Dad. This war is all wrong. I will continue to fight, win my medals and fight the elements and hardships of this country. But that is because I'm a soldier and it's my job and there are other people depending on me. That's my excuse. That's all I have, theories and excuses—no solutions.

Your loving son,
Phil

Sgt. Phillip Woodall, Company A, 1st Battalion, 501st Infantry, 101st Airborne Division, served in Vietnam from December 1967 through July 1969, operating in I Corps. He is now manager of an insurance company in Pineville, North Carolina.

— ☆ —

10 May 68

Dear Mom,

It's official! Today I received my award. But it was more than I had dreamed. Would you believe a *Silver Star!*

I was given the wrong information about a Bronze Star.

To say the least, I'm quite proud of myself! But to be broad-minded about it, as much as it means to me, it is just a rung up the ladder to success. I say this because I have so much more to accomplish—much more.

I'm sorry to rebuke all of you, but I'm no hero. Heroes are for the "Late Show." I was just trying to help a couple of guys who needed help. Keep in mind, I didn't do it alone.

That's all.

Love,
Phil

P.S. You can tell anyone, I mean *anyone* who asks, exactly how I feel about the hero bit. They are only in comic books and television and movies. The so-called heroes over here are the guys trying to do their jobs and get home from this useless war.

Sp/4 Phillip Arterbury was assigned to Company C, 1st Battalion, 27th Infantry, 25th Infantry Division, operating in III Corps from Parrot's Beak to Saigon, between October 1967 and October 1968. He is now a silver trader in Beverly Hills, California.

— ☆ —

August 13, 1968

Dear Steve,

I think perhaps this experience is changing me. Of course, it would —but it is happening not as I expected. Of course, again, I have not found much opportunity to "help" the people, as I once almost romantically rationalized. But I've learned a little here—I've learned to dislike this war more.

It's not that I've seen more atrocities than I anticipated or that I've noticed an oppressed willingness in the Vietnamese to be governed by Ho Chi Minh and Company. What I've seen is the superabundant American economy overflow with its war effort into the Vietnamese peasants' and city dwellers' environment. While most Americans sit in their clubs or tanks or B-52s and scatter their lethal currency over the countryside, the higher-ranking Vietnamese grabble for the rake-off and black-market profits and the rest of the crowd (including the Montagnards) reap the scraps and the burden of the casualties.

Of course, Americans are dying, and I would not belittle anyone who served "with proud devotion" and faith in this enterprise. It may not have been a terribly wrong theoretical idea at one time. But the foreign, introduced offensive, the consequent corruption and then the contempt that developed between people and groups—it makes a mockery of the "noble" words used to justify this war. It belies the phony enthusiasm with which those words may be delivered. It's now a war of survival. . . .

Yours,
Doug

Douglas McCormac, a sergeant with Company C, 5th Special Forces Group, was based in Pleiku and Kontum provinces from May 1968 to May 1969. He is now attending law school at Northeastern University in Boston, Massachusetts. This letter was written to his friend Stephen Tilly.

—— ☆ ——

3 Nov. 68

Dear Merle,

Thanks ever so much for the great picture of Rowe, Whiz Kid, Deb, and Horse, and the books—great! Extremely nostalgic. I am presently in Di An, about 40 miles south of my base camp at Lai Khe. I flew down this afternoon on a helicopter to deliver some reports to Headquarters—a lovely summer evening's flight with only the grim reminder of the hell 500 feet below to put it in perspective. Tomorrow I will fly north again.

The longer I am here, the more my hatred of war grows, but curiously enough I'm no more a pacifist than I ever was, though I know I have stronger leanings in that direction than most. The tragedy is the price that I see reclaimed daily, and my only hope is that someday it can be justified. For us, it probably never will be, but I hope that we will have learned something from it all. Being in a medical battalion, I find myself curiously suspended from "sides" or causes and can only feel the human loss and terror which can never be measured in pretty medals or sweet, patriotic speeches. Humans can be such damned fools.

I look forward to getting home, seeing all of you again, and appreciating the little things which seem so important now. I plan to play the young bachelor at large and will take a first step in this direction by buying a Porsche through the military discount. Hell, I've always wanted one anyhow, and this may be the last time I'll be able to afford one.

My love to you and the urchin,

Rob

Sp/4 John Riggan, author of Free Fire Zone, *was based at Lai Khe from September 1968 through September 1969, assigned to Company D, 1st Medical Battalion, 1st Infantry Division. He lives in Rowe, Massachusetts.*

— ☆ —

26 Nov 68

Dear Vikki,

. . . It's so funny, or should I say weird, to write my little sister with a "Mrs." in front of her name. But I'm very happy for both of you. I hope you will always be as happy as you were on your wedding day.

And you were wrong. I *was* at your wedding, although not physically. I was very much there mentally. I will never forget the way you looked.

They say all brides are beautiful. But you—you were more beautiful than words could express. The happiness in your eyes expressed not only that moment but your whole future.

As for your feeling guilty for me not being there, don't. Your happiness always comes first. I have a far greater task at hand that will ensure that not only my sister, but everybody's sisters can get married in the church of her choice, have children, and instruct them in the religion of their parents, send them to the school of their choice. Until this is done for the whole world, brothers like me can't possibly be at their sister's wedding.

Like me, every one of those brothers are in the chapel, enjoying the festivities and feeling very happy and proud of their sister. My spirit [is] with you and Nick, hoping that your children will not have to see, or do, some of the ugly and terrible things in the world today. I probably have seen the majority of it. Children being slaughtered like cattle. Women being mutilated and raped. The people, who want the best for their family and friends, being strung up and brutally murdered. . . .

No, I'd rather have been here, for the sake of you and Nick, your children and mine, and for the billions of other Vikki's and Nick's in the world that have every right to enjoy life at its best, instead of seeing it at its worst like I do right now.

Please, don't worry about me, but think of the future, the future. Better days lie ahead. Days of love and happiness. Enjoy them while you can. May my blessings and good wishes follow both of you wherever you may go, and may God give you happiness, good health, and fortune. And may God bless you both for as long as you both shall live.

Johnny

PFC John Louis Brown wrote this letter to his sister nine days after her wedding. He had been in Vietnam for six months, assigned to the 586th Signal Company, 43rd Signal Battalion, 1st Signal Brigade, 1st Cavalry Division (Airmobile), An Khe. Today he, too, is married, the father of two children. He lives in Flushing, New York, and is a Port Authority police officer at Kennedy International Airport.

— ☆ —

10 Feb 69

Hi Mom,

Well, I am fine today, and I hope that you are in good shape also. Today, I am at the river swimming, washing and taking in the sun. The beach is great, the sand is white and the sky is clear. Boy, I wish every day was like this. Then I wouldn't have any problems while I'm here.

How is Dad's health? What are you doing, and how are the peace talks? I have to wonder if it is worth anything to be here. Nobody wants us, and yet we still maintain our position. Well, I guess that is what life is all about.

I heard that you and Jo's parents got together. It is about time if I am going to marry her. I do suppose you should get together. I hope you like them because you will be seeing a lot of them when I get married. My plans are already down in my head. All I have to do now is wait till I am home to talk it over with Jo. It will be a wonderful wedding.

Love always,
Jack

Sgt. Jack Calamia, from Glendale, New York, arrived in Vietnam in December 1968 and was assigned to Company D, 3rd Battalion, 11th Light Infantry Brigade, Americal Division, in I Corps. He was killed by a land mine on 20 October 1969. He was 21 years old.

— ☆ —

7 July 1969

[Dear Mom & Dad,]

They think the enemy went back into Cambodia to get resupplied and that he's on his way back. There's talk of the 299th moving again, but they've been talking about it for a couple of months now. The politics behind all the monkey business around here is insane. This gradual withdrawal is going to cause more damage than good. As there become less and less GIs over here, it means that the guys still here will have to depend on the ARVNs. I would not want to have to depend on an ARVN for anything. I don't see how we ever won a war if we are fighting the same way as they fought in WWII. Maybe we will leave soon after all.

George

Sp/4 George Ewing, Jr., served in Vietnam with Company D, 299th Engineer Battalion, between January 1969 and January 1970, stationed at Dak To. He is now a student at Columbia University in New York City.

— ☆ —

24 July 1969

Dear Family,

Things go fairly well here. Monsoon is very heavy right now—haven't seen the sun in a couple of weeks. But this makes the sky that much prettier at night when flares go off. There's a continual mist in the air which makes the flares hazy. At times they look like falling stars; then sometimes they seem to shine like crosses.

At 4:16 A.M. our time the other day, two of our fellow Americans landed on the moon. At that precise moment, Pleiku Air Force Base, in the sheer joy and wonder of it, sent up a whole skyful of flares—white, red, and green. It was as if they were daring the surrounding North Vietnamese Army to try and tackle such a great nation. As we watched it from the emergency room door, we couldn't speak at all. The pride in our country filled us to the point that many had tears in their eyes.

It hurts so much sometimes to see the paper full of demonstrators, especially people burning the flag. Fight fire with fire, we ask here. Display the flag, Mom and Dad, please, every day. And tell your friends to do the same. It means so much to us to know we're supported, to know not everyone feels we're making a mistake being here.

Every day we see more and more why we're here. When a whole Montagnard village comes in after being bombed and terrorized by Charlie, you know. These are helpless people dying every day. The worst of it is the children. Little baby-sans being brutally maimed and killed. They never hurt anyone. Papa-san comes in with his three babies—one dead and two covered with frag wounds. You try to tell him the boy is dead—"fini"—but he keeps talking to the baby as if that will make him live again. It's enough to break your heart. And through it all, you feel something's missing. There! You put your finger on it. There's not a sound from them. The children don't cry from pain; the parents don't cry from sorrow; they're stoic.

You have to grin sometimes at the primitiveness of these Montagnards. Here in the emergency room, doctors and nurses hustle about fixing up a little girl. There stands her shy little (and I mean little—like four feet tall) papa-san, face looking down at the floor, in his loin cloth, smoking his long marijuana pipe. He has probably never seen an electric light before, and the ride here in that great noisy bird (helicopter) was too much for him to comprehend. They're such characters. One comes to the hospital and the whole family camps out in the hall or on the ramp and watches over the patient. No, nobody can tell me we don't belong here. . . .

Love,
Lynda

1Lt. Lynda Van Devanter, 71st Evac. Hosp., Pleiku, and 67th Evac. Hosp., Qui Nhon, 1969–1970.

—— ☆ ——

[August 1969]

Dear Yolanda,

. . . Things are picking up around here. We're starting to train the Vietnamese to do our jobs so they can take over when the time comes for the Air Force to pull out.

The Army's 9th Infantry Division has pulled out already, and the Navy's river patrol force is just about taken over by the Vietnamese Navy. The local people are not very enthusiastic about our leaving because, for one reason, they don't want to lose all the money they are making off the American GIs.

We cannot blame them for wanting a way of life that they have never had, and a continuation of the war is not going to bring any solution. They do not want to fight, they're tired of suffering, and they've finally realized this is more a political war with no gains for the common people. It's a complicated problem. I just can't begin to go into it without ending up with a book. I've always felt that if the North would agree to a peaceful settlement, both North and South could make more progress toward helping their people, whether it be under a communist or democratic system, than by killing each other. I've learned only one lesson from this and that is if man has been fighting his fellow man since the beginning of time, he will continue to do so, and the United States, as powerful as it may be, cannot play the role of God and solve all the problems of the world, and sometimes I wonder if there really is a God.

Well, now, I'll be leaving for Hong Kong on the 14th to REST MY BONES. Really, Yolanda, I need a rest. What I'm really interested in is buying some tailor-made suits and a coat. I'll be getting you your ring in Hong Kong also. I want to see if I can find something special that no one else has. OK? . . .

I'll write again soon. I have to write to the kids.

Love,
Chicky

Sgt. Hector Ramos spent the year from January 1969 to February 1970 with the Air Force's 632nd Security Police Section at the air base in Binh Tuy. He is an electrical designer with an architectural firm in New York City. Yolanda is now his wife.

— ☆ —

2140 hrs, Thursday
30 October 1969
Cu Chi

Dear Mom, Dad, and Tom,

. . . Everybody here is waiting for what Nixon has to say on 3 November. I'm personally skeptical about any idea for a unilateral cease fire, as are most of us here. . . . There was a time when this post used to be hit often—very often—with mortars which are high-trajectory weapons whose range is in thousands of meters, not miles. So I just hope Nixon knows what he's doing. Whether or not we should be here, the fact that 500,000 GIs *are* here means they deserve as much protection as they [can] get.

I read in the paper that [New York City] Mayor [John] Lindsay had the city's flags fly at half staff on the so-called Moratorium Day. After nine months I have mixed feelings about our involvement here. I can say, however, that the so-called Vietnamization of the war, while perhaps overplayed, is coming about. [The ARVNs] are taking more casualties than the Americans these days. . . . Maybe all the time we've bought for these people with American blood will finally begin to pay dividends. In any event, the Vietnamization seems to me the way to get us out of here, not simply to get up and let the VC have this country.

I've philosophized enough on the war. There are so many things here that I've seen that make me proud to be an American, proud to be a soldier. Yet there are times too when I just wonder why things are done the way they are in the war, in the Army. I find myself a witness—and, yes, even, at times, an accomplice—to things I never would have dreamed [of]. I suppose that innocence at best is not permanent, but the end of it is inevitably accompanied by some pain. . . .

Take care. I'll be OK.

Love,
Bobby

1Lt. Robert Salerni, platoon commander, Co. B, 554th Engr. Bn., 79th Engr. Gp., 20th Engr. Bde., Cu Chi, Nui Ba Den, 1969–1970.

— ☆ —

Oct. 1969

Hello Brother,

How are you treating life these days? Have you gotten a grip on those Merrimack students yet? . . .

This place is sort of getting to me. I've been seeing too many guys getting messed up, and I still can't understand it. It's not that I can't understand this war. It's just that I can't understand *war* period.

If you do not get to go to that big peace demonstration [on] October 15th I hope you do protest against war or sing for peace—I would. I just can't believe half of the shit I've seen over here so far. . . .

Do you know if there's anything wrong at home? I haven't heard from anyone in about two weeks, and normally I get 10 letters a week. You mentioned in your last letters that you haven't heard from them for a while either. I couldn't take sitting over [in] this place if I thought there was anything wrong at home.

Well, brother, I hope you can get to your students and start them thinking about life. Have you tried any marijuana lectures lately? I know they dig that current stuff.

I gotta go now. Stay loose, Paul, sing a simple song of freedom and I'll be seeing you come summer.

Feb. 9, 1970

Hello Brother,

How is America acting these days? Are the youth still planning new ways to change our world? I think the 70s will see a lot of things changed for the better.

I'm still trying to survive over here but the NVA aren't making it too easy lately. We've just been in contact with them for three days and things aren't looking too bright. When you have bullets cracking right over your head for a couple days in a row, your nerves begin to fizzle. When you're getting shot at, all you can think about is—try to stay alive, keep your head down and keep shooting back.

When the shooting stops, though, you sort of sit back and ask yourself, Why? What the hell is this going to prove? And man, I'm still looking for the answer. It's a real bitch.

Thanks for that *Playboy* you sent me. I sort of forgot what girls looked like. I think the real personality of Jesus has been sort of hidden from us. Either that or no one's wanted to look for it before. If he were alive today he'd probably be living in Haight-Ashbury and getting followed by the FBI who'd have him labeled as a communist revolutionary. He'd definitely be shaking some people up. . . .

Well, it's time to make my delicious C-ration lunch. Stay loose and stay young. . . .

> The beat goes on,
> Joe

Joseph Morrissey, a staff sergeant with Company C, 1st Battalion, 12th Cavalry, 1st Cavalry Division (Airmobile), served in III Corps from July

1969 to May 1970. He wrote this letter to his brother, Paul, a Roman Catholic priest in the diocese of Brooklyn. He now works as a carpenter in Parkesburgh, Pennsylvania.

— ☆ —

15 May [1970]

Dear Joanie,

I am in the recovery land of penicillin and bandages, but I am a lucky one. I was dusted off by helicopter to the 93rd Evacuation Hospital for a liver infection. The water has gotten to me. Sorry I have not written, but the times have been a bit slow. I passed out during my first blood test —real cute. I am better and ready to leave by Tuesday of next week. I guess I haven't written you for a few days.

Mike Bradley writes of how bad the colleges are. He is very bitter in his letter and is outspoken against the Army. This war has split the country—even I don't know where to stand. We have to clean out Cambodia, yet we are doing other people's jobs for them. Why fight if the GI will do it. Then the campus deaths—what is happening, Joanie? I am really confused about everything. Where does man find the hatred to do the things he does? And many over here don't even care. Where is the life we wanted and talked about? Will we be able to find the pieces?

Please don't worry.

Love,
Mike

From September 1969 to September 1970, Michael Rush was an artillery captain working with the ARVN 5th Division and Company B, 2nd Battalion, 5th Cavalry, 1st Cavalry Division (Airmobile), operating in III Corps and Cambodia. He is now a managing director of Shearson Lehman/American Express in New York City.

— ☆ —

[July 1970]

[Dear Editor:]

This letter I am writing is not only from me but quite a few of my friends. I just thought you might like it.

This letter is from the men who daily risk their lives in the air over the war-wrought land of Vietnam. It is the combined thoughts and beliefs of 1st and 2nd flight platoons, B Company, 159th Aviation Battalion, 101st Airborne Division, and you can believe me that a lot of our descriptive phrases are being omitted due to the grossness and obscenities of them.

The outburst of raw violence and malice spontaneously occurred when the following quotation was read aloud to them from a letter: "We've had some memorial services for them at school and there's a movement for a strike." The quotation was in regards to the recent killings at Kent [State University] in Ohio. We are sorrowful and mourn the dead, but it grieves us no end and shoots pain into our hearts that the "biggest upset is over the kids who got killed at Kent [State]."

So why don't your hearts cry out and shed a tear for the 40-plus thousand red-blooded Americans and brave, fearless, loyal men who have given their lives so a bunch of bloody bastard radicals can protest, dissent and generally bitch about our private and personal war in Vietnam and now Cambodia?

During my past 18 months in hell I've seen and held my friends during their last gasping seconds before they succumbed to death. And not once, I repeat, and not one goddamn time did they chastise our country's involvement in Vietnam. Christ, we cheered when Nixon sent troops to Cambodia—we are praying we'll also see Laos.

And how in the hell do you think that we in Vietnam feel when we read of the dissension and unrest in our country caused by young, worthless radicals and the foremost runner of them all: the vile and disease-ridden SDS. This is what we feel like: We have an acute hatred, an unfathomable lust to maim, yes, even kill. You ask, "Is this towards the NVA and VC?" We answer, "Hell, no, it's for all of you back in the World who are striving to make us feel like a piece of shit for fighting and dying for what we believe in—freedom."

Last month my company lost 12 good men and five more were torn up so bad that they have been sent back to the States. We shed true tears for these men. What did you do? Protest. In your feeble and deteriorating and filthy degenerate minds you have forced and caused these men to die for nothing. Do you place such a low value on our heads? We are trying to end the war so that our loved ones will never have to face the harsh realities of death in our own country.

Do not judge us wrongly. We are not pleading for your praise. All we ask is for our great nation to unite and stand behind President Nixon. Support us, help us end the war, damn it, save our lives. . . .

I am coming home soon. Don't shout and preach your nothingness to me. I am ashamed to be fighting to keep you safe, the rest of the loyal Americans. I am proud to give my life for you members of the SDS and your followers. I am returning to educate you on what it feels like to be in Nam. Yes, I am bringing the war home. We'll see if you're as good in fighting as you are in protesting.

Prepare yourselves—the makers are returning. May your children honor and respect our dead and chastise your actions.

We personally challenge you to come to Vietnam and talk with the VC and NVA in the A Shau Valley. Let us know what they say, if you live.

We the undersigned are in full [agreement] with the forth-put statements. . . .

> With love,
> Greg Lusco
> Phu Bai
> South Vietnam

Sp/4 Gregory Lusco, who served in Vietnam between November 1968 and August 1970, and 19 other soldiers from Company B, 159th Aviation Battalion, 101st Airborne Division, wrote this letter, which was published in the Greenfield *(Massachusetts)* Recorder *on 23 July 1970. He is now in the Navy, stationed in Japan aboard the* U.S.S. Midway.

— ☆ —

28 July 70

Dear John,

It was very good to hear from you. You cannot imagine how important it is to receive mail over here. I have a lot of time to write, and most of my friends have been very faithful in writing. It takes some of the edge off the frustration and bitterness of being here. Especially after a week like last week!

You may have read about Fire Support Base Ripcord, southwest of Hue. The 101st, true to its reputation, had another defeat like Hamburger Hill and Khe Sanh. You will get the whitewashed version of what happened, I'm sure. But let me tell you, we were driven off that hill after overwhelming casualties. We lost over 80 men in KIAs in less than two weeks and over 420 wounded. A full battalion of men. And for what? There is absolutely nothing out there in the jungle but mountains and triple canopy. Nothing but NVA who have built roads and who outnumber us in the province by two or three to one.

Yes, it is no longer a case of the big imperialistic American aggressor killing the pure VC patriots. Instead, the VC are almost completely out of the picture. Instead, we [are fighting] highly trained, well-equipped NVA regiments and divisions. The South Vietnamese are doing very well militarily here. The 1st ARVN Division does as well [as], if not better than, the 101st Airborne Division. The popular and regional forces keep the VC pretty much under control, but the fact remains that we are very much outnumbered and our best weapon cannot be used for political reasons. Napalm is almost out of the picture.

You may be surprised at my seemingly changed position. Talking of napalm, etc. When you see people, Americans, dying for lack of protection, for phony Vietnamization (it's not working because there just are not enough ARVN troops—they lose about a regiment a month in AWOLs and desertion) and for lack of good leadership (the infantry units were needlessly pinned down by the NVA at Ripcord because they stayed in [a] one-night defensive position for five or six nights in a row, which is *never* done. The whole thing is to move around and not let the NVA know where you are. Instead, they sat and took mortar rounds every night, with their 74 KIAs *every* day!). My position has not really changed. There is no reason to be here—and there is even less reason to see Americans dying here. Many of the rear-echelon troops (higher-ranking officers and enlisted men) seem to be immune to their death. It still makes me limp with rage —overcome with sorrow! There seem to be so many people that are insensitive to this killing, even many of the political left who call the American GI "animal," etc. But the fact remains that both sides are suffering a catastrophic loss! I don't know if I've expressed myself very well, but perhaps you can sense my frustrations. . . .

There are so few things here that can keep you sane. Everything seems out of whack. People won't watch *Oliver* or *A Lion in Winter.* They're faggot movies. They only want to see violent Westerns—even when they are surrounded by a violence more real! To maintain some sense of humanity, I've been going out on Med Caps—the medical service taken out to remote villages. I went along as security and got to help treat some of the children. We played games with them, went for a walk to the beach, took pictures, in general just loved them up. They stole my watch, but it really didn't matter, because just before leaving I sang for them (the "Largo al Factotum" from the *Barber of Seville*—you know, "Figaro, Figaro," etc.). They loved it, laughed. But what was most gratifying, they started singing part of it back to each other. I was overwhelmed! They called me "Bee-tho-ven." It was a truly uplifting experience. I became somewhat concerned when the helicopter became lost and it was getting dark, since the area we were in was a VC Rest and Recreation center at one time and still an area of VC infiltration. But we got out safely.

Well, just now I got word that the camp just north of here (12 WIA, 1 KIA) will get it tonight.

Sleep well—

My best to all—
Tom

Sp/5 Thomas Pellaton worked in intelligence while serving with the 101st Aviation Group, 101st Airborne Division, stationed at Phu Bai, from June 1970 to May 1971. He is maître d' at the Carlyle Hotel in New York City.

— ☆ —

I Love My Flag, I Do, I Do,
Which Floats Upon The Breeze
I Also Love My Arms And Legs
And Neck And Nose And Knees.

One Little Shell Might Spoil Them All
Or Give Them Such A Twist.
They Would Be Of No Use To Me
I Guess I Won't Enlist.

I Love My Country, Yes, I Do,
I Hope Her Folks Do Well.
Without Our Arms And Legs And Things,
I Think We'd Look Like Hell.

Young Men With Faces Half Shot Off
Are Unfit To Be Kissed,
I've Read In Books It Spoils Their Looks;
I Guess I Won't Enlist.

—Thomas F. Smith

PFC Thomas F. Smith, who was assigned to the 501st Signal Battalion, 101st Airborne Division, Phu Bai, from June 1970 to April 1971, wrote this poem around 9 September 1970, his sister, Margaret Hogan, recalls. A resident of Forest Hills, New York, and an employee of the telephone company, he died on 11 October 1983.

—— ☆ ——

12 Sept 70

Dear Dad, Bob, & Jean,
    I received your letter of September 7 on the 12th, a Sunday. It really seems funny that the summer is already over in the World. Seems like only yesterday that I was going down to the lake and freezing, waiting for it to warm up so I could go skiing. Damn this Army anyhow.
    I can just picture looking back on this time period in a few years and suddenly jumping to a tropical environment, blanking out my familiar life patterns for 18 months. Before I get off on an anti-Army kick, I'll end this train of thought, because in my mood right now I could get really violent on paper. And after all I'm over here because the gooks "want" us here. I'm really serving an important purpose over here, allowing the lifers to sock away beaucoup money at my expense and that's about it. Vietnam wants to be free. Look, they even have elections. What a fine democratic country. Maybe they'll remember us after we've pulled out . . . . at least until we stop giving them everything they want.
    Well, I didn't suppress all my feelings, because after a while it becomes impossible and they just have to spill out. I don't expect you to swallow everything because you haven't been over here to see the people in action: hooch mates ripping off GIs' clothes and other belongings; ARVN troops refusing to take used serviceable equipment yet demanding new pieces (and getting them); government officials charging the Ameri-

can command for using the land and its resources; local nationals hired to work in the offices running around all day doing nothing and getting paid for it. This is why people get disgusted with Vietnam.

The Vietnamese don't want us over here. All they want is our money. Many of us who see all this can't do anything about it because those higher up are too intent on hauling in more money than they could amass anywhere else in the world for doing as little as they do. After a while all I see just catches up with me and I begin to realize the futility of it all. I really don't want any part of it, so I participate as little as possible in all things Army. I just try to enjoy living with the GIs I'm here with and learn what I can from them. Eventually my tour will be over, and I'll be able to come back to the U.S. . . .

One thing I'll applaud [is] the sincerity and openness of the American enlisted GIs around me. Something in Vietnam releases all the restraints in our people, and you can talk and act freely without fear of retribution. Don't get me wrong. I'd never dream of staying here. But this similarity of situations among most of the GIs is really a unique, moving experience. I will miss this part of Nam. But that's about it. . . .

Peace & Love,
Bill

Sp/4 William J. Kalwas, from Rochester, New York, went to Vietnam in June 1970. He was assigned to the Army Engineer Command at Long Binh. Shipped home in January 1971 to a military hospital in Phoenixville, Pennsylvania, he committed suicide two months later, while on his first leave from the hospital.

— ☆ —

A Relative Thing

We are the ones you sent to fight a war
You didn't know a thing about.

It didn't take us long to realize
The only land that we controlled
Was covered by the bottoms of our boots.

When the newsmen said that naval ships
Had shelled a VC staging point,
We saw a breastless woman
And her stillborn child.

We watched ourselves become insensitive.
We laughed at old men stumbling in the dust
In frenzied terror to avoid our three-ton trucks.

We fought outnumbered in Hue City
While the ARVN soldiers looted bodies
In the safety of the rear.
The cookies from the wives of Local 104
Did not soften our awareness.

We have seen the "pacified" supporters
Of the Saigon government
Sitting in their jampacked cardboard towns;
Their wasted hands placed limply in their laps;
Their empty bellies waiting for the rice
Some district chief has sold
For profit to the Viet Cong
We have seen Democracy on Zippo raids,
Burning hooches to the ground,
Driving eager Amtraks through a farmer's fields.

We are the ones who have to live
With the memory that we were the instruments
Of your pigeon-breasted fantasies.
We are inextricable accomplices
In this travesty of dreams;
But we are not alone.

We are the ones you sent to fight a war
You did not know a thing about.
Those of us that lived
Have tried to tell you what went wrong.
Now you think you do not have to listen.

Just because we will not fit
Into the uniforms of photographs

Of you at twenty-one
Does not mean you can disown us.

We are your sons, America,
And you cannot change that.
When you awake,
We will still be here.

—W. D. Ehrhart

Cpl. William Ehrhart served with the 1st Battalion, 1st Regiment, 1st Marine Division, operating in I Corps, from February 1967 to February 1968. A later version of this poem, which was originally published in 1972, appears in his collection, To Those Who Have Gone Home Tired: New & Selected Poems. *A teacher and poet, he lives in Doylestown, Pennsylvania.*

— ☆ —

7
"We Gotta Get Out of This Place"

In a youth culture dominated by rock 'n' roll, "We Gotta Get Out of This Place," sung by a British group called The Animals, was one of the most popular songs for troops in Vietnam. Its title alone expressed what was on the mind of even the most ardent soldier. In a war in which each of us knew from the day we arrived in country the date on which we could expect to leave, getting out of Vietnam was what almost all of us longed for.

We looked forward to the day when we could consider ourselves "short," when we'd be "two-digit midgets"—have under a hundred days left in country—when we'd need, as we joked, a stepladder to get into bed and a parachute to get out.

Our time in Vietnam, though, was not without its diversions. Letters to and from those we loved were our lifeline to the World. Holidays were emotional anchors that we celebrated as best we could. R&R—five- or six-day jaunts to such places as Bangkok or Hong Kong or Hawaii—were anticipated eagerly. But getting home was our goal.

6 July 1967

My Darling Claudia,

It's raining outside. A damp smell in the air and the raindrops slamming onto the plasterboard roof. Sound of cricket and frog, and the rumble of distant bomb explosions shake the earth here many miles away. Lightning flashes bare the heavens for a brief glimpse at a troubled sky watching over a war-torn land. The area is flooded, and mud clings to boots with a slurp-sucking sound. Soaked uniform hanging on chair to dry and shriveling up into a wrinkled mass. A chilling air is coddled by two ceiling fans and swirled through my body. I miss you, my darling. The night is cold, and you are warm and loving and soft.

At times like this, my darling, I feel as if I would do anything if I could just be back again with you. Sometimes you have to pretend you're not really lonely or else you'd find yourself going out of your mind. But when the day is done, and you're lying alone with your thoughts, then there's no more fooling and that's when it really hurts. The days seem to go by quickly, but the weeks seem forever. Today I have been in Vietnam 73 days, 10½ weeks, a little over 2½ months. The guys who are over here now tell me, looking back, that the time flew by. But right now it seems so very long until you're in my arms again.

Darling, it's midnight, so please forgive the short letter but I'm very tired now. Be careful Dia.

I love you,
Michael

1Lt. Robert Michael Murray, who served with Company A, 5th Special Forces Group, based at Bien Hoa, from April 1967 to April 1968, wrote this to Claudia Johnston. They married in May 1968, two weeks after he returned from Vietnam. He is now an attorney, practicing in White Plains, New York.

— ☆ —

21 May 69

Darling,

Today I can honestly say I did nothing but think about you. I stayed in the company area all day just trying to stay out of trouble and harm's way. I spent most of the morning trying to picture how you must feel. Here I sit in the midst of a group of people who are going through misery similar to mine. For all their short-timing and beer drinking, there isn't one of them who wouldn't be back in the World if they had a chance.

You, on the other hand, are in a world where life goes on around you. People just don't know what misery there is in your heart. They can't sympathize with you because they don't know the loneliness and plain fear in your heart. I want my baby so much. . . .

This morning the sunrise was even more beautiful than the last one I described. It was amplified by the rays of light racing across the waters of the rice paddy, which extends for about a mile in front of our position. The stark black shapes of things not yet inundated in the fluid of light create an unreal character about the scene. Every black barb on our concertina wire a quarter of a mile away stands in sharp contrast with the morning glow. Why aren't you here to see it with me?

Eddie

Sp/4 Edmund Fanning was a combat engineer, serving with Company D, 168th Combat Engineer Battalion, 20th Engineer Brigade, based at Lai Khe and Cu Chi, from March 1969 through March 1970. Janet Bohman, his "darling," is now his wife. They have two children. He lives in Brooklyn and is manager for technical policy development for NYNEX Service Company in New York City.

— ☆ —

13 December '68

My Darling Mic,

Today has been another long day at Moung Soui [Laos], but at least now it is ended and I am that much closer to being with you and Robin once again. You know I actually enjoy this tour as long as I am busy enough to keep my thoughts from wandering back to you—but that is never for very long. It is almost strange that the one who has always made me so happy can now make me sad—because I miss you so much, darling one.

I have been giving some serious thought lately to what else I could be happy doing. You know how much the Army means to me. But then I have only one love and that is for my little family. Mic, it has been so very difficult for me, especially the past few months, to be away from you. And I know that if I stay in, we will eventually be separated again. That thought causes me quite a lot of worry. Baby, for once in my life I just can't make a decision—what do you think? . . .

Still no word on R&R. That is a bitter pill, I know, for we have both been longing so much for it. The only time that really looks hopeful is February—and even that isn't sure. Like you said, if there were anyone I could write to, I would. If I don't mention R&R, don't worry that I have forgotten—it will just be that I haven't heard. Love, I'm so sorry.

The pictures of you and Robin were real morale boosters. You two must be two of God's most precious specimens. Gosh, you both look so good—and that daughter of ours is going to grow up to be as pretty as her mother—almost! Mic, old Joseph still loves you. As you must already know and though the days grow longer, the time grows yet shorter until these lonely arms hold you tight once again.

Your own,
Joe

Capt. Joseph K. Bush, Jr., whose home was in Temple, Texas, never got his R&R. While serving as an adviser to Laotian forces at Moung Soui, he was killed during an attack by North Vietnamese commandos on 10 February 1969. He was 25 years old.

— ☆ —

24 March 68

Dear Dotty and Everybody,

I received your package about a week ago, and couldn't thank you until now. Well, thank you! It was very thoughtful of you all. And, Frankie, thanks a lot for sending me those comic books and magazines. It got my mind off this war—a little bit, anyway. . . .

So far, everything's all right. I'm a little tired but still healthy, like any American. The only problem I got now is that I got eight more months over here. That will be over one of these days. I just can't wait!

I hope everybody's fine back there in Brooklyn. I miss it and all of you, too. I guess you might just say that I miss everything that's back in the U.S.

Well, Dotty, are you still working? I guess you probably are. What else is there to do? But if anything changes, let me know. Maybe I can get you a job over here. (Just kidding, of course.)

And ask Frankie if he personally wants to hear from me—I mean about what I, we, the 101st is really, really doing over here and what we're actually going through. Mostly war stories, that's what I mean. But I'd rather he tell nobody else about what I tell him. Even he might find it hard to believe.

Well, I guess there's not too much more I can say. But this I can say, "It's a beautiful country, but I hate it!"

Well, good-by, everybody. Hope to hear from you again.

Love,
Nick

Sp/4 Nickolas Szawaluk, who lived in Hackettstown, New Jersey, served with Company B, 1st Battalion, 501st Infantry, 101st Airborne Division, operating in I Corps. He was killed on 3 June 1968. He was 20 years old. Dotty is Dorothy Klimasz, a friend.

— ☆ —

Oct. 17, 1968

Dear Gidget,

Well the weather here, believe it or not, has been rainy and cold every day, and I've been working nights on gates and patrols and convoys. Yes, soon I will be home, Gidget. I've got six and a half months yet, and six months over here is a lifetime.

Dear Gidget, you don't know how bad I miss you and Dad. It's awful to stop and think about home once in a while, and realize you've been here ages and still have ages to go. A year is a long time. I can't wait to be my real self again and groove out, but I feel I won't be the same as I was. I just feel messed up inside, but maybe I'll change after I return. Lots of times I think of home, and great times I had, and bad ones. They seem like they were all a dream, though, and that I have been living here all my life. It's really weird, the feelings you get over here. Oh, well, that's life.

I love you, Gidget, and miss you awful. I cried my ass off that morning I left you and Dad. It was horrible. Well, I must go. Write me soon.

Love,
Brother Dan

Sp/4 Daniel Bates was a military policeman with the 504th Battalion, 18th Military Police Brigade. Operating out of Hue and Phu Bai, he spent most of his tour between May 1968 and May 1969 escorting convoys. Today he is unemployed and lives in Daytona Beach Shores, Florida. Gidget is his sister.

— ☆ —

16 June 1968
Marble Mountain

Dad,

Sitting here tonight writing you and Mom of my six months' extension, it just turned midnight. The radio announcer played the national anthem and wished us a Happy Father's Day. Suddenly I realized the day slipped right up on me and I had not written.

You are 50 now. I am nearly 25. We have not seen much of each other in the last three years. But I still feel as close as the days when I was a kid building boats in the garage with your help, the robot man for the science fair, the school elections and the speeches we wrote, the good meals we have enjoyed together at home or out, Camp Compromise, the college fraternity kitchen and the good beer and sandwiches down the street at Eddie Price's Place, and the many great days of scouting and camping.

Over here I enjoy your letters that I get regularly. They arrive without fail, four or five days after you mail them—some war, huh? I have always enjoyed your letters. For seven years now, you have "kept them coming." Amazing how little things like that can mean so much.

Your son,
Rod

*Capt. Rod Chastant, Mar. Air Gp. 13, 1st Mar. Air Wing, Da Nang, KIA
22 October 1968.*

— ☆ —

14 Sept 70

Dear Mom and Dad and my other little family,

It seems that in each of your letters, you've always been on several
little mini-trips to the coast or the Napa Valley, or the foothills or some
idyllic little spot, and it sounds like such a storybook life—eating cheeses
and drinking wines on some grassy knoll overlooking the Pacific. I feel like
some 13th-century peasant trying to conceive of the place called heaven.
Letters from home are like Bibles: they tell of tales so distant from this
reality that they demand a faith before one can actually believe them. Is
there really such a beautiful place, and such a good life on that distant
island, or is my memory based only on some childhood myth that I was
awed into believing?

Yes, the thought of Pete and Mary leaving makes me blue as well.
I'm kind of a cripple when it comes to a close-knit family. My friends and
loved ones are like crutches that need to be in close proximity for me to
be happy, and the thought of their being so far away is a sad one indeed.
It's the one weakness or insecurity in my personality I'm not the least bit
ashamed to have. I cried the day I left my home; I'll cry even harder if
I have to leave it ever again. I guess it's a reflex built into me by our life
in the military. We never had a place we could really call home, and I
think you need such a place when you're young. . . .

Ah hah. Ionto finally got his feet clipped, no more clickety-clickity
around the floor anymore! I'll bet it's a real blessing. I miss that old dog
a lot, and I was thinking on one of my guards last night how he will
monopolize my presence when I get home. He is my dog, and what comes
first in a man's life but his old dog? When I see that red nuisance of a
dog, then I'll *know* I'm home!

We're set up along a creek, a small, rocky, fast-dropping embankment like the one running out of Deer Lake, and there are some huge old
bunkers abandoned by the NVA perhaps a year or two ago down along
the creek, and I often sit and try to visualize the enemy living from day
to day here by this beautiful little gorge, cooking his rice, laughing and
splashing in the creek, listening to it gurgle. And when you think about

it, it's hard to believe that there really is someone out here trying to kill you. And it's even harder to understand why.

Hiding in some rocks nearby we found some rocket-propelled grenades and various medical supplies and ammunition left here by the people who built the bunkers. They were in perfect condition, like new, but the people who made the cache are either long dead or long gone.

The battalion CO got all excited that we'd found a cache, but actually it's silly because we could have left them where they were and they'd still be there a thousand years from now. Anyway, we made a few points in his book, and I got some good pictures of a small part of the cache and the RPGs. It's really interesting to see the stuff and look it over, even if we didn't foil anybody's plans.

Today we get logged and the first mail in 6 days? Oh, boy!

Take care, and write *more* good letters!

Love,
Michael

Sgt. Michael Kelley served with Company D, 1st Battalion, 502nd Infantry, 101st Airborne Division, operating in I Corps, from November 1969 until he was wounded by a booby trap two days after he wrote this letter. He now lives in Sacramento, California, where he is an artist and a real property appraiser.

— ☆ —

Wow Babe,

I'm a daddy! I really can't believe it. Yesterday I got a call from the Red Cross. I was the one to answer the telephone, and after this cat told me you delivered a baby girl, I couldn't remember anything. All I could say was that I had a baby girl. I went down to the Red Cross and picked up the following message:

WIFE INGRID DELIVERED KATRINA 11 JUN 6 LBS 5 OZS 19 INCHES. DR STATES MOTHER AND DAUGHTER FINE.

After I picked up the message, I went to the PX and bought a box of cigars. Wow, did I ever have fun passing out cigars. George, Harvey and I got the rest of the day off, and we drank large quantities of wine and champagne, smoked cigars and talked of babies, mamas and papas. They were very kind and treated me to a steak. I got pretty drunk and was all misty-eyed all day. I can't remember ever being that emotional about anything. I went to bed quite early (7:00) and felt quite contented.

Everyone who came in my room while I was sleeping told me that they've never seen anyone sleep with a smile on his face. I'm so happy, Hon, for both of us. . . .

I have about a million questions to ask you. I really want to know how it was to have a baby. What were the thoughts going through your head while she was coming out? Were you sad because I couldn't be there? Did you get to see her right after she was born? I've always heard that newborns aren't very pretty. Six pounds, five ounces sounds kind of small. I'll bet that she's a real tiny little thing. How come you didn't name her Jennifer? Does she look more like a Katrina? I hope that I get lots of pictures of you and her. What a groovy family we're going to have! Of course, I should have said "already have." I still can't believe it . . . we have a little girl! And just think, Hon, we did it all by ourselves.

I'm going to have to read some books on children. I don't want to be uninformed or misinformed on what's happening in our kid's world. Once I read *Baby and Child Care* by Benjamin Spock, but I've forgotten everything I read.

Please forgive the rambling, Hon. I find it particularly difficult to express my feelings about having Katrina. For all my life I've been saying "Dad" and now Katrina will be calling me that. I really want to be a good father, but I don't have any experience.

I have so many things to say to you, Hon. Please take care, and give my love to Katrina. I love you both, tons and tons.

Love,
Daddy Ron

"Daddy Ron" is Sp/4 Ronald Buehrer, who from November 1969 to November 1970 worked in the personnel office while assigned to Headquarters and Headquarters Company, II Field Force, Bien Hoa. He now works as a data processor in Vallejo, California.

— ☆ —

November 27 [1969]
Thursday

Hi Sweet Thing,

Yesterday I can say it was one of the happiest days in my life. Hearing about the baby. It is one of the best things a man over here can be told. I wish you could have seen the way me and my friends were acting after we heard about it. We were shooting our rifles and making all kinds of noise. The people in the village thought we were going crazy. It was really something to see. I wanted to be home so bad.

Denise, how has the baby been feeling? Is she getting used to being in the world? Does she seem to be happy? How are you feeling after having her? How many times do you have to see the doctor a month? What did the doctor say about your and her health?

Today is Thanksgiving, and I have a lot to be thankful for—a wonderful wife and being able to have a child of ours. I'm thankful to be a father.

All my love,
Bernie
Father of one girl

PFC Bernard Robinson was assigned to the 3rd Marine Division's Civil Action Program 357 in I Corps between June 1969 and July 1970. He now owns a video-rental store in New York City.

— ☆ —

11 Aug 1965

Dear Tracy

I find it very hard to begin this letter. The things I want to say to you can never be fully expressed in words.

I want so much to say the right things. I want to say the things that will make you understand how very much I love you. Before you were born I, like most men, wanted a son. But when I saw you for the first time just a few minutes old, I knew I could never love a son the way I loved you. For a son grows and becomes a man while a daughter is always a child to be loved and cared for. More than anything I want you to know me and love me. I want the love that will grow between us to be one of understanding, just as the love that exists between your mother and I.

The next time I see you, you will be a little lady, walking and talking. Learn how to say "Daddy."

I love you with all my heart.

Love,
Daddy

Marine 2Lt. Tyrone Sidney Pannell, born in West Virginia and raised in New York City, arrived in Vietnam in July 1965, assigned to the 1st Battalion, 7th Regiment, 3rd Marine Division. He was killed on 30 November 1965 near Chu Lai when a land mine exploded. He was 24 years old. Exactly six months earlier, his wife Marlene gave birth to their child Tracy Renee, now a student at Stanford University.

— ☆ —

25 May 69

Hello Princess,

Forgive me for having taken so long to write. The past days haven't been busy ones, only long, hot and very tiring. I feel the quiet tiredness of [them and have] slept-awake through the passing days, not desiring nor doing—being apart. I've taken to looking back boldly on things and sparking forgotten memories: a childhood, a sweetheart, a close friend, a laugh shared, winged, fleeting, uncapturable—it's all so ancient.

Numerous times I've thought of how much your letters have meant to me. Your letters are sanity in an insane world. How much I've relied on getting a note of concern, a phrase that conveys a thought of interest, a word that asks of well-being. Loneliness at one time seemed so much a part of me.

All set for R&R. Next month on the 17th I'll be on my way to Bangkok. It feels as if I've gone and I'm back. Six days is so short a time when it's metered against seven and a half months—seven and a half months bottled and tapped, then poured into six days. Sounds exhausting. Let me know if there is anything you'd like me to send you while I'm there. (I think I told you nothing gives me a joy more than buying gifts.)

Take care.

Clarence

"Princess" is Janet Scarpati, of Jackson Heights, New York. She received this letter from a pen pal, Sp/5 Clarence Jarmon, who was serving with the 42nd Army Postal Unit from May 1967 to December 1969. Jarmon, who hailed from Houston, Texas, was stationed in Phu Bai. He is now an actor and lives in Brooklyn, New York.

— ☆ —

Hi Vern,

Welcome from Bangkok—the undiscovered jewel of the Orient. I'm convinced that the Orient is the place to live. A room for one week—$30.00. A chauffeur 24 hours a day for a week—$30.00. You can stuff yourself in the best restaurants for $3.00. The weather is beautiful. Just a fantastic place. I met a friend from the Delta on the plane and we've been having a ball. He's a real character. We got all dressed up last night, and he left the shoe horn in his shoe. I call him "Mr. World." The sights are fantastic: "Bridge on the River Kwai," Ramakien murals, temples, markets. . . .

I haven't written home for a while, but I'm fine. The best night in San Francisco would cost about $200.00. Here you can see good entertainment (not topless) and spend $10.00. Prices in America are ridiculous for what you get.

I met a Thai girl working in an Italian restaurant who looked like Nancy Sinatra. After four pizzas I finally got a date with her. She had three roommates, and they thought I was Number 1. I'd phone Dong from the hotel, and if she wasn't there her friends would say, "You come home now." *Home* is such a beautiful word. They all liked me, and Dong bought me three ties before I left.

Your brother,
Jim

During 1968, Jim Simmen, from Danville, California, served as a lieutenant with the 5th Battalion, 60th Infantry (Mechanized). He now works as a carpenter for the Coast Guard in Alaska.

— ☆ —

Dec. 14, 68

Dear Gidget,

So very glad to hear from you. I wish you could write more often, but it's all right—as long as I hear from you once in a while. I sent another package with some groovy jungle clothes in it. You can open it and look if you want.

I got my R&R to Australia. Patti wrote and told me about Bruce and the beating those guys [gave him]. I don't know. They go around fighting and shit like that, and think they're bad asses. I wish they'd get over here and see how they like to fight and see how little they are. I'm so mad and disgusted with America—all these riots and fights. And to top it all, men are dying every day over here and fighting their asses off while our country and North and South Vietnam are fighting over what kind of table they should talk peace over. I'll never know. Oh, well, when I return from here I'll have done my share, and the rest of the world can go to hell.

How's my wonderful sister? When I get back, I'll be so happy, Gidget, I won't believe I'm really there talking to you and Dad, and drinking a nice cup of hot coffee in the early morning. Just those small things sound so great to me. It will be so great to look outside and not see dust and choppers and [hear] cannons going off. It's sure been a long time. I'm afraid I'll be a little dumb towards life when I first get back. I'll have to get right in with the swing of things.

Well, honey, be good. I hope you get that operation paid for, and I pray you'll be all right. I love you more than ever.

Love,
Brother Dan

Sp/4 Daniel Bates, 504th Bn., 18th MP Bde., Hue, Phu Bai, 1968–1969.

— ☆ —

27 Nov 69

Dear Mom,

I wrote you a letter this morning, but I just had to write you again and tell you about our Thanksgiving day dinner.

Well, all week I had this funny idea that because I had to be here in Vietnam I had nothing to be thankful for. But then I went to the mess hall to eat. I was really surprised. It was beautiful. They had Thanksgiving decorations all over. There was a white tablecloth on all the tables, Thanksgiving napkins and menus. We walked in and sat down and the dinner was brought to us. Then I realized that it was a symbol of what all of us soldiers had back home. I realized how wrong I was to feel that I had nothing to be thankful for.

When I think of all these poor people here fighting hard to achieve what we Americans already have, I feel obligated.

I can't tell you how proud I feel. I feel very proud. Of course, I'm depressed because I'm away from home. But I know that when my children grow up, the world they live in will be better than the world we live in now, and I will feel content knowing that I helped.

I'm sending you the menu of the meals and a napkin from the meal. I'll say good-by for now, Mommy. I love you.

Love Always

&

Forever,

Henry

Sp/4 Henry Romero was assigned to Headquarters Maintenance Support Company, 1st Supply and Transportation Battalion, 1st Infantry Division, from November 1969 to October 1970, based in Di An. He died in 1982 in an accident at a construction site in Manhattan.

— ☆ —

23 Dec. 69, Mon.

Chu Lai

Dear Mom,

I hear you had some snow at home, and that the weather is very cold. I'll bet it'll be a beautiful Christmas. I hope you, Pop, and Len enjoy it. . . .

Well, I'll be spending Christmas Eve in good old bunker 110. I've got guard duty again. The only Mass we're having here for Christmas is the Midnight Mass. I want to try to go to Mass. I should be able to. There's supposed to be a truce, so I'll be twice as alert!

When I found out I had guard duty on the 24th, I remembered a TV show they had on a long time ago. It was the story of how "Silent Night" was composed. Do you remember staying up with me to watch it? At the end of the show, when it's supposed to be many years after the song was composed, it showed several soldiers in Germany going into a church on Xmas Eve. They were in full combat gear, just like I'll be this Christmas Eve. I always wondered what it must be like to be at war and far away from home at Christmas. Now I know. I can imagine how Pop felt during World War II.

When I go into church tomorrow night I'll be sad because I'm so far from home. But I'll also be happy because by being here I'm making sure that you and Pop and Len can be at home, and safe, and can really enjoy Christmas. Knowing that I'm keeping you safe and happy at Christmas will make my Christmas happy too.

Love & XXXXX,
Ray

Sgt. Raymond Wahl served as a radio teletype operator at Chu Lai for Headquarters Battery, Americal Division Artillery, from March 1968 until April 1969. He is a vice-president of an insurance company and lives in Glendale, New York.

— ☆ —

Bong Son Plains
12/25/67

Dearest Auntie Mame,

It is Christmas Eve in San Francisco—how I wish I could be with you to enjoy it.

A truce has been negotiated, so today we do nothing but lie around. It's raining now, so I am in my tent. Last night one of the Cav's helicopters circled over "the plains" firing different colored flares. It had speakers mounted, so as it flew by I could hear Christmas carols. It was at that time that this intense loneliness hit me. I have saved all the [Christmas] cards I received and just finished rereading them for the third time.

I have, in the past, experienced loneliness, but nothing as intense as the feeling I now have. My heart is crying. I knew that Christmas here would be bad, but not as much as this. Some of the guys are talking to each other, but most are just lying and thinking.

Thank you for the pine branch. When I close my eyes and smell it, I can see your tree [and], in your "penthouse," us together.

I look forward to the day when I board that big jet and come home.

A very Merry Christmas to you, *my* Auntie Mame, and happiest of New Years.

I love you—

Your nephew,
Dave

PFC David Bowman was an infantryman with Company B, 1st Battalion, 8th Cavalry, 1st Cavalry Division (Airmobile), based at An Khe and Phong Dien, from September 1967 through September 1968. This letter was sent to his aunt, Elsa Bowman. He is now a retired police inspector and lives in Petaluma, California.

— ☆ —

26 Dec 1970

Dear Mom and Dad

Well hello there. Wow, Christmas is over—hope you had a nice eve and holiday. All the time I kept thinking about being home, but I couldn't. So I—we—made the best of it here on base. I had off during the day of Christmas Eve but had to work that night. It was only for 2½ hours, so the evening wasn't too disturbed.

The day before the 24th one of the guys in the hooch "procured" a Scotch pine, and it was really great to have a big Christmas tree right at our bedposts. We even decorated it with our own adornments. I was in Saigon most of that day, and many bars were planning eve parties with girls galore. The city was in a festive mood, but I had to work that night so back to the base. After work we opened our Xmas presents and sang a few carols. I had my old standby, champagne, but there was lots of soda, beer, Scotch and whiskey to go around. One of the guys received a Johnny Lightning Jaguar toy and an assembly kit for a Corvette Sting Ray. Well, did I have a ball playing with these toys! Some other guys got super balls and suction guns, so we all acted like kids! (Of course, the champagne helped.) There were fruitcakes all over the place and I sampled them all and concluded that mine was the best. It really is a delicious cake. Where did you buy it?

I received a whole bunch of Christmas cards and care packages from organizations in Huntington and proceded to cover my wall lockers with cards. It looks real good and Christmasy. . . .

I floated to bed on Christmas Eve and missed Midnight Mass in the process. On Christmas the whole company was loaded onto a 2½-ton truck and carted off to Bien Hoa to see Bob Hope! Imagine, I've looked at Hope for years entertaining the troops and never once thought that he'd someday be entertaining me! It was a scorcher of a day, and my arms and face are black tan . . . but the heat was incidental for the show was good and it really made me feel that the authorities in charge of this whole mess sometimes do the right thing. . . .

Love,
Jim

Sp/5 James Schubert spent November 1970 through June 1971 as an illustrator and draftsman with Headquarters and Headquarters Company, 34th General Support Group, based at Tan Son Nhut. He is now an art teacher at a junior high school in Centerreach, New York.

—— ☆ ——

26 Dec '68
Chu Lai

Dear Mom and Dad,

Hi. Well, once again we get ready for a new year. I hope all are feeling well and had a great Christmas and a very happy New Year.

How is everything at home? I sure would like some pictures of the kids getting their presents and of the Christmas tree. I had a pretty good Christmas. I got to see the Bob Hope show, and was it ever something to see. They could only let so many from each company go, and I was one of the lucky ones. We all sang some Christmas carols and had a great time.

Now I'll tell you how I spent Christmas Day. I had to work all day getting the guys out in the field their Christmas dinners. We even had one of our officers dress up as Santa Claus and take small gifts out to the field. Here's the part that is really weird, and, believe me, I don't think I'll ever forget it. After work, about 15 of us got together in my tent and were having a party when from out of nowhere in walked a baby black cat. Well, this was really something because none of us had ever seen a cat over here before. We gave it something to eat, and then it just took off. So we started up with our party again and really didn't think too much of it. About five minutes later all hell broke loose. We were all standing around singing when all these explosions started going off. Balls of fire were shooting through the tent, so we all hit the ground. Man, I didn't know what was going on, but it didn't take long to find out that we had been hit by gas. I don't think I was so scared in all my life. I was never so happy as I was to get my hands on my gas mask. The gas lasted for about half an hour, and then we all waited for Charlie. But I guess all he wanted to do was ruin our Christmas.

Well, Mom and Dad, I'm going to say by for now because I'm so tired that I can hardly keep my eyes open. Tell all I said "Hi" and to be good, and I'll write again real soon.

Love and miss you all,

Your son,
Bill

Sp/5 William R. Stocks, from Glen Burnie, Maryland, 1st Battalion, 6th Infantry, 198th Light Infantry Brigade, Americal Division, was in Vietnam four and a half months when the resupply chopper he was flying in crashed and burned at Chu Lai on 13 February 1969. He was 21 years old.

— ☆ —

January 7th, 1971

Dear Family,

I got all the Xmas packages—at least I think I did. The tree was a huge success. I brought it with me to a small fire base where I spent Christmas Eve and Christmas. We rigged up the lights with dry-cell batteries, and it was the only "formal" tree in the small camp.

Christmas out there was really something. I can hardly tell everything since there was a certain emotion that belies words. At midnight on Xmas Eve, the mortars and tracks and tanks and all the 1st Cavalry artillery sent up an absolutely thunderous barrage of high-altitude flares —all red and green star clusters. Since we were in a valley ringed by 1st Cav positions, it was quite a show. The Cavalry gunners topped it off with a crown of white phosphorus shells fired at an extreme altitude. I believe few people have seen fireworks like these.

Then, when all had quieted and the flares had gone out, the whole area calmed and hushed and we could just hear one of the fire bases start singing "Silent Night." Then it was picked up by the other positions around us and by everyone. It echoed through the valley for a long time and died out slowly. I'm positive it has seldom been sung with more gut feeling and pure homesick emotion—a strange and beautiful thing in this terribly death-ridden land. It is something I will always remember. . . .

Love,
Peter

Sp/5 Peter Elliott was assigned Headquarters and Headquarters Company, 20th Engineer Brigade, attached to the 1st Cavalry Division (Airmobile), based at Bien Hoa. He served in Vietnam from January 1970 through February 1971. He now owns a construction company in Dallas, Texas.

—— ☆ ——

Dear Family,

Hi. How is everything? OK, I hope.

There isn't much of anything new happening over here. Just the same crap. . . .

We got a lot of "Newbies" (replacements) in our company, and it looks funny. All of them walking around with brand-new boots. We always hassle them and tell them how short we are. Wow, I am definitely glad it isn't me who has 363 days left. But I can remember when that was, and it doesn't seem that long ago. This year has gone by exceptionally fast. And I am in favor of that.

Take care, and write soon.

Love,
Eddie

Sp/5 Edward Martin spent December 1969 to December 1970 with the 185th Maintenance Battalion, Long Binh. He now works as an installer for the telephone company in New York City.

— ☆ —

18 July 70

Hi Mom,

How are you, kid? Well, I'm at LZ English now and have been for the past few days. I think the last time I wrote to anyone was when I was at An Khe. Been quite awhile.

I'm under 100 days now, or will be when you receive this. . . . I'm taking a seven-day leave next month in Taipei with three of my friends. It will probably cost me about $450, but I may never again get to see Taipei or all those cute Chinese dolls. . . .

I got a reenlistment talk from the first shirt [sergeant]. He said, "Son, it's time you decided on your future." I told him I was going to join the Navy. He said. "Listen. You're an NCO, a platoon sergeant, senior man in the company, experienced at leadership. We need you." I laughed and asked for my discharge. I thought he was going to cry. Right now I'd rather be a garbage man. I think that if I had [had] more stateside duty I might have signed [on] again. But all I know is Vietnam, so forget it. The Chinese would have to be coming up the Hudson [River] in sampans before I'd join again, and only after the women and children went first. I feel like a civilian already.

I guess I'll take about one week off before I go to work when I return. I don't think I could sit still longer than that. It's hard to make [any] final decision[s] over here, so I gave up trying. I'll get it all figured out later. Bye, Kid.

Love,
Pete

From January 1969 to October 1970, Sp/5 Peter Torrano was a crew chief on a dust-off helicopter with the 498th Medevac Company based near Qui Nhon. He is now a police lieutenant in Norwalk, Connecticut.

— ☆ —

29 Jan 69

Dear Lynne,

Had lunch today with a visiting correspondent from *Newsday*, a Long Island newspaper, who wanted to write an article about psychiatry in Vietnam.

I told him all about the people with "short-time syndrome," that is, people who get nervous or worry about getting killed just before going home. This is a sign of their reluctance to face relationships and responsibilities back home. While it is only reasonable to fear being zapped over here, it is unreasonable to be *more* afraid of being zapped in the last few weeks of one's tour. The fear is actually an unconscious partial wish that something will happen and one won't have to go home. A large number of persons become psychotic at this time, and [some] soldiers do something wrong and get thrown in jail. Still others extend over here over and over again, continuing to put off responsibility.

Another aspect of the syndrome (a collection of symptoms) is a fear that what one has been looking forward to for the whole year won't materialize. Young troops especially expect wives and parents to wait on them hand and foot after such an ordeal. Such indulgence only lasts a few days. Then the folks at home ask the returning hero, "What have you done lately?" Promises made prior to departure in the anxiety of going to war must be kept, and the person no longer has an excuse why he hasn't done this or that to further himself. Actually, the great majority of us only have a little anxiety and are very happy to come home. . . .

Love,
David

Capt. David Forrest was a psychiatrist attached to the 935th Medical Detachment, based at Long Binh, from September 1968 to September 1969. He now has a private practice in New York City. This letter was written to his wife.

———— ☆ ————

September 8 [1968]

Hi! Clara, Tony and Kids,

How are you all? I hope fine and in the best of health. Tell Tony I said hello, and ask him if he's still got that bottle because I'm getting short (four more months). You know, as I sit here now, it seems like just last month I left home for Vietnam. And pretty soon, I'll be home. Thanks for that picture of you, Tony, and the kids. I really enjoyed them when they came—it was great. I can hardly wait to see your daughter and Anthony and Toni. They both look like they're getting so big, but they're still the same as far as faces [go]. Tell Rosie and Annie I said hello.

Right now we're in Quang Ngai. We've been here a week now. There's a lot of NVA and VC over here. Yesterday we got into a fire fight, and one guy got killed and we had eight wounded. But I managed to come out alive again with flying colors. Like I always do. HA!! HA!! Like I told Mom, if you have eight or nine months, you know what's happening. It's mostly the new guys that get hurt. So don't worry about me. . . . Thanks for the Xmas present, and I'll sure be glad to get home and get it. But I'll tell you, you don't have to buy me an Xmas present. My biggest Xmas present will be just being home with my family and seeing you. . . .

Well, there isn't much now for me to say except take care and God bless you all and here's wishing you all health and happiness.

Love,
Richie
XXXXX

Sp/4 Richard A. Sito, Sr., of Kew Gardens, New York, served with Company A, 3rd Battalion, 1st Infantry, 198th Light Infantry Brigade, Americal Division, I Corps. He was killed in action on 16 November 1968, two months after he wrote this letter to his aunt and uncle, Clara and Tony Vaccaro. He was 24 years old.

— ☆ —

7 Apr. 69

Dear Jim,

Hope you had a good journey home and are enjoying your leave.

I'm sorry I'm unable to bring you glad tidings, buddy, but I think you'll probably want to know this news. Of course, there isn't much that can be said or done by any of us.

Our friend, our happy, crazy, almost always laughing pal, Dave Ranson, was killed during a fire fight at 0600 this morning. An RPG took his head, and several others were hurt. Jim, that guy had so much going for him—a beautiful girl to marry in October, school to finish, RELAD [Release from Active Duty] orders, and under 40 days to go. I've been a terrible bitch today as well as overly depressed. This —— war is taking too many good guys. Perhaps I'm selfish, but a few have been friends and I know you've felt the same. There's nothing more to say. I thought you'd like to know. . . .

Jerry

Sgt. Jerome Balcom, H & S Company, 2nd Battalion, 7th Regiment, 3rd Marine Division, spent most of his tour from November 1967 through July 1969 in I Corps. He is now commanding officer of Bronx County Family Court, Bronx, New York, and lives in South Ozone Park, New York. This letter was written to his friend, Jim Buckley, who also served with the Marine Corps in Vietnam.

—— ☆ ——

Dear Civilians, Friends, Draft Dodgers, etc.:

In the very near future, the undersigned will once more be in your midst, dehydrated and demoralized, to take his place again as a human being with the well-known forms of freedom and justice for all; engage in life, liberty and the somewhat delayed pursuit of happiness. In making your joyous preparations to welcome him back into organized society you might take certain steps to make allowances for the past twelve months. In other words, he might be a little Asiatic from Vietnamesitis and Overseasitis, and should be handled with care. Don't be alarmed if he is infected with all forms of rare tropical diseases. A little time in the

"Land of the Big PX" will cure this malady.

Therefore, show no alarm if he insists on carrying a weapon to the dinner table, looks around for his steel pot when offered a chair, or wakes you up in the middle of the night for guard duty. Keep cool when he pours gravy on his dessert at dinner of mixed peaches with his Seagrams VO. Pretend not to notice if he acts dazed, eats with his fingers instead of silverware and prefers C-rations to steak. Take it with a smile when he insists on digging up the garden to fill sandbags for the bunker he is building. Be tolerant when he takes his blanket and sheet off the bed and puts them on the floor to sleep on.

Abstain from saying anything about powdered eggs, dehydrated potatoes, fried rice, fresh milk or ice cream. Do not be alarmed if he should jump up from the dinner table and rush to the garbage can to wash his dish with a toilet brush. After all, this has been his standard. Also, if it should start raining, pay no attention to him if he pulls off his clothes, grabs a bar of soap and a towel and runs outdoors for a shower.

When in his daily conversation he utters such things as "Xin loi" and "Choi oi" just be patient, and simply leave quickly and calmly if by some chance he utters "didi" with an irritated look on his face because it means no less than "Get the h— out of here." Do not let it shake you up if he picks up the phone and yells "Sky King forward, Sir" or says "Roger out" for good-by or simply shouts "Working."

Never ask why the Jones' son held a higher rank than he did, and by no means mention the word "extend." Pretend not to notice if at a restaurant he calls the waitress "Numbuh 1 girl" and uses his hat as an ashtray. He will probably keep listening for "Homeward Bound" to sound off over AFRS. If he does, comfort him, for he is still reminiscing. Be especially watchful when he is in the presence of women—*especially* a beautiful woman.

Above all, keep in mind that beneath that tanned and rugged exterior there is a heart of gold (the only thing of value he has left). Treat him with kindness, tolerance, and an occasional fifth of good liquor and you will be able to rehabilitate that which was once (and now a hollow shell) the happy-go-lucky guy you once knew and loved.

Last, but not least, send no more mail to the APO, fill the ice box with beer, get the civvies out of mothballs, fill the car with gas, and get the women and children off the streets—BECAUSE THE KID IS COMING HOME!!!!!

Love,
Dave

Versions of this letter circulated through various units in Vietnam. This was sent home by PFC David Bowman, Co. B, 1st Bn., 8th Cav., 1st Cav. Div., An Khe/Phong Dien, 1967–1968.

— ☆ —

7 March [1971]

Dear Mom,

. . . This may interest you. The Army is discharging me two months early. I'll be in the States on or near 8 June. As part of Nixon's reduction-in-force policy, all captains and lieutenants with a two-year service obligation are being discharged approximately two months early.

This will change my plans after service life. I'm not sure what I want to do. Europe beckons with its slower pace, peaceful ways, and gentle culture. I want to finish what I started to write when I was in California. Europe might be the place to do it.

My initial reaction to the early-out (as they call it) was anger. I'll be losing a tidy sum of money, and I'll be leaving before I've really had enough of this place. I like Vietnam and the Vietnamese. After a few days' reflection the prospects of not being in the Army in a short period somewhat balances the two disappointing aspects. I was daydreaming about long hair (mine) this morning.

Please. No parties on my return. I am not a war hero, I've no glorious stories to tell, and there are very few people I am really anxious to see outside the immediate family. I'm sure you understand that my sojourn here has been a very personal, very complicated experience for me, and it's going to take time to adjust to the States. What I'm looking forward to is some tranquility so I can reflect on what's happened.

Spring arrives soon. I'm sure the balmy weather will be welcome in New York City.

Love you,
Jim

Capt. James Gabbe spent his tour in Long Binh, serving as MACV command historian, from July 1970 through June 1971. He is now a business and financial writer in New York City.

— ☆ —

Nov. 13, 1968

Dear Mom,

How are you? I received the food package that you sent. It was luscious, and I really appreciated it. Thank you. Happiness is a warm stomach. . . .

I hope you are feeling well. I realize that the wedding is taking much work and expense to prepare for it. I'm already so excited about coming home that I've been having trouble getting to sleep at night. So I had to go to the medics to get some sleeping pills. I'm a light sleeper and a heavy thinker, I guess, and there are so many things that I have to get done and we're needed in so many places that it drags me down sometimes.

This may sound strange, Mom, but I worry more about the war back home than I do about my own life over here. What good is the peace that we accomplish here if we don't have peace in our own backyard? If you only knew the horrors that arguments and hate can bear upon people as I've seen here. We can't hate righteously, we can only try to understand —to work with people rather than to destroy. Darwin's eat or be eaten works well with animals, but what are we? Do we speak of God and hate the "ungodly"? Are our brothers just the next-door neighbors or all of humanity? Or is the alien who walks from his flying saucer shot before he speaks because he doesn't look like us? You may not know it, but you taught me the answers. But, Mom, have you forgotten?

I'll have to sign off now. A special "Take Care" to Grampa, Al, Elaine, Jeff, Auntie Riva and Family from me. Only 31 days left to go. Miss you.

Love, your son,
Howie

Sp/4 Howard Goldberg, assigned to Headquarters and Headquarters Company, 11th Light Infantry Brigade, Americal Division, was stationed at Duc Pho from December 1967 to December 1968. He works as a mail clerk and lives in Minneapolis, Minnesota.

— ☆ —

6 Oct [1969]

Hi—

Three days from now I'll be all through playing this silly game. Three more patrols and I'll be off the river and have nothing to do but pack up for Hong Kong. Following that I'll have nothing to do but get ready to depart beautiful Vietnam.

With every week this thing gets more ridiculous. With the force nearly half turned over this month, they are starting a new operation in the U Minh Forest area of the Ca Mau Peninsula in the southern Delta. It has been a VC base area since before the French were here, when they were the Viet Minh. The U.S. has *never* before been there except for air strikes. No one is there now except for 10 PBRs [which] began patrolling two days ago and have already lost two boats and one killed and 10 wounded. At this stage it's just insane—it's suicidal for the boats and can never be pacified by 10 little boats. The Army won't touch it. I'm glad I'm through with it all. . . .

The rain's beginning to slack off and should be stopped altogether by the latter half of October. With any luck I'll be home for Thanksgiving!

Carolina won yesterday—how about that miracle!

Love,
Ed

Lt. J.G. Edward Vick, Jr., served two tours in Vietnam—August 1967 to May 1968 and December 1968 to November 1969—with the Navy's River Patrol Flotilla 5, Riverine Division 534 and 551, which operated in the Mekong Delta. He is now executive vice-president and chief operating officer at Ammirati and Puris, a New York City advertising agency.

— ☆ —

16 May 1968

Dear Sue,

I'm writing this letter with the full knowledge that it will reach Minneapolis after me. I just wanted to see what one of my own letters looks like when it arrives.

At the moment, I'm in the Transient Officers' Barracks at Tan Son

Nhut AFB, Saigon. Hopefully, it will be one of my last days in this country. If everything goes according to schedule, I leave at 0910 on the morning of the 18th. I thought I heard some mortar rounds falling into Tan Son Nhut late last night. However, they were pretty far off. All I'd need now after a full year in Vietnam is to have a damn mortar round or L-22 minirocket fall in on top of me.

By the time this arrives, I will have told all my hairy war stories and shown you my scar. (Wow!) One thing that worries me—will people believe me? Will they want to hear about it, or will they want to forget the whole thing ever happened? I'm pretty proud of my last year. I did a lot over here: I saw a lot of combat, and got a few results. But they mean very little to any one outside of that group of Americans who have been over here and who have been through it. I know *you* could never understand the thrill of hearing rounds sing over your head and of shooting back. It's going to take a while to get over the nervous anticipation one gets from being constantly under the gun, so to speak. I'll hear a car backfire, and I'll reach for a machine gun.

Be seeing you in a very short time.

Love,
Dick

This was the last piece of correspondence sent by Lt. J. G. Richard Strandberg to his wife Sue. He spent May 1967 to May 1968 with River Patrol Sections 533 and 522, operating along the Mekong River and its canals. They now live in Mesa, Arizona, where he is an artist.

— ☆ —

20 April 1970

Hi doll,

I don't know who will get home first, me or this letter. But I thought I would write anyway. It was so good to hear your voice [last night]. The connections were weak, but still the same you sounded great. I can still hear you saying, "I can't believe it." You sounded so happy, and it sounded like you did not believe that I only busted a few bones.

I got a call through to my parents a little while after I talked to you. My mother did not believe that I was coming home. But I finally got through to her. And, boy, was she happy. She said she was sorry that I got hurt, but also glad—you know, glad that it was only this and not something worse.

You don't know how close I have been to getting killed or maimed. Too many times I have seen guys near me get hit and go home in a plastic bag. Like I have said before, someone was looking over me.

Well, it is all over now. Now it's time to forget. But it's hard to forget these things. I close my eyes and try to sleep, but all I can see is Jenkins lying there with his brains hanging out or Lefty with his eyes shot out. You know these guys—we have lived with them for a long time. We know their wives or girlfriends. Then you stop to think it could be me. Hell, I don't know why I am writing all this. But it feels better getting it out of my mind.

So, doll, in titi time I will be with you again. . . .

Well, honey, I will close for now. Until I see you again,

I love you.

> Your,
> Pete

Sp/4 Peter Roepcke, from Glendale, New York, was an infantryman with Company A, 3rd Battalion, 506th Infantry, 101st Airborne Division, from September 1969 until April 1970, when he sustained a broken leg while jumping from a helicopter. He died of a heart attack in October 1981.

—— ☆ ——

Air Force Major Edward Alan Brudno, assigned to the 68th Tactical Fighter Squadron, was shot down over North Vietnam on 18 October 1965. He was a prisoner of war for seven and a half years before being repatriated in 1973. The following are photocopies of letters he was permitted to send home to his wife, Deborah.

Debby, my dear honey-cake:

My health is much better now. The more I dream of the love we have shared, the more I love you. These dreams make me feel as if I'm still with you. Debby, I'll surely have much love and lots of joy with you in our future. I'll remember your youthful and lovely face always; our love shall live forever. Please keep a full and complete diary so we can reminisce. I sure hope you have had much happiness at home. Only a very true love like ours will bring you ever greater happiness in future.

Please pray for me, Debby,

Alan

NGÀY VIẾT (Dated) ....

6 Oct. 1969

GHI CHÚ (N.B.) :

1. Phải viết rõ và chỉ được viết trên những dòng kẻ sẵn *(Write legibly and only on the lines).*

2. Trong thư chỉ được nói về tình hình sức khỏe và tình hình gia đình *(Write only about health and family).*

3. Gia đình gửi đến cũng phải theo đúng mẫu, khuôn khổ và quy định này *(Letters from families should also conform to this proforma).*

NGÀY VIẾT (Dated) 25 June 1970

I often ponder over our petty misunderstandings of the past, while dreaming of the future. It's so hard to shut such regrettable memories from my mind. Surely, it is not good to dwell on such things; but the heartaches we shared & my failings as a husband, hang heavily on my heart. I can only hope & pray that you harbor few regrets over the many long years you've wasted, waiting for me. I'll make it all up to you some day, Debby, I swear. When I return, you'll find me older, wiser, & far more capable of being the husband you deserve. Please keep faith in me, darling. —— Alan

GHI CHÚ (N.B.) :

1. Phải viết rõ và chỉ được viết trên những dòng kẻ sẵn (*Write legibly and only on the lines*).

2. Gia đình gửi đến cũng phải theo đúng mẫu, khuôn khổ và quy định này (*Notes from families should also conform to this proforma*).

NGÀY VIẾT (Dated) 23 February 1972

Debby, though I have not yet given up all hope, the possibility that we may never again see each other becomes more apparent with each passing year. I simply can no longer hide from that hard reality. Like unlucky players at a game of chance, we may some day have to make the difficult decision to call it quits. It's just not fair to you, that I should ruin your entire life, Debby—I'm not worth it, believe me. You are still young—with many good years ahead of you. For your own future happiness, perhaps you should consider the possibility of re-marrying. Please write, and tell me what you really feel. I'll always love you—

Alan

GHI CHÚ (N.B.):

1. Phải viết rõ và chỉ được viết tren những dòng kẻ sẵn (Write legibly and only on the lines).

2. Gia dình gửi dến cũng phải theo dúng mẫu, khuôn khổ và quy dịnh này (Notes from families should also conform to this proforma).

30 November 1972

Merry Xmas, my darling—indeed, for me, a very merry Xmas this year. Merry for all the blessings I've re-discovered, for all the hopes & dreams I've repossessed. My values have changed over these many long years; future plans have come & gone, and, from time to time, I've faltered. But my new values, my new dreams, will bear delicious fruit—I assure you—for they've matured well these past months. I've searched very carefully for lasting happiness—for what life really means to me—and I've found it. I've found it in a family & a home—the dream home we'll soon build together. I've found it in the beautiful New England that I loved so well—that I miss so much. But most of all, Debby, I've found it in you. And I've searched for a realistic career worthy of my talents—fascinating & challenging. And I've found that, too—in scientific research. Everything—even school, now—is calling me back to Boston, to Franny, to a fulfilling & rewarding life. On top of all that, I'll add a pipe-dream or two—But my old ambitions have ceased to be a prime factor in my life—only the frosting on my cake.—Life will begin in Hawaii, Debby, no matter how or when I return—we must start there! Begin now arranging for the most perfect three weeks there possible. Let's spend most of it on two of the outer islands—first, in the privacy of a simple beach cottage, with all services provided, then at a plush resort hotel. Honolulu will be last, & we'll return to San Francisco by luxury liner. Reunion with Bob next—then home for six weeks: to see the family, to find the perfect homesite, to begin our house plans, & to prepare for our flings abroad (including shopping trips to Denmark & Sweden for furniture & accessories).—I dream every day, my darling, of that magic moment when at last we will meet: There, at ebb tide, I'll find you standing at the water's edge—your back to me. As I approach with pounding heart, I'll whisper your name, & you'll turn. Few people have known, or will ever know, the incomparable joy we will share then. And there as we stand, face to face, hand in hand, and we gaze into glistening eyes—at last we'll find peace. And til time should ever cease, for us there'll be no more good byes.

Alan

On 3 June 1973, four months after his release and one day before his 33rd birthday, Major Brudno committed suicide. The week before his return home he penned the following two "dream-sheets," lists of things about which he had been "dreaming" at the time. He wrote them in ink he made himself.

I. IMMEDIATE

ADDRESSES - DEB, BOB, STEVE
TELEGRAM TO DEB; BOTH FOLKS } PLAN!
PHONE DEB - ESTABLISH R-V
TELEGRAM CLOSE FRIENDS, FAMILY
SPEC. DELIV AIRMAIL - DEB + FAMILY (FOR INFO,
   REQUESTS, GIVE PLANS)
CAREER: GET INFO ON HANSCOM, LOGAN, SCHOOL
   EST: LEAVE, CIV. SCHOOL (BOSTON)
   P. PCS → HANSCOM
   FLY W/ ANG
   SPACE PROG. - 3 PRIORITIES
   SPECIAL (1976 LV, OVERSEAS SPENDING)
STEREO CLUB - TAPE POEM, CK STEREO EQUIP.
BK: WATCH, PEN, LIGHTER, BASIC CLOTHES, GIFTS
TYPE POEM
LAW OFF. - APPROVAL, COPYRITE INFO
   U.S. CUSTOMS INFO
PHOTO CLUB - CK NEW EQUIP, EST. NEED
GET CASH
WRITE REJECTIONS - DAWN
NOTEBOOK / DIARY (UNDATED PAGES)
PERSONAL AFFAIRS OFF - FINANCE
T.I. CAR3
GIFTS ⟵ PERHAPS BOOKS

II. HONEY/MOON

SOME CLOTHES, GIFTS (CK HICKAM) FLOWER
ORGANIZE FAMILY / FRIEND REUNIONS OR
   HAVE FOLKS DO IT
PERSONAL HYGIENE / HABITS - CONSCIENTIOUS!!
SHAVE TWICE A DAY, BATHE OFTEN

III. HOME ⟵ NOTE C. GREENE, LANGYEL

CAREER- VISIT MANG, HANSCOM, SCHOOLS
   CK. NASA (PHOTOS, INFO, NEEDS)
LAND- SHOP FOR HOME / SUMMERHOME PROP.
   CK. LOCAL ORDINANCES / TAXES.
   BLM REVIEW - BUREAU OF LAND MANAGE-
   MENT MAILING LIST - U.S.G. PRINT OFF
FINANCE: CK TAXES (MASS., U.S.)
   EST. CREDIT, BANK, CHECKING ACCT.
   EST. ALLOTMENTS.
   PAYOFF DAD - $ OR HOME IMPROVEMENT
   INVEST. INFO: DAD, DAD-IN-LAW, BROKER
   KIPLINGER NEWSLETTER
   "CHANGING TIMES"
   FORBES MAG / WALL ST. JOUR.
   LOCAL FEB. RESERVE BANK BULLETIN
LAWYER: GET EST. W/A GOOD ONE
   ESTATE PLAN, WILL, COPYWRITE
   CK HOW TO AVOID LAWSUITS; INSURANCE

DENTIST
REGIS. OF MOT. VEHICLES - PLATE, LICENSE
INSURANCE - LIFE (TERM - ESTATE CONCEPT)
   CAR (? WAIT)
   PERSONAL LIABILITY
   HOME ITEMS (PETS, PROPERTY)
   HOUSEHOLD
RESIDENCE - EST. IN MASS.
HOUSE - EST. BASICS; CK BOOKS, MAGS
   ATTEND OPEN HOUSE
   SEE CARNEY
FURNITURE - SEE INTER. DECOR. FOR U.S. STUFF
   CK: KNOLL FOR FAMILY RM. (C.C. GREENE
   DUX (U.S.?) CHAIRS + OTHER FURN
   HERMAN MILLER ; SARANAN
   CHARLES EAMES
   MELS VAN DER ROHE
   HANS WAGNER (DANISH) "TEDDY BEAR"
V.A. BENEFITS : CK.
VOTING REGISTRATION - CHANGE
LTRS TO SENATORS / REP?
LTRS OF APPRECIATION; CORRESPONDANCE Ⓐ
MY STORY - SEND COPIES (BETTER THAN MIMEO)
POEM - BOUND - LIMITED EDITION
   HAIR STYLIST, PROFESS. DRESS ANALYST
   GRAD. RECORDS EXAM (FIND OLD, TAKE NEW)
   SMALL TAPE AT BEDSIDE
LOVE ADVICE: M.D., RECOMMENDED BOOK(S)
CK. INTO READING GLASSES
[PERSONAL RESUME, FAMILY BIOGS (TAPED)]
GENEOLOGY: L.D.S. ARCHIVES } S.L. CITY
   GENEALOGICAL SOC. } (JAY)
   CK. LIBRARY FOR FORMS
CATCH-UP PROGRAM: LIBRARY!
   YEARBOOKS; LIFE SPECIALS
   CK LOCAL COLLEGE POLISCI DEPT.
CK ON FUTURE PURCHASES: WRITE TO
   STEREO BIG NAMES, SCM (LOG ITO)
   DOUG FL. FOR IBM SELECT.
   SEE LOCAL CAR DEALERS (RIV. & CORVETTE?)
SEND FOR "ESTATE PLANNING" TEXT
   FM AFA LAW - ECONOM. DEPT.
WRITE SONY - IDEAS, TX, INFO - SCIENTIFIC AM.
BEGIN SCRAPBOOKS - ON FAMILY, ON INTERESTS
KEEP BODY SIZES - (DEB & ME) FOR FUT. CLOTHES
OLD PUBLICATIONS - AD IN BK. SECTION, SUN. TIMES
   W.D. COMICS
   CK DAD FOR NAT. GEOG
   [OLD AMERICAN HERITAGE & SPECIALS]
PERSONAL HYGIENE / GROOMING / CLOTHES
   SEE ADDITIONAL SHEET

PRE-EUROPE PLANNING:
CK: PASSPORT / VISA / MEDICAL REQ.
CK: NEW ITALIAN LINERS
CK: SST ROUTES
BERLITZ - POLISH FRENCH, LEARN BITS OF
   OTHERS (TOURIST GUIDES) - PHRASE BKS.
   KNOW SOMETH. AGT COUNTRY!
   USE TRAVEL AGENCY
EST. MAJOR PURCHASES:
   FURNITURE
   CHANDELIER ? VENICE
   SCREENS - SPAIN
   STAINLESS "SILVER SERVICE?"
   "   CHESS
   OKREFORS CRYSTAL (DANISH)
   STAINLESS / CRYSTAL (CHINA ETC (SILV)
   SETTINGS FOR 2-4-6
GUIDES TO WINES
CREDIT CARD (AMER. EXPRESS, DINERS CLUB,
   CARTE BLANCHE) CHOOSE 1.
ETIQUETTE / PROTOCOL GUIDE
CK. MILITARY BENEFITS ABROAD (FACILITIES)
   LEARN INTERNATL SIGNS.
   BUY DANISH FURNITURE IN GERMANY (AT BX)
STAMPS: EST. ACCT. AT J. MARSH
   BEGIN 1st DAY COVERS, DUCK STAMP
   CK. GEN ; TRAVELS
COINS: EST. "NEW U.S." COLLECTION +
   FOREIGN FM TRAVELS
CREDIT CARDS: GAS, PHONE
MICHELIN & FIELDINGS TRAVEL GUIDES
   CAN DIET BK ON EACH COUNTRY
   ALSO "EUROPE ON $5/DAY" - FOR KICKS
EXERCISE PROG - BRING SIMPLE GEAR ABROAD
GRAPEFRUIT JUICE DIET - CK. MAYO CLINIC
WALDORF CAKE

IV. TRAVELS

CK. EUROPEAN RAIL TICKET (EURORAIL)
   AROUND-T-WORLD AIR TICKET
   (MOSCOW - NEW DELHI, SYDNEY)
HONG KONG: (VICTORIA IS., KOWLOON)
   PENINSULA H. (VERY OLD) (KOW.)
   HILTON (V.I.)
   GLOUCESTER H. - CHINESE REST. ON TOP
   PRINCESS GARDENS REST. - NATHAN RD.
   PRESIDENT (KOW) - SIAM (ESE) REST.
   ON TOP - GREAT VU - GET WIND. SEAT
   CHINA FLEET CLUB
   INCL. "PEOPLES RADIO LTD"
   "LANE CRAWFORD LTD"
   SIBERIAN FUR CO - SUPPLIES SAKS
AIR EUROPE - $300/MO.

IV CONT.

CK INTO RENTING CAR
NITE CRUISE ON SEINE - PARIS
TOUR D'ARGENT (ACROSS FRM N. DAME)
CROSS - US → CAL. → JAP → H.K. → CROSS U.S.
USE CHAMBERS OF COMMERCE/AGENCIES
GET OF FREEWAY - SEE AMERICA
OUTINGS; TRIPS TO HISTORIC PLACES (BOSTON)
  KNOW BOSTON!!
VISITS: TO FACTORIES (STEUBEN)
  A/C CARRIERS - "DEPENDENTS CRUISE"
    (CK. PROTOCOL)
SAFARI - MOZAMB. (PHOTO) - C. GREENE
CARIB. CRUISE BY SAILING SHIP - JAMAICA
GUEST FARM IN FALL (SUNSET, ETC.)
USE TOURS (GUIDED, TOO!)
SEWING/KNITTING MACHINES + LESSONS
COOKING SCHOOL IN PARIS? OTHER SCHOOLS
TRAINS: GREAT NOR. PACIFIC/HOKKAIDO SPECIAL

V SELF-IMPROVEMENT

ETIQUETTE (CK. MILITARY PROTOCOL)
  EMILY POST/AMY VANDERBILT
  ESQUIRE (MORE SUITED FOR MEN)
  COURSES - "CHARM SCHOOL" FOR BOTH
I.Q. TEST - CK. COLLEGE PSYCH DEPT.
  1) STANFORD - BENET 2)?
SPEEDREADING - EVELYN WOODS COURSE
  SELF-TEACH (LIKE READERS DIGEST)
  (PERHAPS ON VACATION TOO)
PUBLIC SPEAKING - DALE CARNEGIE
"HOW TO DEVEL A SUPERPOWER MEMORY"
DANCING LESSONS (TUTOR @ HOME)
PROFESSIONAL ADVICE - ALL MATTERS
"HOW TO WIN FRIENDS -". DALE CARNEGIE
  GUITAR LESSONS
WFF-N-PROOF - CK. SCIENTIFIC AMERIKAN
"THE ART OF THINKING" ERNEST DIMNET
"PWR OF POSITIVE THINKING" - N.V. PEEL
"MODERN RHETORIC" ROBT. PENN WARREN

VI EDUCATIONAL INTERESTS

GET INTERPRETER RATING (USNA?)
- ASTRONOMY - PHOTOJ FM PALOMAR (400"ER)
- NUC PHYSICS, CHEMIS. (ORGANIC), ANTIMATTER
  BIOLOGY - ORDERS
  ARCHITECTURE, ARCHEOLOGY, MAN
  GEOPHYSICS - CK. NASA (SPACE RESULTS)
- BERNARDS STAR
- T.V. CK ON 3-D/STEREO/RESOLUTION

RELIGION, BIBLE, TALMUD,
STUDY JEWISH CULTURE - ALL ASPECTS
VISIT + STUDY OTHER CHURCHES.
RELIGIONS OF THE EASTERN WORLD (AJM)
FIND OUT ABT FREEZ-DRY & OTHER PROCESSES
  LIFE SPECIAL
COURSES: ART & MUSIC APPRECIATION
  U. OF CHICAGO: BA W/ GREAT BOOKS
  SLEEP-LEARNING

VII POLICIES, PROGRAMS (SEE BELOW)..

GO-OUT-PROGRAM:
  MOVIE ~ 1/WK
  EATING &/OR DANCING - 1/2 WKS
  OTHER ENTERTAINMNT., TRIPS, SPORTS
    THEATER, SHOWS, CONCERTS, ETC.
EST. LIKES & DISLIKES - TALKS THINGS OVER
JOIN SYNAGOGUE - BE ACTIVE
HUMOR
SMOKING: NOT BEFORE BREAKFAST, LOVE
DON'T OVERLOOK QUALITY BARGAINS:
  REA WAREHOUSE, FACTORY 2NDS
  USED, RE-POSSESSED, AUCTIONS, DAM-
  AGED, UNCLAIMED, FIRE SALES, SALES
  DAILY BULLETIN
BE JEWISH! EST. A PHILOSOPHY/RELIGION
DINING POLICY: MAKE IT BEAUTIFUL, FANCY,
  AN OCCASION
  KISS & GRACE
  NO T.V., READING
  EST. WORTHWHILE CONVERSATION
  SPECIAL NITES - SEMI-FORMAL, FRENCH
  EVENING DESSERT BREAK
  DISCOVER WORLD OF WINES
  GO OUT - HAVE FRIENDS OVER
FOOD PURCHASING: KNOW GRADES
  MAIL ORDER (WISCONSIN CHEEZE PAKS,
    FRUIT BASKETS, PECANS, ETC.)
  QUANTITY BUYS
  AVOID BUYING FOR THE PACKAGING
    (ESP IN TINY AMTS)
  ROADSIDE FARM STANDS
  SPECIALTY SHOPS
  TRY ALL BRANDS - HAVE PLAYOFF
COOKING: TREAT AS ART; ENCOURAGE DEB
  INTERNAT'L CUISINE
  HOME BAKED BREAD/PASTRY
SOMETHING NEW POLICY -- TRY IT!
.. GOP - TRY A DOG, FLOWER SHOW ...

VARIETY - SPICE OF LIFE
BE CONSCIENTIOUS, PRECISE
BE HEAD OF HOUSE, WEAR PANTS
DEMAND RESPECT
EST. CHALLENGES - & MEET THEM
JOIN COMMUNITY: SCOUTS, MASONS
  COUNTRY/YACHT CLUB
EXERCISE/WGT BUILDING PROG.
CORRESPONDANCE - BE ORGANIZED
TV - ELIM TRASH (USE TIME WELL)
GIFT POLICY FOR FRIENDS/RELATIVES - EST
GIFTS + FLOWERS → DEB
HOLIDAYS: CELEBRATE ALL - GIVE MEANING
  MAKE-UP PROGRAM
XMAS POLICY: CELEBRATE!
  MAKE DECORATIONS
KEEP PHOTO ALBUM - FAMILY YEARBOOK

VII FOOD

* WALDORF CAKE RECIPE (ART H., DWIGHT S.)
  GERMAN CHOCO. CAKE/WHITE CHOCO.
  KNORR. SOUPS - SWISS
  USINGENS-MILWAUK.-SAUSAGES (BAND.)
  FUTURE GARDEN, FRUIT & NUT TREES
    CK. DEPT OF AGRICULTURE
    USG PRINT. OFF.
* CHERRIES JUBILEE - "SADDLE & SIRLOIN"
    IN MANDARIN H. (H.K.)
  GADGETS: CHOPPER/DICER ETC.
    FRIED POTATO CHIPS
  BOOKS: JOY OF LIVING ('64 BEST SELLER)
    GOURMET -2 VOL. (CHER)
    OFFICERS WIVES
    AL LURIE - JEWISH
    ESQUIRE/PLAYBOY GOURMET CB
    FRENCH HAUTE CUISINE VIA
      MODERN MEANS
    LOW COUNTRY CB (S. CAROLINA)
    RIVERROAD CB (LOUISIANA)
    DUNKIN HINES GUIDE
  CK: WATERLESS COOK WEAR

TONY AND.

APT. LIVING OR CHEAP HOTELS IN EUROPE
WHAT EVERY YOUNG MAN SHOULD KNOW - ESQUIRE
PSYCHIATRIST/ANALYST
PARK LANE HOTEL NYC. CALIF. ZEPHYR → DENVER
PUBLISH AGENT

IX MILITARY

UNIFORM: MIL. TAILOR/SUPPLY
MORREY LUXEMBOURG - N.W.E.
(BEST WHEEL HAT)
AIR OFFICER'S GUIDE / REGS
PENTAGON: STAY AT "MARRIOT" MOT.
VOQ BOLING →Q VIA BOAT
INTERAGENCY MOTOR POOL - ON ORDERS
PERSONNEL - RANDOLPH
A.F. LIBRARY (INCL. FILMS + PROJECTOR)

X SPORTS/GAMES/PROJECTS/HOBBIES

SAILING ON CHARLES
SKI (LESSONS), SOARING, RALLIES
FLY (PRIV. LISENCE)
CK: HANDBALL, TENNIS, GOLF?
EVENTS - GOP: TRY ICE HOCKEY
SKATING - LESSONS?
ORIGAMI - PAPER
VEGAS GAMES/POKER/BRIDGE (DEB)
MILKY WAY PROJECT
OIL PORTRAIT OF DEB
MOSAICS/TROPICAL FISH
RE-DO SLIDES/CK. USED QUESTAR
PAINT-BY-NUMBER WALLPAPER

XI HOME ENTERTAINMENT

THE BAR: GOOD BAR GUIDES FOR
BASIC SETUP, KNOW GOOD LABELS!
KEEP 2 STOCKS: 1 FOR BEST FRIENDS
PLAYBOY/ESQUIRE
SO. COMFORT RECIPE BK
"AMER. BARTENDERS GUIDE" - DEMPSEY
SPIKED HOT DRINKS: IRISH COFFEE,
HOT BUTT. RUM, GLUG (SWEDISH)
MUSIC, PIANO, ELECT. PIANO + GUITAR
JAZZ "WHAT IS JAZZ" - L. BERNSTEIN.
W. COAST JAZZ BASICS (SEE ①)
RECORDS: OLD 45 COLLECTIONS
RECORD CLUB OF AM. - LANCASTER, PA.
A MUSIC DICTIONARY
8 DAYS OF CHANUKAH

XII SPECIAL PURCHASES

PLAYBOY KEY?
PISTOLS: REMINGTON XP-100 (TGT/VARM)
WALTHER: PPK (SELF-DEFENSE)
LESSONS FOR BOTH
GLOBES - CK. NASA, NAT. GEOG.
WATCHES - EVERYDAY + DRESS + (POCKET?)
ROLEX - BEST VALUE
GERRARD PEREGEAUX
OMEGA
PATEK PHILLIPE - BEST
HAMILTON (U.S.)
LONGINE (U.S.) - BEAUTIFUL
LIGHTERS: GERRARD PEREGEAUX
"KREISLER" - U.S. / "MONOPOL" GERM.
CANDLES: HOUSE OF CAN. - LA JOLLA, SAN D.
(IN OLD TOWN - SAN DIEGO)
CK. BUTANE
LUGGAGE: CK. LOUIS VUITTON ($ $ $)
PEN: "CROSS" CK. IN NYC
PAINTINGS: SCI-FICTION
LINEN/TOWELS: VARIETY, BEST
DOG
QUESTAR/COGITO? WRITE
STEUBEN FROG

XIII BOOKS ▽.

CK. REVIEWS IN SAT. REV/ATLANTIC,
HARPERS/N.Y. TIMES
NY TIMES: SUNDAY BK SECTION: BUYS
CK: BEST SELLER LIST; GREAT BOOKS
YR BKS: GREAT BKS/ENCYCLO/LIFE
GREAT BKS & ENCYCLO (USED)/ATLAS
LIFE SPECIALS
HOUSEHOLD ENCYCLO.
HOW-TO-DO-BKS: POP. SCI./BETTER HOMES
HOW TO AVOID PROBATE COURT
ROGET'S THESAURUS
"BARTLETT'S FAMILIAR QUOT." - 2 VOL.
"LEAVES OF GOLD" - QUOT., SAVINGS ETC.
"GOLDEN NUGGETS OF THOT" - 2 VOL.
"THE DEVIL'S DICTIONARY" - BIERCE
A SUMMARY OF ENG. LANGUAGE AUTHORS
AND THEIR WORKS (2 VOL.)
"MASTERPIECES OF WORLD LIT" - 2 VOL.
"THE ART OF FICTION" - W.S. MAUGHAM
UNDERSTANDING POETRY - A.F.A. PROF.
"HIST. OF T. ENG. SPEAKING PEOP" - CHURCHILL
"HIST. OF WESTERN CIV." - B. RUSSELL
"JOHN BROWN'S BODY" STEVE GINET (POEM)
AMERICAN HERITAGE, INC. SPECIALS
"10 DAYS THAT SHOOK T. WORLD"
"RISE + FALL OF 3RD REICH" - SHIRER
"WAR THRU THE AGES" - LYNN MONTROSS
"1000 DAYS" - SHLESSINGER JR.
MAKING OF A PRESIDENT
"GOALS FOR AMERICANS"/PROFILES IN COU.
"YOU ARE NOT T. TOT" - LAURA HUXLEY
THE "ANNOTATED ALICE" (IN WONDERLD)
IRVING STONE'S WORKS
"THE PROPHET"
"WALDEN" + OTHERS - THOREAU
"THE TRUE BELIEVER" - ERIC HOFFER
• WANDERING JEW/
GORKI - "CHILDHOOD" + OTHERS
TOLSTOI (RESURRECTION IN GR. BOOKS)
J. MISCHNER (RESURRECTION IN GR. BOOKS)
KON-TIKI - THOR HYERDAHL
AYN RAND
G. ORWELL - ANIMAL FARM - 1984
J. VERNE
H.G. WELLS: "OUTLINE OF HISTORY" + SCI-FI
"A-B-C'S OF RELATIVITY" - B. RUSSELL,
GIVE BOOKS FOR GIFTS:
"GIFT FM T. SEA" (FOR WOMEN?)
VANCE PACKARD - STATUS SEEKERS/HIDDEN PERSUA.
U.S. NEWS + W.R. BOOKS PROGRAM (STOCKS/MUTUAL F.

XIV OTHER PUBLICATIONS

XMAS CATALOGS - SEE ②
CONSUMERS GUIDE/DIGEST
NATIONAL GEOG.
A/W, M&R, A.F. & S.P. ASTRONAUTICS
SCIENTIFIC AMER.!! (WRITE THEM) BOOKS, FILMS
FORTUNE/HOLIDAY/ARIZ. HIGHWAYS
CLASSIC COMICS $25
COMIC STRIP BOOKS/COLLECTIONS
IN FRENCH: READ. DIGEST, FASHION, RÉALITÉ?
U.S.G. PRINT OFF. (JON H. BROTHER WORKS TR)
J.B.'s POEMS
"NATIONAL REVIEW" - WM. F. BUCKLEY JR.
SUNDAY TIMES (LONDON?) ...

XV CLOTHES/GROOMING (BASIC)

DARK EVE SUIT; SOMEWHAT LIGHTER IN COLOR (CAN BE WORN IN DAYTIME & TO CASUAL EVE ENGAGEMENTS - DINNER IN A REST., DANCING; A LIGHT CASUAL SUIT ONLY FOR DAYTIME. 1 EACH IF ABOVE FOR SUM. + WINT. WGT. NOT HVY - MORE FOR FALL. THE DARK EVE SUIT CAN BE USED FOR SOMBER OCCASIONS (FUNERAL). INSTEAD OF TRADITIONAL BLACK/MIDNITE BLUE IT MIGHT BE A BLENDED COLOR (CHARCOAL ETC)
MED-LO (90-120)   M-MED-HI (120-175)

HART SCHAFFNER + MARX	BROOKS BROS.
CRICKETEER	GREIF
BOTANY 500	KUPPENHEIMER
THE BROOK	HICKEY-FREEMAN

EXPEN. (175+) - BROOKS BROS. ALL THESE HAVE OTHER PRICE CLASSES, BUT CONCENTRATE ON ABOVE. MANY FINE SHOPS HAVE OWN LABELS.

SPORT COAT/BLAZER; CASUAL DAY SUIT CAN BE WORN ANY TIME S.C. IS APPROPRIATE (NEITHER AFTER 6PM) ∴ THE S.C. ISN'T MANDATORY. TK OF IMAGE!! IF NOT SPORTY, CASUAL, BUT MORE CONSERVATIVE - LITTLE NEED FOR IT. ONE SUM, ONE WINT. S.C. — SHORTER SKIRT; SQUARE SHOULDERS ETC; METAL BUTTONS, USUALLY SOLID COLOR. ABOVE FIRMS MAKE S.C.'S. "HARDWICK" IS BIG IN BLAZERS. THE SUIT COAT DOES NOT DOUBLE AS A S.C.! MED-LO (55-75), MED TO MED-HI (75-125) EXPEN. (125+)

SLACKS - MIN. OF 4 PR SUM., 4 PR WINTER. 2 OF EACH GROUP SHOULD COMPLEMENT S.C. CONSIDER BELT VS BELTLESS, CUFF VS CUFFLESS, SLASH VS STRAIGHT POCKETS, SLIMNESS OF CUT (PREFERENCE &/OR PHYSIQUE. ABOVE FIRMS MAKE GOOD SLACKS. "DAKS LTD" OF LONDON GREAT. VALUE. MED-LO (22-30), M-MH (30-50), HI (50+)

SHOES: DON'T SKIMP!! CONSERVATIVE WEAR ONLY STRINGS W/TIE. (SOME SAY DRESS LOAFERS OK W/ S.C.). EYELETS DETERMINE FORMALITY: 4-6 EYELETS - DAYTIME/CASUAL SHOES (WITH HEAVIER CONSTRUCTION); 3 OR LESS, WITH LIGHT WGT. - EVE SHOES. BLACK SHOE WITH BROWN SUIT - NO! (NOR VICE V!).
MED-LO (18-26)   MED (26-35)

JARMAN	BOSTONIAN
NUNN-BUSH	FLORSHEIM
CROSBY SQUARE	BRITISH WALKER
FRENCH SHRINER	

MED-HI (35-50)   HI (50+)
BALLY   JOHNSON & MURPHY

BROWNS & GRAYS CAN BE MIXED IN 1 BASIC COLOR OR SCHEME. — 3 PR MIN (EXCLU. UNIFORM SHOES, OPERA PUMPS ETC.): 1 PR DRESS LOAFERS, 1 PR DAY STRINGS, 1 PR EVE STRINGS. KEEP TREED IF NOT IN USE; USE WOOD TREES THAT FILL ENTIRE INSIDE. LET DRY 1 DAY FOR EACH DAY OF USE. CALF, ITALIAN CALF VERY SOFT. CORDOVAN (HORSEHIDE) WON'T CRACK, BUT STIFF.

OUTER GARMENTS - 1 DAY, CASUAL TOPCOAT, 1 DARK EVE TOPCOAT, 1 RAINCOAT, 1 CARCOAT FOR 1 COLOR SCHEME. CARCOAT CAN BE WORN W/ COAT & TIE ON SPORTY/VERY CASUAL OCCASIONS. "LONDON FOG" IS ONLY A RAINCOAT "ALLIGATOR" - FINE NAME IN RAINCOATS: ((75-150). LOOK TO MAJOR SUIT CO'S FOR TOPCOAT. EXPECT SAME PRICE AS SUIT. CARCOATS 30-100: "WHITE STAG", "McGREGOR", "PENDLETON"

SWEATERS- CONSIDER PHYSIQUE/IMAGE! WEAR TO SPORTY/VERY CASUAL OCCASIONS. MED-LO (17-30), MED (30-50), MED-HI (50-75)

SOCKS - ONLY CALF LENGTH OR OVER - T-CALF, SOLID COLOR W/ SUIT OR S.C. (COLOR AT LEAST AS DARK AS TROUSERS). "BRITISH BYFORD", "EXECUTIVE", "SUPPHOSE" 3-5. ANKLE LENG. SOLID COLOR OK. W/SPORT SHIRT + SLACKS. "GOLD CUP", "EXETER" 1.75   BILLFOLD

ACCESSORIES - BREST WALLET! HIP IF NECESSARY, BUT THIN! WALLET & BELT MATCH IN COLOR, TEXTURE. BELT: LEATHER ONLY. - NOT FOR HOLDING UP PANTS. $10+ NEVER MIX WHITE + YELLOW GOLD. TIES - SELECT FOR A PARTICULAR SUIT. - 5 FOR EACH SUIT & S.C. TIES HAVE SIZES. "COUNTESS MARA" "CHRISTIAN DIOR". MED (5-15), HI (15-100).
CUFFLINKS - FRENCH CUFF ONLY. NEVER IN DAY. PREFER ONLY W/ DARK EVE SUIT.

HATS: WEAR ONE! DARK SOLIDS FOR EVE, LIGHTER CHECKS OR TWEEDISH OK FOR DAY/CASUAL. WEAR SQUARELY - DON'T TILT. TOUCH BRIM IF MEET LADY ON ST. - TAKE OFF IN ELEVATOR. "ADAMS", "DOBBS", "STETSON IN THAT ORDER. A GOOD HAT HAS PRESSED EDGE ON BRIM.

FORMAL: EVE - WHITE TIE & TAILS; DAY - MORNING COAT. - LITTLE NEED.

SEMI-FORMAL - SUMMER TUX (EASTER TO LABOR DAY): WHITE DINNER JACKET, TUX PANTS, TUX SHIRT, STUDS + CUFF LINKS, BLACK TIE + CUMBERBUN, OPERA PUMPS. WINTER TUX SAME, BUT BLACK TUX JACKET. OUTER GARMENTS INCLU: "HOMBURG HAT", "CHESTERFIELD TOPCOAT", COLORED DINNER JACKET W/SUM. TUX: BECOMING POP, NOT YET ACCEPTED (1965). OCCASIONS: DINNER IN FINE REST, THE THEATER, SEMI-FORMAL ENTERTAINING. PRICES SAME AS SUITS. ("AFTER 6"—CHEAP!). OPERA PUMPS-PATENT LEATHER - $50+.

TIPS
KNOW KNOTS, HOW TO WEAR CLOTHES (CUFFS)
COLORFUL UNDERWEAR
DON'T SKIMP ON ANYTHING'
AVOID BEING TOO COOL (CK. 10 WORST-DRESSED)
FIND A CLOTHES IDOL/USE A THEME
BECOME A REGULAR CUSTOMER, BROWSE.
ASK QUESTIONS, INTRO YOURSELF, BE OBSERVANT OF OTHERS
USE ONLY FEW COLORS/STYLES
BETTER QUALITY - LESS QUANTITY
THE CONSERV. DRESSER WON'T GO OUT OF STYLE QUICKLY.
DON'T BUY EVERYTHING AT ONCE/ROTATE
BE CONSCIENTIOUS TO DETAILS
PLEASE MYSELF FIRST
THERE'S A REASON FOR PRICE DIFFERENCES
SOURCES: GQ, ESQ, PLAYBOY, N.YORKER
        (LATTER IS CITY-ORIENTED).
SVANK: CATALOG OF ACCESSORIES
"CLOTHES MAKE THE MAN" BOOK
TOILET ITEMS: ENGLISH LEATHER
        (K. CANOE, AVON
SOAP: "PEARS" (ENG) } TRANSPARENT
       "ICE-O-DERM"
SUITS ③ KNOW HOW TO WEAR, BUTTON, HOW TO USE POCKETS, ACCESSORIES HOW TO KEEP (AIRING, HANGING)
BUTTON COAT!
HALF-LINED COAT + TROUSERS
★ USE SILENT VALET, LINT ROLLER HOW TO DON COAT AVOID FREQ. CLEANING
ROTATION - WEAR ALL (EVEN WEAR) - STAY IN STYLE - MAINTAIN SIZE OF WARDROBE
TWEEDS - BEST FM SHETLAND ISLANDS
TAILOR MADE UNIFORM + SHIRTS (DRESS)
SWEATERS - AVOID ORLON, CASHMIRE AIR, STORE IN BAGS.

24 May 67
Di An

Dear Mom & Dad,

. . . It sure is going to be different being around clean things again. I hope I can take it. It's going to take a while to get used to stateside living. Guess I'll have to watch my manners.

You know, when you get over here all you think about is getting back to the World. But when your time gets near, it sort of scares you because you know in your heart that you're not like the people back home. It's a funny feeling to be afraid to go home, but everyone over here feels the same (except the [rear-echelon troops]). There are a lot of mixed emotions —worrying about hurting the people close to you, or maybe your dreams about the States will shatter when you get home. And then there's always the way you regret leaving your buddies in this hell hole. We all joke about "Put your time in," but in our hearts we wish we could all go home together. . . .

All my love,
Butch

Sgt. John Hagmann spent two tours in Vietnam—February to October 1965 and July 1966 to July 1967—with the 337th Radio Research Company, 1st Infantry Division, based at Di An. He is now a manager for the telephone company and lives in Ballson Lake, New York.

— ☆ —

8
Last Letters

. . . I can tell you truthfully, I doubt if I'll come out of this war alive. In my original squad I'm the only one left unharmed. In my platoon there's only 13 of us. It seems every day another young guy 18 and 19 years old like myself is killed in action. . . . All of us are scared cause we know a lot of us won't make it.

Like 58,000 others, Private Raymond Griffiths, who wrote these words, didn't make it. He was killed in action in 1966, on the Fourth of July.

The letters which follow are, in many respects, unremarkable —except for the fact that they are the last letters written by GIs who within days would become statistics in the body count. Unlike Ray Griffiths, none of those who wrote these letters foresaw imminent demise, at least not in their final letter home. They did, however, go home sooner than they had imagined, and not as they had hoped.

04 Feb 68

Hello All,

Once again I haven't written but I haven't had too much time. Today is the 4th, 14 days left in the field and then I should be headed back to CONUS (Continental United States).

By the way, did you receive my $134.00 check I sent about Jan. 3rd? I can't write too long, we are going out in about an hour for an ambush. Here is a $159.00 check plus my W-2. I'll tell you—it's a hard way to make $1,206.00

Love,
Jim

PFC James J. Rice, from Newtonville, Massachusetts, served with Company K, 3rd Battalion, 3rd Regiment, 3rd Marine Division. In action near the DMZ on 7 February 1968, he was killed while attempting to rescue a friend who had been badly wounded. He was 21 years old.

— ☆ —

Tuy Hoa
7 Feb 66

Dear Mom,

I know you must be worried to death from not hearing from me, but at least it was unavoidable this time. We moved out about a week ago from our base camp at Tuy Hoa and replaced a unit of ROK [Republic of Korea] marines. I was right in the middle of a letter when we got the word to move, and I had to pack it away. These ROKs we replaced were dug in defensively in the middle of a rice paddy. They had been hit by two battalions of VC a few nights before, suffering 48 casualties and killing over 100 VC. They hadn't been sending out patrols or recon, so when they dropped us out here we had no idea what the situation was.

Since we've been here we've suffered pretty heavy casualties. Yesterday the count stood at 2 dead and 15 wounded. But last night B and C Companies got into it with a battalion of VC, and at last count there were 6 dead and many wounded. By the time you get this I imagine you will have heard about the 101st on the news. We've killed a lot of VC and captured a lot of weapons, and that's what counts.

I got into it pretty heavy a few days ago, and it was a miracle that I'm alive. I can give you the date and time and see if there was any indication of extreme danger at that time on my chart. It happened on the 4th of February. There were about 12 of us with the lieutenant out on a routine patrol and a half mile from the hill the rest of the company was on. We were searching through an abandoned village looking mainly for chickens, eggs and mats to sleep on. We were crossing a dike between two houses when we were opened up on by about 10 VC with automatic weapons. I was carrying the radio, which made me a prime target. That's not my usual job. On this particular day I ended up with it.

We started returning fire, and my weapon jammed on me on three different occasions. This whole fight was being observed by our men on the hill. We received instructions to try and maneuver and push the VC, which we were able to do fairly successfully, and were told that help was on the way. The guys on the hill said they could observe about a platoon of VC moving away from us. Anyway, they entered a tree line as we were coming out of a another tree line with about a 300-yard open rice paddy between us. We were about halfway across when they opened up from the tree line again. We were laying in about six inches of water and a foot of mud. We held back for an air strike and artillery. These helped some, but they didn't follow through.

We were told to begin pushing again. When we stood up, they wounded two men, and when the lieutenant ran over to one of them, they killed him. This put us without a leader because the platoon sergeant was way around to the left trying to flank them. About this time the company was coming up behind us and they didn't know where we were exactly. The fire from the VC was going over us and into them and the company was firing back at us. So we were receiving murderous fire from both sides. They were so close that when one of us would try and stand up and tell our guys they were firing at us we could hear them yelling, "There's one! Get him! Get him!" We ended up with one seriously wounded by our own fire, and the other one we're not sure who got him. It was about 2:30 P.M. when they first fired on us and about 4:30 P.M. when we finally met up with the company and pushed the VC to the river. When you check your chart, be sure to allow for the time difference.

You probably can't tell too much from what I'm writing, but I'm mainly interested in getting this letter off to ease your worry. As you can see I'm writing this on the back of one of Shawn's letters. I carry all your letters in the top of my helmet, and I was able to scrounge up an envelope. I'll close this now and [it] will go out on the resupply chopper.

Don't worry, and I'll write first chance I'll get.

Love,

Johnny

PFC John R. Price, from Norfolk, Virginia, who arrived in Vietnam in December 1965, served with Company A, 2nd Battalion, 502nd Infantry, 101st Airborne Division, based at An Hoa. He was killed in action on 9 February 1966 before this letter to his mother, Mrs. Dorothy Dobrinsky, was mailed. He was 21 years old.

— ☆ —

5 Feb '69

Dear Mic,

Time really seems to be going by now. Of course, next week I'll probably think it is creeping but at present it seems to be going pretty fast. Only two and a half more months to go! From all that is happening in little Laos it seems that I will keep quite busy, so that will help also.

Baby, as you have probably guessed by now, R&R looks doubtful. Maj. McManners has the mid-February quota, and there is a quota open for March. Either me or Lt. Col. McLean, my boss, will get it. He hasn't made up his mind yet. I realize that is only a month before I would be home, but it would be worth it to me. How about you?

I think the R&R setup for us is a dirty shame: 12 quotas a year for Hawaii for 72 people. Sweetheart, I know that worrying about it has caused you a lot of heartache, but Joe has done all he could to try to get to Hawaii. I sort of feel like the U.S. Army has let us down on this one.

The past few days here have been so cold I had to wear a field jacket all day. At night I just freeze. Gosh, won't it be nice to have someone to snuggle with again! Not just someone, but you! The idea really excites me, to put it mildly. Baby, I need your lovin'. Poor Robin, what will she ever think of her father—always taking Mommy off and locking her up in the bedroom three or four times a day.

Well, baby, it looks like I will have about six new ribbons on my

uniform when I come home. All of that is classified, but if all the paper-
work gets completed I will have received a little recognition for a generally
thankless job. Also it is a little consolation that I have been asked to extend
by our office, which I politely refused to do, and ordered to extend by the
local commander—an order that, thank goodness, he cannot enforce!
Don't worry, old Joseph will be home to his wife and daughter in April
as planned even if he has to swim the Pacific.

Keep smiling, darling, for Joe thinks of you and loves you every
minute of the day.

Your own,
Joe

*Capt. Joseph Kerr Bush, Jr., whose home was in Temple, Texas, was
serving as a military attaché and adviser to Laotian forces at Moung Soui.
He was killed during an attack by NVA commandos on 10 February 1969.
For his actions he was posthumously awarded the Silver Star. Capt. Bush
was 25 years old.*

— ☆ —

2 May 1968 (?)

Dear Mom and Dad,

I am now sitting in a little hooch in a village in which we're operating. Company A is still situated on LZ Sue, securing the artillery battery
which supports our battalion. The way things are working is that two
platoons secure the hill while the third goes off into the villages on patrol.
Each platoon stays down for three days and then moves back up to get
relieved by another. On Sue it's relatively safe with large, strong bunkers
[and] several layers of barbed wire around the outside.

We still have to man the perimeter at night, which means not much
sleep, and we're always subject to mortar attacks, but Charlie would need
a fully equipped battalion-sized force to take it, so I don't think he'll try.
Basically, being on Sue means a rest and security, so it's good to be there.
Right now, though, we are on our three days down in the field, and I have
to tell you that ever since we hit that minefield I am nervous all the time.
My platoon is way under strength right now, and I feel that we are too
small a force to be operating as independently as we do. My authorized

strength is 43. I had 36 when I first joined the platoon and am now operating with 20. That minefield cost me several people, plus I am hit with a rash of people on profile [medically excused from duty because of a physical ailment] and people on R&R at this time.

Last night I split my element into two ambushes. I took one, and my platoon sergeant took the other. Sgt. Western's patrol was in position about an hour and a half when some dink sneaked up and threw a grenade into their perimeter. Sgt. Western saw it come in and managed to grab it and throw it back out where it exploded harmlessly. It was, needless to say, an awfully close call. I put him in for a Silver Star today for his courageous action. . . .

Despite losing people and being scared all the time, I find being an infantry platoon leader an exhilarating, exciting, and, yes, rewarding job. I have ambitions to go higher, even in my short two years in the Army, but I don't really want to because platoon level is the last at which I still can have close working contact with my men. I think I've developed a pretty good relationship with my people, one in which they depend on me for leadership, but they know that I must be able to depend on them too. It's very healthy and, as I say, rewarding. I am doing all the politicking I can to get a staff job, but if I do get one, I will hate to leave my men (not enough to turn it down, though!). . . .

I have a couple of requests which I wonder if you would mind filling. (1) Have you been able to change the address of the *Newsweek* subscription you said you ordered? I live in quite a vacuum for news over here, and *Newsweek* seems about the best and easiest way to pull myself out. (2) Could you check the status of my bank account and send me a report? (3) Could you send me half a dozen black mechanical grease pencils. I use these to mark my maps, which are covered with acetate. (4) Could you keep me supplied with felt-tip pencils (blue) like this one. About two a month should do me fine. As you can probably tell, it's a cold day in hell (or Vietnam, for that matter) when I get a chance to get to a PX.

This is all for now (both requests and deathless prose). More soon.

Love to all,
Mike

P.S. You might tell any friends you have in Washington to get off their fat asses, quit quibbling, and start talking about ways to end this foolishness over here. Aside from being opposed to the damn war, it really gives me a case that LBJ, who claims to want peace and who says he'll go anywhere any time to talk peace, has taken over a month without being able to find an acceptable site. Anywhere, according to his promise, ought to be "acceptable."

During a night ambush near Quang Ngai on 3 May 1968, 2Lt. Robert C. Ransom, Jr., called "Mike" by his family, was leading a platoon from Company A, 4th Battalion, 3rd Infantry, 11th Light Infantry Brigade, Americal Division, when he was seriously wounded by a mine. His death on 11 May, two months after he arrived in country, was officially attributed to peritonitis and pneumonia resulting from his wounds. He was born and raised in Bronxville, New York, the eldest of six sons. He was 23 years old when he died.

—— ☆ ——

December 12, 1967
Monday

Dear Family,

I thought I'd drop this picture to you. I'll send some more when they come back from the developers. By the way, it's a [picture of a] flag I pulled out of a tunnel I found the other day. I got mucho goodies out of it. I got to keep this NVA flag and a Chicom M-1 rifle in mint condition. Now all I have to do is get it back from my CO who said that it had to go to intelligence first. It better. The rotten, selfish, thieving skunk. Oh, well.

So goes another day in the Land of Make Believe.

Much love,
Your son and brother,
Stephen

P.S. I'll try and write a letter soon.

PFC Stephen W. Pickett, from Jackson Heights, New York, served with Company C, 4th Battalion, 23rd Infantry (Mechanized), 25th Infantry Division, based in Chu Chi. He was killed on 14 December 1967 during a search-and-destroy mission. Two days later, his brother Douglas, who was serving with the Navy off the coast of Vietnam, wrote home: "We are near Vung Tau, right off the Saigon River, so I guess I am closer to Stephen than I think. Who knows, maybe we shall get to see each other. I doubt it, but who knows, maybe we will." "They did," writes their sister, Mrs. Victoria Miano. On 22 December, Douglas escorted Stephen's body home. Stephen Pickett was 20 years old when he died.

— ☆ —

4 June 1969
Wednesday

Dear Mom & Dad,

Got your letter of 28th, Mom, yesterday, 3 June. Today I got Dad's of 26th April. Never know what is going on with the mail. Haven't gotten the package yet. Heaven only knows when they will arrive and in what condition.

Worked in ICU [Intensive Care Unit] again today. Was lucky, got to 102° today, and ICU is air-conditioned. They have a lot of really sick patients. Had three die yesterday. They still have four on respirators. None too good, either.

One of the GI's who died yesterday was from Ward 8, medical. Had malaria. During the previous night he had been nauseated and kept getting up to the latrine to vomit. Got up at 2 A.M. and was running to the latrine. Fell really hard and cracked his head on the cement floor. The nurse who was on duty said you could *hear* his skull fracture. He immediately started bleeding from ears and nose and stopped breathing. Then had cardiac arrest. They got him going again and transferred him to ICU but he died anyway yesterday. Had severe brain damage. Other death was [a] GI with multiple fragment wounds from a mine explosion. He was there two weeks ago when I worked that other day in ICU. Also a Vietnamese died. Don't know what was wrong with him.

Census hit the 10,000 mark yesterday. This unit, the 312th [Evacuation Hospital], has treated 10,000 patients since [we] arrived last September. Unbelievable. Registrar office had a poll going as to what time and what date the 10,000th patient would be admitted. Was yesterday morning. Haven't heard who won the money yet.

They put plastic or rubber? floor tile down in the mess hall the evening before last. Looked real nice until yesterday noon when it got hot. The tar came up between the tile and it got tracked all over the place.

Couldn't move your chair at all. It was stuck to the floor.

How did the home-made ice cream turn out? Start "nights" tomorrow so don't have to get up early tomorrow. Nice thought.

Still very quiet around here. Haven't gotten mortared for couple of weeks now. We are getting some new nurses this week. They are from the unit who will take over when the 312th goes home in September. Their hospital is farther south somewhere. They are handling 80% Vietnamese casualties now so are turning their hospital over to the Viets and coming here to take over. Supposed to get the new chief nurse tomorrow. So the unit will change names in September. However, they are supposed to be an RA [Regular Army] group. Not a reserve unit like the 312th is. Things are supposed to get a lot more "strict Army style." No one is looking forward to it.

Read a book last night and missed a good Lee Marvin movie at the mess hall.

Had a movie star visit here the second or third week I was here. Named Ricardo Montalban? Ever hear of him? Forgot to mention it previously. Some of the older people here remembered him. Said he was in movies with Esther Williams.

Will stop for now. Getting sleepy.

See you sooner.

                                                            Shar

2Lt. Sharon A. Lane, a nurse from Canton, Ohio, arrived at the 312th Evacuation Hospital, Chu Lai, in April 1969. Two months later, on 8 June, she was killed by shrapnel during a rocket attack. She was one month short of her 26th birthday.

—— ☆ ——

Dear Mom and Dad,

I got your package today, and it came at a very good time. We are in the fire base, and I can take my time and enjoy it.

I'm very sorry that I haven't been writing very often, but I've been pretty tired lately. But I've got some good news for you. After a lot of consideration, I've decided *not* to extend my tour here. I will have to serve five months (until December) in the Army, but that time will be spent in the States.

I don't want to spend any more time over here than I have to. I'm really starting to get homesick, and I want to get back to the people that I love.

I'm seriously considering going back to school. I probably won't start until the June quarter, which will give me a lot of time to get adjusted again. I want to take things slow at first so that I don't mess anything up.

How is the VW running? You haven't mentioned anything about her in a long time. The way things look, that car may have to last me until I quit school. What is the mileage now? I'll bet that in the six months before I start school, I'll bring it up to about 100,000.

We are getting a lot of new guys in the company now. When you're just responsible for yourself, everything is easy, but when you've got to watch out for a bunch of kids, then the going gets rough.

I'm not afraid of the responsibility, and, in fact, I'm sort of enjoying it. The thing that bothers me the most is that one mistake on my part could cause one of them to get hurt. I guess I owe at least that much to them, because I was treated that way when I first got here.

The unit I'm in, though, has a big problem that most units don't face. The other units that are here—like the 101st Airborne, 1st Air Cavalry Division, the Americal, the 1st Infantry Division—all have a full division here. That's made up of two to five brigades. Each brigade has a one- or two-star general as head, and each division has usually a three-star general. They also have numerous support units assigned to them, such as engineers, aviation, medical, etc.

The 82nd is a divided unit. Out of four brigades, three are in Ft. Benning, South Carolina. (The 4th Brigade just recently made a mock combat jump near Seoul, South Korea.) The lonely 3rd Brigade, of which I am a member, is stationed in Vietnam. It's the only unit in the Army which is divided up like this, and so it's sort of a novelty being in it.

But the novelty wears thin when one realizes that the highest ranking man which the 82nd has here is just a one-star general. One of the biggest problems that is created by this lack of higher authority is poor resupply.

As far as base necessities are concerned, we're OK. Food and ammo and mail have to be taken care of for a unit to exist. But as far as anything extra, we are in bad shape. It didn't affect us too much before, because we got used to it. But now, since everybody is leaving the company to go home, we're running into one of our worst problems. We're not getting enough replacements. The company strength should be approximately

120 to 130 men in the field. Right now ours fluctuates between 75 and 85.

They are starting to bring more replacements in, but we are always last on the totem pole to pick them. Less than two months ago my platoon leader and platoon sergeant were both brand new. They were very scared about being here, and neither one of them would take any advice from their squad leaders or anyone. Our old platoon leader, who I've mentioned to you before, extended his tour for six months, with the intention of having an easy job in the rear. But when he saw the predicament we were in, he gave up the easy job that he had worked for months to get and came out to the field because he said that he owed his friends a little more than they were getting. He got rid of the new platoon sergeant by getting him a rear-echelon job, and filled the position with a 20-year-old man who just made sergeant. The two are the best team in the company.

But as far as the other platoons go, they are in trouble. All the men that we get sent to us are new, because all of the old-timers are taken up by the other units. This leaves us with a sticky problem of not only breaking in the PFCs but also the leaders, and some of them are rather obstinate about it.

I don't want to sound like a war-torn hero, because I'm not. What I'm mostly talking about are the practical things that we're not taught in a class. It's the same thing that a mother and father try to show a belligerent son to keep him from making mistakes. But over here, one mistake, especially by a leader, could cause him and other people to get hurt.

I guess I'll just have to bear with it for another two and a half months, and then I'll be home for good. See you soon.

Your son,
Jimmy

P.S. If I didn't tell you about the Bronze Star that I sent home, it is just like the other medal I received. It's for "meritorious service," which means that I was here for my tour and very little more.

Sp/4 James H. Wilson, from Sparta, Tennessee, was assigned to Company B, 1st Battalion, 505th Infantry, 3rd Brigade, 82nd Airborne Division. He was killed near the Cambodian border on 31 March 1969, two days after receiving the Bronze Star with a Presidential Citation for meritorious achievement in ground operations against hostile forces. He had been in Vietnam since 16 June 1968. He was posthumously promoted to sergeant. He was 21 years old.

—— ☆ ——

24 Feb 68

Dear Jeanene, Bob & Billy,

You are all fine, I'm sure, and working harder than you should be. Of this I'm also very sure. You know that [it] is Saturday night, and here I sit stone-cold sober. Mainly because of the lack of booze! Can't think of why there is such a shortage other than maybe they think chow and ammo is more important or something. Every day that comes and goes brings one just a little closer to seeing you again in a more friendly place than this. How is every little thing at home? I suppose that Mom and Dad are working their heads off. I hope that you are keeping a close eye on them, and making sure that they are hacking it all right.

We're just sitting here waiting for all hell to bust loose. With each day that goes by, the incoming increases and the 3rd Platoon digs deeper. We are all ready for them, in my opinion, but no matter how well prepared you think you are, there is always something more you can do. We have been lucky so far, and I hope that the good fortune holds for us. Although my platoon has had 30 wounded since January 21, none have been too serious and the majority of the men are still on duty and all healing. One or two have made it home early, but that is all to the good. For they have done their part. They seem to think that Khe Sanh will be the turning point to the negotiation tables. I hope so. But if not, we will go on until this is over one way and the only way.

Well, I'm sure old Billy is getting to be a big boy and more and more of a nuisance. That is to be expected from any little guy. I just hope we can do our part well enough so that your Billy and Mark or Matt don't have to follow us over here in years to come.

This little guy, J.D. Carter from Florida, a real little farmer with that southern accent and everything that goes with it, got hit today, not bad, but there he [lay] on the ground in the trench bleeding and he looked up at me and said, "I'm OK, Lieutenant, fine and dandy! Nothing can get me. I'll just head over to the aid station and get me one of them there bandages and be right back!" They're all like that. You know that little guy, 17 years old, got half way over to the hospital on his own, and remembered he had forgotten his magazines for his rifle and came all the way back for them. Crazy kid. Well, not much more except I'm fine and still kicking. I'll write again soon.

Love, Brother
Don

2Lt. Donald J. Jacques, from Rochester, New York, platoon commander with Company B, 1st Battalion, 26th Marines, 3rd Marine Division, was killed in an ambush during the siege at Khe Sanh on 25 February 1968. He was 20 years old.

— ☆ —

24 July 1969

Dear Brian,

Well, I'm still here in Vietnam, but should be home by mid-August, barring something out of the ordinary.

Hope you did well in your bar exam, but you probably do not have the results yet. Best of luck anyhow.

Diane has been doing outstanding at West Chester. She'll be looking forward to my return so she can vacation for a while prior to returning to school this fall. She'll probably be going to University of Maryland in that I received my orders to return to the Naval Academy to teach Chinese to first-semester students. That'll prove to be a ball for me and work into a lot of plans that I have.

I'm glad the Army satisfied your desires and is giving you until January 20 before they take you away. Don't fret Vietnam, that is, seeing it. The thing will be over before you'd have the opportunity to come.

I've got many plans and none. You know how it is; I'll probably just stay in the Marine Corps and rest well in security and hope for another war somewhere to do "my thing." It is all the time an experience. I couldn't have done it any other way, and will never regret the past 13 months. Your not desiring to come is rather immaterial in that if you're assigned, you go, or if you feel strongly against doing so, resist. At either rate, you are definitely the man of decision if dictated so by your principles. Yet if you came as a lawyer you'd never be faced with killing, or

defending those that have done so in excess. Really, it isn't all that bad
—war, I mean. In the large sense disgusting, but in the smaller sphere,
combat is a happening. At least we know this is at last "the war to end
all. . . ."

I really have no perspective.

When I get home next month, maybe you can "tune me in" and
perhaps, just perhaps, "turn me on."

Until later—

> Your friend,
> Michael

*Capt. Michael Charles Wunsch, Company A, 3rd Tank Battalion, 3rd
Marine Division, was killed in a rocket attack near the DMZ on 28 July
1969, 10 days before he was to return home to Feasterville, Pennsylvania.
He received the Silver Star for his actions during the operation, called
Idaho Canyon, in which he was killed. He was 25 years old. This letter
was written to his friend, Brian Baker.*

— ☆ —

> May 19, 1968

Dear Mom and Dad,

How is everyone? I hope fine. When you receive this letter, May will
be just about over. I will be down to *six months* and a couple of days left
in December which amounts to nothing. I'm going to have a big celebration when I leave Vietnam. And when I get back to the World, I won't
forget to keep the seventh day open to the Lord.

I guess the time is passing by fairly fast for you, because you're pretty
busy. "But not for me." Received all your letters, Ma, and I'm *always* glad
to hear from a squared-away mother, as the Army would say it about a
Number 1 soldier. It all just comes to the heading—you're the *best* in my
books, Ma.

Also heard from Aunt Flo. I know you will thank her for me, about
writing to me, it was nice of her. So far you're doing good, Ma, about
writing. Keep up the good work. Now I want to let you know you will
always be Number 1 mother in my books.

Heard you got Nancy a portable hair dryer. I think it was nice of you to always look out for the other person. But, remember, stay like you are, and don't let them take advantage of a well-natured mother. Also, keep up the good work, and keep the letters flowing in. Say hi to everyone.

Love,
Rick

P.S. Watch my return address. I'm all over—everywhere.

Sp/4 Richard A. Carlson, a medic attached to Company D, 2nd Battalion, 8th Cavalry, 1st Cavalry Division (Airmobile), operating in I Corps, had been in Vietnam four months when he was killed while ministering to the wounded during an ambush on 24 May 1968. "Doc, I'm a mess," he said to a fellow medic. "Oh, God, I don't want to die. Mother, I don't want to die. Oh, God, don't let me die." These were his last words. He was 20 years old.

—— ☆ ——

[Dick,]
. . . Let me describe to you events of the recent past. . . .

I left for Utapao, Thailand, which is a little over 300 miles south of here on the coast. I had no clear idea as to what was going on, but we felt as though it had something to do with Saigon for the obvious reason that the military and political situation there was deteriorating rapidly.

The next morning, which was a Sunday, I went to an intelligence briefing. They told me that I was going to fly my airplane . . . to a Navy carrier. Well, that was not really a surprise because Utapao is on the ocean and we knew that the Seventh Fleet was doing some weird thing out there.

But I didn't know that the goddamn carrier was 500 miles away— off the coast of South Vietnam.

Well, obviously I did manage to find the carrier, the *U.S.S. Midway.* I assure you that they are not as large when they are on the ocean as they appear to be when they are tied up at the dock.

I landed on the carrier and was quickly indoctrinated into the way of the Navy. I didn't like it one goddamn bit. We went to daily intelligence briefings, and basically the situation was this: We were there to evacuate American citizens, selected Vietnamese and other delegated third-country nationals at the last possible moment if the situation deteriorated to the point that they couldn't use Tan Son Nhut airfield, which serves Saigon. . . .

I made four sorties into Saigon. The situation with 150,000 [enemy troops] around the city, of course, was not the most salubrious situation in which to take a big, lumbering aircraft with nothing but defensive weapons to take people out.

And, of course, Tan Son Nhut was closed.

I could tell you about how real the fear was that I felt, since from the time we crossed the Delta and made the run into Saigon we were over enemy territory. We were being fired upon by anti-aircraft guns. The VC had commandeered Air America Hueys and they were flying them around, which simply made for a very interesting chess game.

I mean, it was bad. We thought that they were going to call off the operation when it became dark, because we never expected them to send us into such a bad situation to begin with, even if it was daytime. But, as you probably know, they continued the mission until nearly 5 o'clock in the morning. The night sorties were the worst, because we flew lights out. The tracers kept everybody on edge. To see a city burning gives one a strange feeling of insecurity.

Tan Son Nhut was being constantly shelled, and when I see you I will show you some pictures of where I was going in relationship to what was happening. And you can judge for yourself that it wasn't the best of all situations.

I learned something . . . oh, that's the wrong way to say it. I was given something, as a result of this trip—the answer to the question: Why did I come?

It isn't very easy for me to even tell myself what the motivation was to come here. It was more the feeling than something concrete. I have been repaid. And that's possibly a funny way of saying it, but that's the way I feel.

There is a disadvantage to this. [The] task which I had outlined for myself [and] felt that I had to accomplish is over. And I cannot assure myself this time that I am prepared to make any kind of decision as to what I am going to do next. I have been seriously considering—in regard to this uncertainty—simply leaving the Air Force. I don't think it has much to offer me any more. . . .

I went into this thing searching for something. I have it now. . . .

Let me throw a couple of facts your way, which may conflict with what you have been reading in the papers. I call them facts in that I saw them happen. I will throw them out for whatever they are worth. Number One: At approximately 9 o'clock on the morning of the 29th [of April, 1975], which was the day that the mission was executed, a Vietnamese Huey flew out towards [the] sea, and found a carrier.

It was nearly out of gas. It made an emergency landing on the carrier. [At that time,] anybody who had an ability to fly anything commandeered aircraft from whatever source [out of Vietnam]. They flew out their families and their children and in some cases select individuals.

This aircraft that landed—landed about 50 feet away from mine— and the man who got out of this aircraft [had been] quoted approximately a week earlier as saying that any South Vietnamese who left the country [was a] coward and that everybody should remain in South Vietnam and fight to the bitter end. This very same man was the first person to arrive on the *U.S.S. Midway* and, to my knowledge, the first to be recovered by the 7th Fleet. This man was General [Nguyen Cao] Ky [vice-president of the Republic of South Vietnam]. Now I really don't have any personal feelings about the war over here. I really don't care one way or the other in regard to who is right and who is wrong, because that's a waste of time, a waste of thinking. But I did find myself feeling that I wish he had been shot down. . . .

We pulled out close to 2,000 people. We couldn't pull out any more because it was beyond human endurance to go any more. . . .

I am back now. I got back today. I am in bits and pieces, fairly incoherent only because it's been such a fast pace. I assure [you] that I am in one piece. It could have been a different story. But I may have told you before that I am somewhat fatalistic about believing that I shall never come to serious harm in the military. . . .

I can envision a small cottage someplace, with a lot of writing paper, and a dog, and a fireplace, and maybe enough money to give myself some Irish coffee now and then and entertain my two friends. . . .

I don't think it will be too terribly long before we are together again.

I wish you peace, and I have a great deal of faith that the future has to be ours.

Adios, my friend.

Air Force 2Lt. Richard Van de Geer, from Lorain, Ohio, a helicopter pilot assigned to the 21st Special Operations Squadron, based at Nahom Phnom, Thailand, participated in the evacuations of Phnom Penh, Cam-

bodia, and Saigon in 1975. When the Cambodians seized the S.S. Mayaguez, his unit was again called into action. As his chopper, filled with Marines, flew into the inland of Koh Tang, it was blown out of the sky by enemy forces. There were no remains. This is an excerpt of a tape Lt. Van de Geer sent to his close friend Richard Sandza, who received it on the morning of 15 May 1975, the day Lt. Van de Geer was killed. Officially, Richard Van de Geer was the last American to die in the Vietnam War.

— ☆ —

WILLIAM E STAINER • ODELL STO
CZYK • HENRY VALENZUELA Jr • T
POLINAR • HARRY R BARTHOLOM
ON • ANDY A CABRERA • JAMES T C
ONROD • CLAUDE DARDEN Jr • D
GLESSING Jr • ALLEN B GLINES • RO
ES • KENNETH R LANCASTER + RO
NNON Jr • THOMAS D O'CONNO
AY • CLARENCE ROBINSON • EDWA
RER • JERRY D SCHROEDER • JERRY
ON • DONALD F WEBB • MELFORD
BIN Jr • COY G STAYTON • REGINAL
EAU • GREGORY E COX • KENNETH
MAN • MEREDITH A GABRIEL • BILLY
• ROBERT C HENDERSON • LARRY
MAN • CURTIS L KENNEDY • ROGER
MINNICH Jr + DENNIS E MONTAC
ETERS • CLIFTON P PIERCE • GENE
OSE • JAMES W ROY III • DAVID L SIM
Jr • EUGENE F SWEET Jr • FRANK O
RK • PAUL H VILLAROSA • ROBERT V
BAKER • DONALD W BORNMAN
ALBERT M CARWITHEN • ARTHU

Epilogue

"Remember, Mom, if something should happen to me please don't be too sad because at least I will have done my share of good in life. So be proud, not sorrowful." Although he was wounded in Vietnam, Hospital Corpsman Gary Panko survived his tour. Billy Stocks did not.

Mrs. Eleanor Wimbish, of Glen Burnie, Maryland, is the mother of William R. Stocks. She leaves letters to him—her dead son—under his name on the Vietnam Veterans Memorial in Washington, D.C. For her, he will always be more than a name etched on a wall.

For Vieterans, and for others, like Mrs. Wimbish, the pain and anguish of the war linger on, scarring our souls, a stain on the national psyche. No memorial can fix this. "Maybe the war will end soon," Navy Lieutenant Richard Strandberg wrote to his wife Susan in 1968. "Wishful thinking? Yes. The Vietnam War will never end."

Dear Bill,

Today is February 13, 1984. I came to this black wall again to see and touch your name, and as I do I wonder if anyone ever stops to realize that next to your name, on this black wall, is your mother's heart. A heart broken 15 years ago today, when you lost your life in Vietnam.

And as I look at your name, William R. Stocks, I think of how many, many times I used to wonder how scared and homesick you must have been in that strange country called Vietnam. And if and how it might have changed you, for you were the most happy-go-lucky kid in the world, hardly ever sad or unhappy. And until the day I die, I will see you as you laughed at me, even when I was very mad at you, and the next thing I knew, we were laughing together.

But on this past New Year's Day, I had my answer. I talked by phone to a friend of yours from Michigan, who spent your last Christmas and the last four months of your life with you. Jim told me how you died, for he was there and saw the helicopter crash. He told me how you had flown your quota and had not been scheduled to fly that day. How the regular pilot was unable to fly, and had been replaced by someone with less experience. How they did not know the exact cause of the crash. How it was either hit by enemy fire, or they hit a pole or something unknown. How the blades went through the chopper and hit you. How you lived about a half hour, but were unconscious and therefore did not suffer.

He said how your jobs were like sitting ducks. They would send you men out to draw the enemy into the open and *then* they would send in the big guns and planes to take over. Meantime, death came to so many of you.

He told me how, after a while over there, instead of a yellow streak, the men got a mean streak down their backs. Each day the streak got bigger and the men became meaner. Everyone but *you*, Bill. He said how you stayed the same, happy-go-lucky guy that you were when you arrived in Vietnam. How your warmth and friendliness drew the guys to you. How your [lieutenant] gave you the nickname of "Spanky," and soon your group, Jim included, were all known as "Spanky's gang." How when you died it made it so much harder on them for you were their moral support. And he said how you of all people should never have been the one to die.

Oh, God, how it hurts to write this. But I must face it and then put it to rest. I know that after Jim talked to me, he must have relived it all over again and suffered so. Before I hung up the phone I told Jim I loved him. Loved him for just being your close friend, and for sharing the last days of your life with you, and for being there with you when you died.

How lucky you were to have him for a friend, and how lucky he was to have had you.

Later that same day I received a phone call from a mother in Billings, Montana. She had lost her daughter, her only child, a year ago. She needed someone to talk to for no one would let her talk about the tragedy. She said she had seen me on [television] on New Year's Eve, after the Christmas letter I wrote to you and left at this memorial had drawn newspaper and television attention. She said she had been thinking about me all day, and just had to talk to me. She talked to me of her pain, and seemingly needed me to help her with it. I cried with this heartbroken mother, and after I hung up the phone, I laid my head down and cried as hard for her. Here was a mother calling me for help with her pain over the loss of her child, a grown daughter. And as I sobbed I thought, how can I help her with her pain when I have never completely been able to cope with my own?

They tell me the letters I write to you and leave here at this memorial are waking others up to the fact that there is still much pain left, after all these years, from the Vietnam War.

But this I know. I would rather to have had you for 21 years, and all the pain that goes with losing you, than never to have had you at all.

Mom

Glossary

AFVN: Armed Forces Vietnam Network radio station
AIT: Advanced Individual Training; specialized training taken after Basic Training, also referred to as Advanced Infantry Training
AK-47: Soviet-manufactured combat assault rifle
Ammo dump: a safe location where live or expended ammunition is stored
AO: a unit's area of operations
APC: an armored personnel carrier, a track vehicle used to transport troops or supplies, usually armed with a .50-caliber machine gun
APO: Army Post Office located in San Francisco for overseas mail to Vietnam
Artie/Arty: shorthand term for artillery
ARVN: South Vietnamese Regular Army; officially the Army of the Republic of Vietnam
AWOL: Absent Without Leave; leaving a post or position without permission
BAR: Browning Automatic Rifle; a .30-caliber magazine-fed automatic rifle used by U.S. troops during World War II and Korea
Base camp: also known as the rear area; a resupply base for field units and a location for headquarters units, artillery batteries, and air fields
Basic: Basic Training
Battalion: a military unit composed of a headquarters and two or more companies, batteries, or similar units
Battery: an artillery unit equivalent to a company
B-52: U.S. Air Force high-altitude bomber
B-40 rocket: an enemy antitank weapon
Big Red One: the nickname for the 1st Infantry Division
Body bag: a plastic bag used to transport dead bodies from the field
Boo koo: bastardized French from *beaucoup,* meaning "much" or "many"
Boom-boom: slang for sex
BOQ: Bachelor Officer Quarters; living quarters for officers

Bouncing Betty: a land mine that, when triggered, bounces waist-high and sprays shrapnel

Brigade: a tactical and administrative military unit composed of a headquarters and one or more battalions of infantry or armor, with other supporting units

Bronze Star: U.S. military decoration awarded for heroic or meritorious service not involving aerial flights

CA: Combat Assault

Cache: hidden supplies

CAP: Civil Action Program; working with Vietnamese civilians to improve their lives

Carbine: a short-barreled, lightweight automatic or semiautomatic rifle

Cav: Cavalry; shortened term for 1st Cavalry Division (Airmobile)

Chicom: Chinese communist

Chieu Hoi: the "open arms" program promising clemency and financial aid to enemy soldiers who stopped fighting and returned to South Vietnamese government authority

Chinook: a CH-47 cargo helicopter

CIB: Combat Infantryman's Badge; an Army award for being under enemy fire in a combat zone

Claymore: an antipersonnel mine which, when detonated, propelled small steel cubes in a 60-degree fan-shaped pattern to a maximum distance of 100 meters

CMH: Congressional Medal of Honor; the highest U.S. military decoration awarded for conspicuous gallantry at the risk of life above and beyond the call of duty

CO: Commanding Officer

Cobra: an AH-1G attack helicopter; also known as a gunship, armed with rockets and machine guns

Commo: shorthand for "communications"

Company: a military unit usually consisting of a headquarters and two or more platoons

Concertina wire: coiled barbed wire used as an obstacle

CONUS: Continental United States

Coxwain flat: the area where the coxwain—driver—stands when he steers a boat or ship

CP: Command Post

CQ: Charge of Quarters; an officer officially in charge of a unit headquarters at night

C-rations: combat rations; canned meals for use in the field

Cyclo: motorized rickshaw

DEROS: Date of Expected Return from Overseas

Didi: slang from the Vietnamese word *di,* meaning "to leave" or "to go"

Didi mow: Vietnamese for "go quickly"

Dink: derogatory term for an Oriental; also "gook" and "slope"

DMZ: Demilitarized Zone; the dividing line between North and South Vietnam established in 1954 by the Geneva Convention

D-ring: a D-shaped metal snap link used to hold gear together

Dust-off: medical evacuation by helicopter; also called medevac

E-5: lowest-ranking noncommissioned officer; sergeant

82 mm: a mortar used by the enemy

Elephant grass: tall, razor-edged tropical plant indigenous to certain parts of Vietnam

EOD: Explosive Ordnance Disposal; a team that disarms explosive devices

Evac'd: evacuated

50-cal: .50-caliber machine gun

51-cal: a machine gun used by the enemy

FAC: Forward Air Controller; a person who coordinates air strikes

Fire base: an artillery firing position usually secured by an infantry unit; also, fire support base

Fire fight: a battle or exchange of fire with the enemy

Flechette: a small dart-shaped projectile clustered in an explosive warhead

FO: Forward Observer; a person attached to a field unit to coordinate the placement of direct or indirect fire from ground, air, and naval forces

Gook: derogatory term for an Oriental; also "dink" and "slope"

Gunship: an armed helicopter

Hand frags: a fragmentation grenade thrown by a soldier

Hooch: a hut or simple dwelling

Hot LZ: a landing zone under enemy fire

HM: Navy Hospital Corpsman; a medic

Howitzer: a short cannon used to fire shells at medium velocity and with relatively high trajectories

Huey: nickname for the UH-1–series helicopters

I Corps, II Corps, III Corps, IV Corps: the four military regions into which South Vietnam was divided, with I Corps the northernmost region, and IV Corps the southernmost Delta region

Immersion foot: condition resulting from feet being submerged in water for a prolonged period of time causing cracking and bleeding

KIA: Killed In Action

KP: Kitchen Police; mess-hall duty

LBJ: Long Binh Jail; a military stockade on Long Binh post

LCM: a medium-sized landing craft; a boat used to transport troops from ship to shore

LP: Listening Post; a two- or three-man position set up at night outside the perimeter away from the main body of troops, which acted as an early warning system against attack

LRRP: Long Range Reconnaissance Patrol; an elite team usually comprised of five to seven men who would go deep into the jungle to observe enemy activity without initiating contact

Lt: lieutenant

LZ: Landing Zone; where helicopters land to take on or discharge troops or supplies

MACV: Military Assistance Command/Vietnam; the main American military command unit that had responsibility for and authority over all U.S. military activities in Vietnam; based at Tan Son Nhut

MG: Machine gun

MIA: Missing In Action

Marker round: the first round fired by mortars or artillery used to adjust the following rounds onto the target

Mechanized platoon: a platoon operating with tanks and/or armored personnel carriers

Med Cap: Medical Civil Action Program in which U.S. medical personnel would go into the villages to minister to the local populace

Medevac: medical evacuation from the field by helicopter; also called a dust-off

Million-dollar wound: a noncrippling wound serious enough to warrant return to the United States

Montagnard: a Vietnamese term for several tribes of mountain people inhabiting the highlands of Vietnam near the Cambodian border

Mortar: a muzzle-loading cannon with a short tube in relation to its caliber that throws projectiles with low muzzle velocity at high angles

M-79: a U.S. military hand-held grenade launcher

M-16: the standard U.S. military rifle used in Vietnam; successor to the M-14

M-60: the standard lightweight machine gun used by U.S. forces in Vietnam

NCO: Non-Commissioned Officer; sergeant

NVA: North Vietnamese Army

Number 1: the best

Number 10: the worst

105: a 105-mm howitzer

OP: Observation Post

OR: Operating Room

P (piaster): Vietnamese money; one piaster was worth one cent or less

PBR: river patrol boat

Perimeter: outer limits of a military position; the area beyond this belongs to the enemy

PFC: Private First Class

Platoon: a subdivision of a company-sized military unit, normally consisting of two or more squads or sections

Point man: the first man or element on a combat patrol

Pop smoke: to ignite a smoke grenade to signal an aircraft

Post-traumatic stress disorder: The development of characteristic symptoms after the experiencing of a psychologically traumatic event or events outside the range of human experience usually considered to be normal. The characteristic symptoms involve reexperiencing the traumatic event, numbing of responsiveness to, or involvement with, the external world, exaggerated startle response, difficulty in concentrating, memory impairment, guilt feelings, and sleep difficulties

Profile: a prohibition from certain types of military duty due to injury or disability

PT: Physical Training

Purple Heart: a U.S. military decoration awarded to any member of the armed forces wounded by enemy action

PX: Post Exchange; military store

Quantico: Marine training base in Virginia

Ranger: soldier specially trained for reconnaissance and combat missions

R&R: Rest and Relaxation; a three- to seven-day vacation from the war for a soldier

Recon: reconnaissance; going out into the jungle to observe for the purpose of identifying enemy activity

Regiment: a military unit usually consisting of a number of battalions

RPG: a rocket-propelled grenade; a Russian-made antitank grenade launcher

RTO: Radio Telephone Operator; the man who carries his unit's radio on his back in the field

Rules of Engagement: the specific regulations for the conduct of air and surface battles by U.S. and allied forces during the Vietnam War

Satchel charges: pack used by the enemy containing explosives that is dropped or thrown and is generally more powerful than a grenade

SeaBees: Navy construction engineers

79: an M-79 grenade launcher

Shrapnel: pieces of metal sent flying by an explosion

Silver Star: a U.S. military decoration awarded for gallantry in action

SKS: Soviet semiautomatic rifle

Slope: derogatory term for an Oriental; also "dink" and "gook"

Sp/5: Specialist Fifth Class; equivalent to a sergeant

Sp/4: Specialist Fourth Class; an Army rank equivalent to a corporal

Spider hole: a camouflaged enemy foxhole

Squad: a small military unit consisting of less than 10 men

Staff sergeant: an E-6, the second lowest noncommissioned-officer rank

Stand down: period of rest for a military unit when all operations other than security are curtailed

Starlight scope: an image intensifier using reflected light to identify targets at night

Titi: slang for "a little"

Tet: Buddhist lunar New Year; Buddha's birthday

Tet Offensive: a major uprising of Viet Cong, VC sympathizers, and NVA characterized by a series of coordinated attacks against military installations and provincial capitals throughout Vietnam. It occurred during the lunar New Year at the end of January 1968

Tracer: a round of ammunition chemically treated to glow or give off smoke so that its flight can be followed

Tracks: any vehicles which move on tracks rather than wheels

Trip flare: a ground flare triggered by a trip wire used to signal and illuminate the approach of an enemy at night

Victor/Victor Charlie/Mr. Charles/Chuck: the enemy

Vietnamese Popular Forces: South Vietnamese local military forces

Vietnamization: U.S. policy initiated by President Richard Nixon late in the war to turn over the fighting to the South Vietnamese Army during the phased withdrawal of American troops

Ville: Vietnamese hamlet or village

WIA: Wounded In Action

Willy Peter/Willy Pete/WP: white phosphorus; an element used in grenades or shells for incendiary purposes

Wood line: a row of trees at the edge of a field or rice paddy

World, the: the United States

Xin Loi: a Vietnamese idiom meaning "sorry about that"

Zippo raids: military operations which involved burning down Vietnamese villages; often Zippo cigarette lighters were used to ignite the hooches

About the Editor

BERNARD EDELMAN, born and raised in Brooklyn, New York, was drafted into the Army in 1969 and served in Vietnam as a broadcast specialist and correspondent in 1970. He has been curator of several exhibits of Vietnam art and now works as a reporter, photographer, and editor in New York City.

Index of Contributors